WHAT
WENT
WRONG

★ ★ ★ ★ ★ ★ ★ ★ ★ ★ ★ ★ ★ ★ ★ ★ ★

WHAT WENT

THE INSIDE STORY OF THE GOP DEBACLE OF 2012... AND HOW IT CAN BE AVOIDED NEXT TIME

JEROME R. CORSI, PH.D.

#1 *NEW YORK TIMES* BESTSELLING AUTHOR OF *THE OBAMA NATION*

WHAT WENT WRONG

WND Books, Inc.
Washington, D.C.

Book designed by Mark Karis

WND Books are available at special discounts for bulk purchases. WND Books, Inc., also publishes books in electronic formats. For more information call (541) 474-1776, email sales@wndbooks.com, or visit www.wndbooks.com.

First Edition

Hardcover ISBN: 9781938067044
eBook ISBN: 9781938067051

Library of Congress information available

Printed in the United States of America
10 9 8 7 6 5 4 3 2 1

FOR PHYLLIS SCHLAFLY

With great respect and appreciation
for her decades of inspiring dedication
and resolute leadership
of the conservative movement
in the United States

CONTENTS

PREFACE

NO SURPRISE

All political thinking for years past has been vitiated in the same way. People can foresee the future only when it coincides with their own wishes, and the most grossly obvious facts can be ignored when they are unwelcome.
—George Orwell, *London Letter,* December 1944

MITT ROMNEY NEVER SAW IT COMING. His top advisors assured him it wasn't possible.

Yet Romney's shocking loss to Barack Obama on November 6, 2012, was no surprise to those really in the know. The Democrats in Chicago saw it unfold exactly as planned.

Democratic strategists surrounding Obama have been building a political machine and demographic coalition designed to rule America for decades, and Obama's reelection is but the first triumph in what many leftists believe will be the new dawn of Democratic dominance in Washington.

Yet *now*, while the GOP establishment is reeling to understand where it went wrong, *now*, while the Democrats are basking in overconfidence, *now* is the time for true conservatives to learn how and why Romney lost, so in 2016 *they* can serve up the surprise instead.

This book is no mere history of the election of 2012, but an analysis of the strategy behind its battles. I did not aspire to write a version of Theodore H. White's The Making of the President series. What I did aspire to accomplish is to understand and explain the dynamics of the 2012 election in the terms of the political science, sociology, and demographics that were fought out by the key advisors of both candidates.

Going into the presidential election, the Democrats enjoyed distinct advantages. Their key advisors were young enough to understand computer and social media technology and educated to take advantage of the social science and psychology they had been taught in universities. The Democrats developed voter-intelligence computer technology that gave their party a decade's head start over the Republicans in the critical get-out-the-vote, or GOTV, ground-game stage of a long election campaign. The Democrats have further perfected the art of voter fraud at a systematic level, having developed the ability to run a nonstop effort between and within campaign cycles to gain through subterfuge enough extra votes to ensure victory in virtually any close election, including the presidential election of 2012.

If left unchecked and unexposed, Democrats have every reason to believe many more election victories lie ahead.

Republicans, on the other hand, grossly miscalculated by nominating yet another GOP establishment favorite in Mitt Romney. In 2012, the Republicans went back to their traditional game of nominating the also-ran, second-place runner-up from the last presidential campaign. But like John McCain, so, too, Mitt Romney was an easy target for cutthroat Democratic operatives eager to frame him as a rich guy out of touch with the people and to neutralize his arguments, armed with research on his centrist track record. Romney was hampered from the start by having introduced "Romney-care" as governor of Massachusetts before Obama had a chance to do so as president. He was hamstrung by his support of the lesbian, gay, bisexual, and transgender, or LGBT, agenda to the point of advocating the Boy Scouts accepting homosexual members even before Democrats advanced the idea on a national scale.

Once Democratic operatives had a chance to frame Romney for the voting public, Republican operatives were unable to convince voters that Romney's experience as a businessman and as governor of Massachusetts proved he could work with Democrats, reduce budget deficits, and create jobs. Skillfully, Democratic operatives undermined Romney's appeal to the Republican base by painting him as a moderate Republican, while eliminating any appeal he might have to Democrats by painting him as willing to cast social justice aside for a Bain Capital payday.

In preparing to write this book, I resolved to see the 2012 presidential election up close and in person. I attended the Republican National Convention in Tampa. After attending the second presidential debate at Long Island's Hofstra University, I rode as traveling press with the Romney campaign on the Romney campaign airplane straight though until Election Day, ending up at Romney campaign headquarters in Boston on Election Eve.

The long days of early-morning airplane flights and late-night hotel check-ins gave an opportunity to see the Romney campaign firsthand, with direct access to top campaign advisors. The daily chance to sit on the airplane in the press rows behind those reserved for the Secret Service and pool reporters offered the opportunity to observe not only Romney, his family, and his closest advisors, only a few feet away in the front of the airplane, but also to observe the reaction of my colleagues in the mainstream media to a Republican presidential campaign that most found ideologically offensive. Reporting for WND from within the Romney camp on the campaign trail provided insights into Republican Party strategy I could have gained no other way. And in the "spin alleys" of the last two presidential debates, I jostled with the other reporters to record firsthand how Obama's top advisors were positioning their efforts and measuring their success.

Even though my methodology differs from that employed by Theodore White, I have great appreciation for an insight he shared when writing his first book of The Making of the President series, the book chronicling how JFK beat Nixon.

In *The Making of the President 1960*, White wrote on the first page of his author's note preface: "For no man can tell it all—either now or much later. The transaction in power by which a President is chosen is so vastly complicated that even those most intimately involved in it, even those who seek the office, can never know more than a fragment of it."[1]

I agree with that statement wholeheartedly. But knowing even a fraction of it can make the difference between a president delivering an acceptance speech and an also-ran offering a concession. Hopefully, this effort to go beyond the election's history and into its strategy will illuminate those who plan to contest for the presidency once again . . . in 2016.

1

A CRUSHING DEFEAT

The problem of choosing an able President is one about which we have been disturbed almost without rest since the election of 1796.
—Clinton Rossiter, *The American Presidency* (1987)[1]

EVEN ON ELECTION DAY, November 6, 2012, the Romney team was confident of victory.

During the last airplane flight of the long 2012 presidential campaign, flying to Boston from Pittsburgh, where Romney met one final time with campaign officials in a local Romney office, Stuart Stevens, the campaign's chief strategist and speechwriter, came back to the press section of the Romney airplane and told me he was confident Romney would be the next president of the United States because "a positive campaign message trumps a good ground game every time."

Stevens had put his finger on the central calculation that led him to roll the dice, focusing the Romney campaign on delivering a free enterprise message that promised to revive the US economy and reduce the burgeoning federal deficit with a small-business, job-creation program validated by Romney's claimed success at building businesses in his years working as an investment banker with Bain Capital.

Stevens assumed the campaign message focusing on James Carville's famous saw, "It's the economy, stupid," would resonate with the electorate across the nation, easily trumping any computer-driven, Internet-based get-out-the-vote strategy the technological geeks running the Obama campaign could devise and implement.

Stevens was wrong.

THE HOME STRETCH

In the last month of the campaign, Romney had maintained a hectic pace, holding three and sometimes four different rallies a day in as many different cities. Typical days on the campaign trail began with a 6:00 a.m. breakfast for the press traveling with the candidate, followed by the day's first flight an hour or so later, and ending as late as midnight or one o'clock the next morning, with the Romney campaign airplane touching down in the city where a rally was scheduled early that day.

This way the traveling press, the Secret Service detail assigned to fly with the candidate, the campaign brain trust, and Mitt Romney himself crisscrossed the battleground states, logging in thousands of miles and seemingly endless hours of time at 35,000 feet every day.

On the last day before the election, Monday, November 5, the Romney campaign had five campaign appearances scheduled, while Obama had only three. Romney began the day with an 8:00 a.m. rally at Orlando's Sanford International Airport.

"Don't you just love this guy?" Stevens quietly asked me, particularly satisfied with how Romney had delivered a stump speech modification Stevens had just engineered. Stevens had a point. With every campaign rally, Romney gave the appearance of looking more comfortable and more presidential.

A noon rally at the Lynchburg Regional Airport in Lynchburg, Virginia, followed Orlando. From Lynchburg, the Romney airplane traveled to Dulles

International Airport for a 3:15 p.m. rally at the Patriot Center at George Mason University, in Fairfax, Virginia. An enthusiastic crowd of ten thousand cheering supporters packed into the Patriot Center. Several thousand supporters, who were prevented by fire regulations from being allowed inside, stood on the roadway to the university to cheer Romney's motorcade as it wound its way to the George Mason campus.

By 4:55 p.m., everybody packed back aboard the Romney airplane for a flight to Columbus, Ohio, and a 6:15 rally in the Landmark Aviation hangar at the Port Columbus International Airport, at which the Oak Ridge Boys and the Marshall Tucker Band appeared in person to play warm-up to the rally's start. With a crowd of thirty-five hundred people packed into the airport hangar, the Romney campaign airplane, with "Believe in America" and "MittRomney.com" painted in blue on the white fuselage, eased into the hangar, accompanied by the playing of Aaron Copland's "Fanfare for the Common Man" over the loudspeaker. From the door at the nose of the airplane, Ann Romney—looking radiant in a rose jacket with scarf—emerged and preceded her husband down the stairs, with Mitt Romney wearing a Leading Edge jacket with a white shirt and tie.

Romney broke the sustained applause by saying, "Let me introduce to you the next First Lady of the United States."

Both waved to the crowd, smiling radiantly, apparently confident that the next day, Romney would be voted to the White House.

"One more day," the crowd chanted, certain Barack Obama was about to become a one-term president.

At the end of the rally in Ohio, the Romney plane headed to Manchester, New Hampshire, for the campaign's final rally at the Verizon Wireless Arena. The auditorium was packed to the rafters, with the enthusiasm built to a crescendo prior to the candidate's arrival by a rock concert headlined in person by Kid Rock, whose song "Born Free" had become Romney's unofficial theme song.

"We ask you to stay with us until tomorrow, when victory is clear," Romney said from the speaker's platform at the opposite end of the auditorium from the stage set up for the rock concert. "Then we begin a new tomorrow. Change cannot be measured in speeches; it must be measured in results."

A banner printed in white letters on a blue background positioned behind the speaker's platform reinforced the theme, reading: "REAL

CHANGE on Day One."

Romney aides insisted "real change" was a legitimate Romney theme, pushing back repeated attempts by Obama supporters masquerading as mainstream media among the traveling press to question at every available opportunity why Romney felt he had a right to appropriate the "Change" theme as his own. The insistent questioning from the press traveling on the Romney airplane implied Romney was so lacking a campaign theme of his own that he had no choice but to heist his final 2012 message from Obama's 2008 "Hope and Change" mantra.

Monday's campaigning ended at 1:15 a.m., nineteen hours after it began, when the Romney bus caravan finally arrived at the Westin Copley Place in downtown Boston, where the traveling press was deposited for the night.

Rather than being exhausted from the heavy travel and rally schedule of the past month, Romney appeared to feed on the enthusiasm of the large crowds he had been drawing in the final weeks of the campaign. As the campaign headed into the final week, Romney appeared more positive and energetic than ever. At campaign appearance after campaign appearance, he basked in the applause, responding with broad smiles to the crowd's faithful chanting in their enthusiasm to oust Barack Obama from the White House, "Mitt! Mitt! Mitt!"

On the flight from Orlando, Florida, to Lynchburg, Virginia, Romney campaign spokesmen refused to confirm or deny reports circulated by Fox News that the campaign was planning to go back out in the field on Election Day. Reporters suggested this was a nontraditional move in that presidential candidates typically stay close to home on Election Day, so as not to detract from or interfere with the campaign's ground-game effort to work the precincts and get out the vote. But when the campaign bus pulled up to the Westin Copley Place, reporters were told to sign up right then on their computers if they intended to go back out into the field yet one more time on the candidate's plane.

ELECTION DAY, NOVEMBER 6, 2012

The idea of campaigning on Election Day seemed to derive, in part, from Romney's reluctance to get off the campaign trail to spend a nervous day in Boston, pacing his suite at the Westin Copley Place and waiting for election results, when he could be out on the campaign trail, mixing with campaign workers.

Peppered with questions from the largely Obama-supporting mainstream media traveling with the campaign, the Romney campaign denied that it was acting in a desperate fashion, arguing instead it was reasonable to want to work right until the polls closed.

Stuart Stevens privately explained to me that the Romney campaign had the resources and the time to campaign on Election Day, and the decision was made to take every possible step to win, even if campaign rallies in the field on Election Day were considered unorthodox.

For Mitt and Ann Romney, Election Day began at 8:15 a.m., when they arrived at the Beech Street Center polling place in Manchester, New Hampshire, to vote. At the polling place, Governor Romney and his wife were greeted by a fairly large crowd, including one woman inside who was holding a sign that read, "Mitt and Ann—Enjoy your new White House."

Picking up the voting materials from poll workers seated at a table in the front of the room, Mitt and Ann walked over to two of the twelve voting booths in the room to cast their votes.

Leaving the polling place, a reporter asked Romney how good he felt about Ohio.

"I feel great about Ohio," Romney responded enthusiastically.

Romney wore a blue suit and tie, while Ann wore a long teal jacket, a black top, a brown belt, and black boots. The Romneys exchanged a kiss, as Mitt bid Ann goodbye for the day, and Mitt climbed into the back of a black SUV to head for the airport.

At 9:15 a.m., Romney arrived at the airport outside Boston for a day rallying the ground troops getting out the vote in Ohio and Pennsylvania. Stuart Stevens and Kevin Madden, another top Romney advisor, accompanied Romney on the airplane.

"We are going to win Ohio," Stevens told reporters. "We always close strong."

Asked to respond to Democrats who said Romney's trips to Ohio and Pennsylvania smacked of desperation, Stevens countered, "I never thought that going out and talking to voters and working was anything but what we are supposed to do."

Romney's campaign plane touched down in Cleveland at 11:15 a.m., and Romney stayed aboard the plane on the tarmac, waiting for running mate and vice presidential candidate Representative Paul Ryan of Wisconsin to arrive. Not to be outdone by the Obama campaign, within minutes of Romney's arrival, while Romney's campaign airplane was still on the tarmac waiting for the arrival of Ryan's vice presidential campaign airplane, *Air Force Two* unexpectedly descended upon Cleveland.

Ryan's plane joined Romney's shortly thereafter, providing an unusual, high-noon spectacle: Romney's and Ryan's planes positioned yards from each other, with Joe Biden's *Air Force Two* visible in the distance. The two planes looked majestic together, a matching set of customized MD-80 chartered aircraft, with Ryan's airplane nearly identical to Romney's, distinguished on the outside by being painted all-white, lacking the blue-underbelly customizing that distinguished Romney's presidential aircraft.

Ryan crossed the tarmac and bounded up the ramp to join Romney for a quick, final-day conference in private. If anyone doubted the importance of Ohio to the 2012 election, that question should have been settled by 12:12 p.m., when Romney and Ryan's motorcade headed toward Cleveland, only twenty minutes on the heels of Vice President Biden's campaign armada. Biden's *Air Force Two*, a Boeing C-32, modified version of the 757, was clearly visible across the tarmac. Seen from the Romney-Ryan aircraft parked side by side, it looked elegant and regal with the boldly painted "United States of America" dominating the white fuselage, its trimming and underbelly a more subtle, paler shade of blue than the royal blue of Romney's campaign plane.

The Republicans drove to a local campaign office in a strip mall in Richmond Heights, a Cleveland suburb, arriving at 12:50 p.m. The office was located next to an Indian restaurant and a local branch of a national banking chain. Signs on the inside walls of the office read: "Vote Today!"; "Ohio Loves Romney"; and "Romney for America." More than two dozen volunteers were making calls from a phone bank when Romney and Ryan arrived. The Romney-Ryan caravan arrived back at the Cleveland airport at around 2:00 p.m., and by 2:35, the Romney plane had departed for Pittsburgh, leaving Ryan at the airport in Cleveland.

Arriving in Pittsburgh, Romney deplaned, surprised to find a group of several hundred supporters standing outside the airport's chain-linked fence, lining the street in front of a two-story parking lot, with people standing and waving from both of the parking lot's double decks. The surprise was that the campaign staff had made no effort to assemble a rally. Seeing the impromptu gathering, Romney walked across the tarmac and waved both hands in the air to acknowledge the supporters.

Asked by reporters as he walked away what he felt about the greeting, Romney said, "Well, that's when you know you're going to win."

In Pittsburgh, Romney visited the Green Tree victory center, where some thirty volunteers were making calls from a telephone bank. A sign on the wall read, "Obama isn't working."

When Romney entered the office, a woman volunteer began chanting, "Twelve more hours! Twelve more hours!"

Romney encouraged volunteers to be positive in making phone calls.

"The president has run a strong campaign," he said. "I believe he is a good man and wish him and his family well. He is a good father and has been a good example of a good father. But it's time for a new direction. It's time for a new tomorrow."

On the airplane from Pittsburgh to Boston, Stevens told me before takeoff he was confident the campaign had won Ohio. "Obama did not get enough votes in early voting to tip the balance in his favor," he argued.

Once in the air, Romney came to the back of the campaign plane and spoke with reporters. With confidence equal to that of his campaign manager, Romney told reporters he felt so certain he would win that he had not drafted any concession speech. He said he looked forward to the next few weeks, when he would be heading the transition team and selecting key members of his new administration, including making the necessary Cabinet appointments.

Back in Boston around 6:00 p.m. on Election Night, the Romney bus caravan headed to the Boston Convention Center, where a ballroom was set up for supporters to gather and television cameras to cover what the Romney campaign fully expected would be a jubilant celebration capped off by a nationally televised acceptance speech.

Instead, long before midnight, the unexpected happened.

Romney lost every swing state in contention except North Carolina. When the key states of Ohio and Florida fell into the Obama column, the night was over, and so was the GOP's hope of unseating a president who had presided over one of the most severe and prolonged economic downturns in United States history.

Obama won reelection in a close vote that was still so decisively in

Obama's favor that a charge of voter fraud was unpersuasive and a recount on the scale of the 2000 effort in Florida was unimaginable. Romney lost, despite every expectation the campaign had—down to the last minute of voting—that he had won.

By 10:00 p.m. Eastern on Election Day, it was all over. Romney suffered a crushing and unexpected defeat. His campaign staff was devastated, his top financial supporters stunned to learn that, in spite of the campaign's heavy spending (and theirs), their candidate had lost.

THE MATHEMATICS OF DEFEAT

The GOP entering into the 2012 presidential election was confident this was a year in which Barack Obama could be defeated.

The historical precedent was Jimmy Carter, a one-term president who was repudiated out of office in 1980, as Ronald Reagan swept the nation with his conservative agenda. Like Carter, Obama had presided over four severe years economically. Carter's presidency was plagued by a Middle East oil embargo that caused long lines and high prices at gas pumps around the nation, compounding the pain of a stagnant economy saddled with mounting inflation and double-digit interest rates, producing the unusual configuration professional economists labeled "stagflation."

Similarly, Obama's presidency was marked by a stubborn unemployment rate at 8 percent or higher—a rate artificially lowered by complicit econometricians at the Bureau of Labor Statistics throwing out of the labor force entirely the millions of chronically unemployed who simply gave up looking for work.

Like Obama, Carter went into his reelection campaign plagued by foreign policy debacles. The Iran hostage crisis that began in 1979 lasted ultimately 444 days, ending only on the day Carter's successor took the oath of office.

For Obama, the problem was an Arab Spring the administration had spun positively as a rebirth of democracy in the Middle East, only to find the US ambassador to Libya, Chris Stevens, along with Americans attempting to defend him, all murdered brutally in a terrorist attack at a US compound in Benghazi. Iran was threatening to develop nuclear weapons, a war in the Middle East looked inevitable—as Hamas in the Gaza Strip was preparing to lob Iranian-built missiles into Israel, and rebels supported by al-Qaeda terrorists were waging a full-scale war to topple nations all across the Middle East and North Africa.

Still, the reality of the Electoral College mathematics presented the GOP a daunting hill to climb. As most students of politics know, presidential elections are settled on Electoral College votes, not the popular vote. Currently, there are 538 electors, based on there being 435 members of the House of Representatives, 100 US senators, and three electors from the District of Columbia. The numbers of electors are allocated to the states based on the number of members of the House that state has, plus 2 senators for each state. An absolute majority of 270 electoral votes is required to win the presidency.

But from the get-go, Democrats began the Electoral College race at an advantage.

The last time California went for the Republican candidate in a presidential election was in 1988, when George H. W. Bush beat Democratic challenger Michael S. Dukakis, the former governor of Massachusetts. The last time New York went for a Republican candidate in a presidential election was in 1984, when Ronald Reagan won his second term by taking every state except Minnesota, beating Democratic challenger Walter F. Mondale, a former US senator from Minnesota.

In 2012, Barack Obama could safely calculate that he would carry California, with 55 electoral votes, and New York, with 29 electoral votes, for a total of 84 electoral votes, without any necessity to campaign in either state. The 2012 Electoral College calculus began with this huge advantage for Obama, who by winning these two states needed only 186 electoral votes to win the election, while Romney needed to find 270.

The assumption Obama would win both California and New York was then extended to distinguish the total number of "blue" states certain to vote for Obama and the total number of "red states" certain to vote for Romney. This analysis allowed each political party to eliminate states where the presidential candidate would have to campaign, either because the party's candidate was certain to win that state, or because the party's candidate was certain to lose that state.

Table 1 lists the red and blue states that were "locked in," assumed certain to vote for one candidate or the other, along with their accompanying electoral votes. The following table examines the geographical United States by moving roughly west to east, and north to south.

Table 1
Electoral College Math 2012
Red States vs. Blue States

Alaska	3	Hawaii	4
Montana	3	Washington	12
Idaho	4	California	55
Wyoming	3	Oregon	7
Utah	6	New Mexico	5
Arizona	11	Minnesota	10
North Dakota	3	Wisconsin	10
South Dakota	3	Illinois	20
Nebraska	5	Michigan	16
Kansas	6	New York	29
Oklahoma	7	New Jersey	14
Texas	38	Pennsylvania	20
Missouri	10	Maine	4
Arkansas	6	New Hampshire	4
Louisiana	8	Vermont	3
Indiana	11	Massachusetts	11
Kentucky	8	Connecticut	7
Tennessee	11	Rhode Island	4
Mississippi	6	Delaware	3
Alabama	9	District of Columbia	3
West Virginia	5	Maryland	10
South Carolina	9		
Georgia	16		
Total "Red" State votes	**191**	**Total "Blue" State votes**	**251**

Table 1 makes clear Obama entered the 2012 presidential campaign calculating he could win as many as 251 electoral votes in blue states that Romney had no chance of winning, regardless of how hard the Republican Party campaigned. Obama needed only to pick up 20 electoral votes from the states yet in contest, while Romney needed 79 electoral votes, approximately four times as many.

Granted, calculating whether a state was "locked in" or not came for both camps to be viewed as an electoral Rubik's Cube game, where calculations could change simply by placing one or more of these states into a swing-state status.[2] For instance, should Romney have picked up one or more of the states Table 1 placed in the Obama column, such as Michigan, Wisconsin, or Pennsylvania, campaign strategy for both camps would have shifted dramatically. The same held for Romney. Losing a state like Utah or Missouri could cost the election.

Truthfully, the calculation shown here of certain red and blue states may only look certain in retrospect. Yet, this is the final configuration both campaigns considered likely as Election Day approached. Given the desire to spend each dollar in the campaign for maximum benefit, placing states in a swing-state category was a costly decision, especially if the campaign took the argument seriously enough to allocate tens of millions of dollars to campaigning in the state, with a resolve to grab a victory from the competitor's "locked-in" column.

Adding the locked-in red states to the locked-in blue states, only 96 electoral votes were considered still in play.

This analysis reveals there were only three states west of the Mississippi River that the candidates needed to visit or otherwise expend precious campaign resources on: Nevada, Colorado, and Iowa. No Midwest states were in contention. The only Great Lakes state the candidates needed to contest was Ohio. On the Eastern Seaboard, only Virginia, North Carolina, and Florida could be considered up for grabs.

For all practical purposes, the presidential election of 2012 was reduced from the start to the seven states listed in Table 2 as "swing states."

Table 2 Swing States Presidential Election 2012	
Swing State	**Electoral Votes**
Nevada	6
Colorado	9
Iowa	6
Ohio	18
Virginia	13
North Carolina	15
Florida	29
Total	**96**

Needing only 20 electoral votes from this list to win, Obama could reclaim the presidency simply by taking Florida and its 29 electoral votes. If Obama lost Florida, he could win by picking up Ohio, plus one other state—a calculation that also held true for Virginia and North Carolina.

The electoral calculation was much more difficult for Romney, given that he needed to pick up 80 of the 96 electoral votes yet in play in the seven swing states. Florida was a "must win" state that Romney could not afford to lose without losing the election. The next most important state to win was Ohio, with 18 electoral votes, the second-highest state total among the seven swing states.

If Romney lost Florida, however, Obama would have to suffer serious and unexpected erosion in one or more of the more populous blue states. Perhaps the most at-risk blue states were Pennsylvania, Wisconsin, and New Hampshire, although when the Republican and Democratic National Conventions were completed at the beginning of September, these three states still appeared solidly in Obama's camp. If Romney won both Florida and Ohio, in addition to North Carolina, he would have gained a 253 electoral vote total, needing only 17 more electoral votes to win.

The electoral calculations determined the dynamics of the campaign in that both camps focused on the swing states to secure a victory. Romney began at a serious disadvantage in that the Republicans could not lose any of the swing states without risking almost certain defeat. Going into mid-October, the only one of the swing states that looked almost certainly to go to Romney was North Carolina. Even a quick look at the Romney travel schedule from a few sample days in October makes clear Romney spent the majority of his personal campaign time in Florida, Ohio, Virginia, Iowa, Colorado, and Nevada, in that order, with the focus on the states that had double-digit electoral votes.

As an indication that the Romney campaign considered North Carolina a likely win, consider that in October, Romney was not scheduled to make a single campaign stop in North Carolina, while several days were spent entirely in either Ohio or Florida. On Wednesday, October 24, 2012, for instance, Romney flew to rallies in Reno, Nevada; followed by Cedar Rapids, Iowa; and ending in Cincinnati, Ohio. The next day, Thursday, October 25, 2012, Romney attended three rallies in Ohio, beginning with Cincinnati at 11:00 a.m., followed by a rally in Worthington at 3:25 p.m. and ending at a football field at Defiance High School at 7:15 p.m., where twenty-five thousand people attended in the dark and cold of evening. The campaign ended the day with a bus caravan back north, to Toledo.

On Friday, October 26, 2012, the Romney campaign flew to Des Moines, Iowa, where Romney delivered a major economic policy address at 11:55 a.m., with the campaign flying from Des Moines back to Ohio for a 6:00 p.m. rally at Canton that was attended by some ten thousand people.

Near the end of the campaign, Obama put on an extraordinary display of energy, attesting to his concern about the same swing states that were the focus of the Romney campaign. *New York Times* reporter Helene Cooper noted that on Wednesday, October 24, 2012, *Air Force One* landed in Davenport, Iowa, at 9:00 a.m. central to begin a two-day round-the-clock schedule of rallies that would not end until the 747 touched down at Andrews Air Force Base just before midnight eastern that Thursday.

"During the 38 hours in between, Mr. Obama will hit a whopping eight states in a hard-charging opening burst to try to accelerate ahead of Mitt Romney in the last two weeks of this dead-heat campaign," Cooper wrote. "So focused is Mr. Obama on gaining ground that he will be making calls to swing-state voters from the air, and he will spend Wednesday night not in a comfy hotel bed, but on his plane, on a red-eye flight to Florida."[3]

Obama told the crowd of thirty-five hundred in Davenport, "We're gonna pull an all-nighter! No Sleep! We're starting in Iowa, then we're gonna go to Colorado, then Nevada, California, then we're gonna go to Florida, then Virginia, Ohio, and then we're going to Illinois to vote."[4]

Cooper noted that the furious pace of the Obama campaign was a sign of the tight race she believed would be won or lost by focusing the campaign solely on the seven or eight swing states believed still in play.

Different electoral calculations varied by placing various states in the "toss-up" stage or in the "leaning" to Obama or "leaning" to Romney, rather than portraying such states as solidly red or blue. Real Clear Politics, for instance, a website that pooled various estimates to produce a composite result, calculated the Obama-Biden ticket had 201 solid electoral votes, with the Romney-Ryan ticket garnering 191 solid electoral votes.[5] Real Clear Politics differed from an estimate by WND by including Michigan, New Hampshire, Pennsylvania, and Wisconsin among the swing states, in addition to the seven states WND identified. The Real Clear Politics estimate was thus more favorable to Romney, even though all the additional states Real Clear Politics considered "toss-up" ultimately went to Obama-Biden.

Going into Election Day, Republican strategist Karl Rove calculated there were twelve "toss-up" states: Minnesota, Nevada, Colorado, Iowa, Wisconsin, Michigan, Ohio, Pennsylvania, New Hampshire, Virginia, North Carolina, and Florida.[6] Rove believed Romney and Obama were essentially tied when solid blue and solid red states were calculated, with each candidate estimated to be at 191 electoral votes. Rove predicted Romney would win seven of the "toss-up" states: Florida, North Carolina, Virginia, New Hampshire, Ohio, Iowa, and Colorado. He predicted Minnesota, Nevada, Wisconsin, Michigan, and Pennsylvania would go to Obama. Thus, Rove went into Election Day predicting Romney would win a close contest with 285 electoral votes, compared to 253 electoral votes for Obama.

Political consultant Dick Morris was even more confident Romney would win, going on the record in repeated television interviews predicting Romney would win the election in "a landslide," ending up with as many as 325 electoral votes.[7] Morris went so far as to say on the eve of the election that the chance Romney would win was 90 percent certain and the probability the Romney victory would be a landslide was a 60 percent certainty.[8]

With the enthusiasm exhibited by Morris exceeding the bright forecast given by Rove—the reputed elections genius George W. Bush had dubbed "the Architect"[9] after the 2004 presidential election—the Romney campaign had every reason to go confidently into Election Day on November 6, 2012, certain Romney would emerge as president-elect, with Obama relegated to Carter's status of a one-term, failed presidency.

STUNNED BY THE RESULT

On November 6, 2012, however, when the final vote was tallied, the Romney campaign was blindsided.

Despite the campaign's best efforts, Romney lost every swing state except North Carolina, collecting only 206 electoral votes, compared to 332 electoral votes for the victorious Obama-Biden ticket.

Obama also won the popular vote, with 65,909,451 votes, 51.02 percent of the total votes cast, compared to 60,932,176 votes for Romney, 47.16 percent of the total votes cast.

Remarkably, Romney barely topped John McCain's total in 2008 (59,950,323), and thus failed to win in 2012, despite Obama's campaign losing roughly 3.5 million votes from its peak in 2008, when Obama was running as the first US president of African descent, a man who had conducted an emotionally uplifting campaign as a relative newcomer to the national political scene.

Obama's diminished popular vote total suggests the Romney campaign had been correct in concluding four years in office during continuing economic hard times had made Obama vulnerable to defeat in 2012.

The problem was Romney had failed to devise and execute a campaign to take advantage of Obama's troubles managing the economy, leaving the American public more willing to continue with a struggling incumbent than to switch leadership to a challenger who had failed to close the case that he should be president.

To win, the Romney campaign needed to grab hold of Republican voters who were lukewarm on McCain and fell through the cracks in 2008. Instead, Romney and McCain join a long list of establishment GOP presidential candidates who failed to capture the imagination of the American public sufficiently to merit their elevation to the highest elected position in the land.

A DEEPER MATH AT WORK

Despite Barack Obama's 2008 campaign promise to unite the country if he were elected president, the 2012 election showed the United States continues to be a deeply divided nation, and in truth, it has very little to do with "red states" and "blue states."

The 2012 presidential election map, broken down by counties, makes clear Obama's voting strength came predominantly from the cities, not from the suburbs or the less densely populated rural areas of America, *regardless* of "red state" or "blue state" distinctions.

As Map 2 indicates, remove about a dozen major cities from the United States, and the presidential voting strength of the Democratic Party practically evaporates. Even in a solidly blue state like California, Democratic voters tend to cluster along the Pacific Coast, in the urban corridor from San Francisco to Los Angeles to San Diego.

Similarly, a postindustrial string of Rust Belt–influenced cities stretching from Minneapolis–St. Paul through Detroit, Milwaukee, Chicago, Cleveland, Pittsburgh, and New York City drives the fortunes of the states in the area. Isolating these cities dramatically changes the political party orientation of eight northern states from Minnesota, Wisconsin, and Michigan along the Great Lakes, continuing through Illinois, Indiana, and Ohio into Pennsylvania and New York. Were the urban areas cut out, these solidly "blue states" convert immediately to securely "red."

Even in Florida, the Democratic Party strength centers around Miami on the Atlantic Coast, Orlando in the central part of the state, and the Tampa/St. Petersburg area on the Gulf side.

A second observation is that the strength of the Republican Party remains impacted by the realignment of the vote toward a resurgent GOP in the Southern and Western states—what became known as Richard Nixon's "Southern Strategy"—first identified by Kevin Phillips in his classic book titled *The Emerging Republican Majority*. Phillips detailed how the New England base of the GOP during the 1932–1968 span of the New Deal era switched orientation from the establishment Northeast, including "the Yankee and industrial bailiwicks of New England, upstate New York, Michigan and Pennsylvania" to the South and the West.[10]

"The Republican Party had been moving its reliance South and West since the beginning of the New Deal cycle in 1932," Phillips wrote. "The 1968 election [in which Republican Richard Nixon beat Democrat Hubert Humphrey] confirmed the general Southern and Western impetus of 1964 [in which Republican Barry Goldwater lost to Democrat Lyndon Baines Johnson]—only the Deep South parochialism had been an aberration—and set a cyclical seal on the partisan re-alignment."[11]

But by 1972, when Nixon won every state except Massachusetts in defeating Democratic pacifist candidate George McGovern, the realignment of the Deep South away from its traditional support of the Democratic Party was complete. By then, the so-called New South embraced the GOP's religious and moral appeal, finally abandoning to 1968 Democratic Party presidential aspirant Governor George Wallace the last vestige of the tight hold the Democratic Party had retained on the South since Reconstruction.

From the presidential elections of 2000–2012, the hold the two parties had on the various states was almost identical. The Democrats could expect to win California and increasingly had a hold on Oregon, Washington, and New Mexico. By 2012, Nevada and Arizona were more inclined to vote Democratic for various reasons, including the union base in the casino towns of Reno and Las Vegas, the influx of Hispanic immigrants from across the southern border with Mexico, and the exodus from California of residents seeking to avoid high taxes and an ever-expanding state government.

The rest of the Western states were reliably Republican, as far east as the Minnesota border. But from the Minneapolis–St. Paul metropolitan area through the Great Lakes to Ohio, extending to Pennsylvania and New York, Democrats were reliably in control of presidential voting, as we have just seen, largely because of the Democratic hold on the major cities. Finally, New England is solidly Democratic, and the South is solidly Republican.

Thus the battle lines have been drawn. The same handful of toss-up states have decided the last several elections.

The 2000 election was settled in the debacle of the Florida recount. The 2004 election was settled when Ohio went for George W. Bush, narrowly rejecting John Kerry. In 2008 and 2012, Obama went to certain victory the moment Ohio and Florida settled in his column on Election Night.

But losing six of the seven battleground states in 2012?

When Romney lost, the candidate and the campaign's top advisors were dumbfounded. Truthfully, until the moment the results began to be tallied on Election Day, those closest to Romney and Romney himself could not imagine Obama would win. The final results left Romney and his top advisors in a daze. That night, Romney gave a short, respectful concession speech to a nearly deserted ballroom in the Boston Convention Center, which at the time felt like a morgue.

The next day, Romney retreated into seclusion. Reducing his staff immediately to what seemed only one assistant, Romney shut the door and did not answer phone calls. From the devastating and unexpected emotion of losing when he felt he had climbed the mountain a second time—this time to win—was almost more than Romney and those closest to him could bear. Few had any doubts Romney would now withdraw once and for all from presidential politics, having been beaten in the primaries in 2008 by McCain, and now losing to a remarkably resilient Obama, who simply refused to lose.

Romney can afford now to withdraw from politics completely, but the Republican Party cannot afford the same luxury. The moment Romney lost, the Republican postmortem on 2012 began, prompted in large part by the ten most generous donors to the campaign, who now demanded to know how the Romney campaign had managed to spend $1 billion, including hundreds of millions of their money, only to come up short.

What Romney's defeat in 2012 confirmed was that the Democratic Party still retains enough electoral power to win a presidential election even with a candidate like Barack Obama, who approached reelection with diminished expectations from the height of his euphoric arrival on the political scene in 2008, and despite an economy that persistently resists robust recovery.

Twice Obama defeated the Republican Party, each time with narrow but clear margins of victory, margins so clear that claims of voter fraud could never explain why Romney lost all but one of the swing states the campaign had worked with such singular dedication to win.

On November 7, 2012, the day after the Romney debacle, there was no assurance the Republican Party could reemerge without fundamental changes the party may or may not be able to make.

What was certain was that there are at least two questions Republicans must address if the party is to have any hope of regaining the White House in 2016: (1) What went wrong? and (2) What must be done differently in 2016 to win?

2

NO ORDINARY ELECTION

There is nothing wrong with this country that a good election cannot cure.
—Richard Nixon, 1968[1]

ON THE DAY following Barack Obama's second inauguration as president of the United States, House Speaker John Boehner told attendees at a Republican luncheon that Obama in his second term was aiming to "annihilate the Republican Party."[2]

Boehner was dead serious. The Republican House Speaker issued a startling message, putting the GOP on notice that President Barack Obama this time around had no interest even in pretending to deal respectfully with the Republican Party as the loyal opposition.

Obama, Boehner insisted, recognized that he cannot achieve his agenda if blocked by the GOP majority in the House of Representatives, the only stronghold of the federal government the Republican Party could claim after the 2012 general election. Boehner averred that the president intended to resolve this problem by waging war on the Republican Party, advancing his agenda with the goal of crushing not only Republican opposition in Congress, but also the Republican Party itself.

"In our meetings before Christmas, the President was so tired of me talking about when we were going to deal with an entitlement crisis that he looked at me and said: 'Boehner, we don't have a spending problem. We have a health-care problem.' It gives you some idea of the challenge that we're facing," Boehner said. "For a guy who's run up the deficit 60 percent—60 percent of the deficit has occurred under his watch—when you see this, and then you hear him say, 'I am not going to negotiate on the debt limit. I am not going to deal with the debt limit. That's Congress's problem!' . . . Frankly, I think it's irresponsible."

Speaking in a level tone, Boehner continued, recalling the words of Obama's second inaugural address the day before.

"And given what we heard yesterday about the President's vision for his second term, it's pretty clear to me that he knows he can't do any of that as long as the House is controlled by Republicans. So we're expecting over the next 22 months to be the focus of this Administration, as they attempt to annihilate the Republican Party," Boehner said. "And let me just tell you, I do believe that is their goal—to just shove us into the dustbin of history."[3]

The presidential election of 2012 was no ordinary election in that it marked the arrival of a new coalition of voters that have formed a Democratic majority Barack Obama would like to make permanent. To that end, Obama has steadily worked to move America toward a socialist state that the self-interest of his coalition will *never* allow to be dismantled, even after he has left the White House.

The newly emerging Democratic coalition was first identifiable during the 2000 election, even as the predominant Republican coalition—the "Southern Strategy" coalition first identified by Kevin Phillips in his 1969 book, *The Emerging Republican Majority*—began to fade.[4]

Phillips envisioned a Republican majority centered on a coalition of aging white workers angry at welfare spending, and evangelical Christians disgusted by the disobedience, disrespect, and violence of the New Left in the Nixon years.

Reagan rode the Phillips coalition to victory twice. It took the incompetence of the Democratic Party to give the "Southern Strategy" a last gasp under George H. W. Bush and his son George W. Bush.

Even during the Bush era, however, the seeds of Obama's new coalition were starting to sprout. At best, Bush Sr. and Son were RINOs—"Republicans in Name Only"—who under architect Karl Rove's tutelage expanded the social welfare state through a myriad of measures, including government-funded prescription drugs and an international effort—through the Security and Prosperity Partnership of North America, for example—to push the USA toward continental integration emulating the European Union. Even the Republicans, it seems, have been playing into the left's hand.

Yet with his reelection in 2012, Obama is making the mistake many second-term presidents have made after the Twenty-Second Amendment was ratified to the Constitution in 1951. Obama imagines that he has crafted a coalition that will persist beyond his presidency, creating for the first time in US history a permanent Democratic Party majority capable of crushing the Republican Party as viable opposition.

In many ways, Obama has calculated correctly. Under the leadership of John Boehner in the House and Mitch McConnell in the Senate, the Republican Party today is dominated by a GOP establishment that, led by Karl Rove, fancy themselves big-government conservatives, or in terms of a previous era, "Big Tent Republicans," inclusive of diversity even on social issues key to conservatives, such as same-sex marriage and abortion.

The contradiction inherent in the term "big-government conservative," however, reveals the problem. "Big-government conservatives" have nothing in common with the forces behind a Reagan Revolution that espoused government *as* the problem, not the solution. The "Big Tent Republican" approach tends to include those who are conservative only on fiscal issues, while opening the party up to a range of opinions and participants mirroring the Democrats on social and moral issues, ranging from the "GO-Proud" advocates of sexual diversity to open-borders enthusiasts who desire to see passed comprehensive immigration reform bills, including DREAM Act provisions.

The GOP establishment has always been internationalist, since the days when the GOP establishment was led by Nelson Rockefeller and referred to by conservatives derisively as the "Rockefeller wing" of the Republican Party, a term that served as code for the bankers, Wall Street tycoons, and big-business boards that viewed the Republican Party as if it were an exclusive country club. Under the Rockefeller wing, the Republican Party forwarded a series of losers as presidential candidates, including Wendell Willkie in 1940 and Thomas Dewey in both 1944 and 1948. Dwight Eisenhower broke this trend in 1952 and 1956, but only because he was by then a grandfatherly hero most Americans attributed with having won World War II.

Pulitzer Prize–winning author and historian Garry Wills was right when he concluded in his famous 1970 book, *Nixon Agonistes,* that Nixon's election in 1968 marked the end of the New Deal.

"The Democrats have been the majority party over the last three decades, so durable was that coalition," Wills wrote. "But in 1968, Nixon claimed, history was accomplishing another of its large realignments—that year would be for Republicans what 1932 was for Democrats."[5]

Quoting from a pamphlet titled "A New Alignment for American Unity," authored in Nixon's name during the run-up to the 1968 election, Wills identified the following five groups "aligned" in Nixon's new majority:

> These were (1) the traditional Republican—i.e., the proponent of free enterprise, (2) the new Liberal, asking for "participatory democracy" which puts "personal liberty ahead of the dictates of the State," (3) the new South, "interpreting the old doctrine of states' rights in new ways," (4) the black militant who wants opportunity, not the dole, a "piece of the action," not degrading welfare, and (5) "the silent center, the millions of people in the middle of the American political spectrum who do not demonstrate, who do not picket or protest loudly."[6]

Nixon's particular genius was always his ability to identify and speak to a "silent majority," who, like Nixon himself, felt deep resentment toward the type of power and privilege that was best demonstrated in the Kennedy family. This brand of authority and license led Democrats of privilege, including FDR, into what Nixon believed was an inauthentic identification with the poor as a way to assuage guilt. In Nixon's eyes, this resulted in nothing of lasting economic value ever done for the poor, except to exploit them for the advantage of the Democratic Party upper class. Perhaps not surprisingly, with his Ivy League education, Barack Obama, who, much like

FDR and JFK, rose to power championing the poor (but having never held a significant job in the private economy), falls into this category.

Obama's *new* Democratic majority coalition, as we will see in a later chapter, is cobbled together out of modern-day elements of FDR's original New Deal coalition. Based on African Americans who almost universally vote for Obama, the coalition also includes:

- Hispanics looking for citizenship and economic advancement in their new home;
- single women and radical feminists concerned about advancing against men in the workplace and managing the needs of childbearing without a husband;
- union workers, and especially government union workers, who cling to the Democratic Party fearing the labor movement is fading into irrelevancy; and
- youths of the Millennial generation coming of voting age, desperately concerned that they will not be able to pay off student loans or find employment equal to their level of education.

All these groups look to big government to set the regulatory table unfairly in their advantage and to pay them generously from the public treasury to compensate for their economic plight.

Obama correctly calculates that he can count on big-government Republicans in Congress to sympathize quietly with the massive federal welfare state he is intent on building. Clearly, House Speaker Boehner, Senate Minority Leader Mitch McConnell, and their Republican friends in Congress loathe the idea of being blamed in public opinion polls for refusing to raise the debt ceiling and shutting down government, with the resulting stoppage in government-issued checks otherwise sent routinely and reliably to various constituents within the Obama coalition. Even though Congressional Republicans make noises about containing government spending, Obama knows that by refusing to make concessions, he guarantees Boehner and McConnell will cave in, giving last-minute approval to Obama to borrow and spend whatever he wants. Obama further calculates that he can ultimately force Boehner and McConnell to pass the massive taxes needed to fund a social welfare state beyond the dreams even of FDR or LBJ, simply because the big-government Republicans do not have the will to say no to groups "Big Tent Republicans" feel they must include to gain electoral victory.

Truthfully, Obama has decided he can disregard a Republican-controlled House of Representatives because he knows he can crush big-government and Big Tent Republicans in the polls, if Boehner and McConnell were somehow to discover the courage to force a fiscal showdown over spending.

The risk Obama runs is common to all socialists. Margaret Thatcher is widely credited with saying it best: "Eventually you run out of other people's money [to spend]."[7]

But Obama shows no signs of worrying that the United States will borrow its way into financial insolvency under his management. The economists advising the Obama administration and the Federal Reserve under the leadership of Ben Bernanke act as if they truly believe the ability of the United States to borrow and spend money without adverse economic consequences knows no limit. The last line of defense against Obama remains those few Reagan conservatives yet active politically and a Tea Party that so far has resisted being completely co-opted by the Republican establishment.

Ironically, although Reagan conservatives and Tea Party members see the Republican Party as their natural home, the GOP establishment loathes both groups, simply because both groups challenge the reliance the GOP establishment has on expanding government to pay themselves. In the end, the Democratic Party establishment, now consisting of the former revolutionary New Left radicals of the 1960s, agrees fundamentally with the GOP establishment that the political game in the United States remains about what it was always about—money—and about power to a lesser degree, but only because power can be translated into money. In the era of billion-dollar presidential campaigns, the establishments of both parties agree the goal is not necessarily winning the White House or Congress, but about being able to raise $1.5 billion for the next presidential election cycle. Meanwhile, the establishment center of neither party shows any inclination to exert the type of courage and determination needed to reduce the burgeoning entitlement state if the United States is to have any real chance of ever again balancing the federal budget. Ironically, the other solution to the problem—namely, growing the economy so as to generate higher tax revenue without having to raise tax rates—remains a remote possibility as long as the only alternative to borrowing is to raise taxes one way or another in a political environment where no politician wants to say no.

The ultimate problem Obama faces is that nothing in US politics lasts forever, including the modern-day New Deal alignment he has cobbled together. FDR's original New Deal coalition lasted for decades, arguably from 1932 until 1968. The Democratic Party has a long way to go to repeat that feat with Obama's majority coalition.

In 2016, provided the nation still respects the Constitution enough to demand the enforcement of the Twenty-Second Amendment, Obama must leave the White House. A lame duck president by definition, Obama can expect to have a rocky time as members of his own party jockey for position to succeed him.

What broke up the New Deal coalition as much as anything was resentment white workers and evangelical Christians felt for being taxed to pay social welfare benefits for minorities and those considered of insufficient moral character because they accept reliance upon the government for sustenance, instead of working whatever jobs were available or relying on charity until they could recover their economic footing.

By the time Nixon was elected in 1968, his majority Republican coalition felt enough time and precious tax revenue had been spent on LBJ's Great Society and War on Poverty to assuage everyone's guilt.

In analyzing Reagan's rise to power, Garry Wills made an important observation: "[California] is a state with a million more registered Democrats than Republicans, which swept Reagan into office by a million votes."[8]

Reagan, like Obama, had charisma. And Reagan, like Obama, was a celebrity.

How ironic it was that the conservative hero, Ronald Reagan, should have arisen out of leftist Hollywood. Obama arose out of leftist Chicago, much the birthplace since the 1930s of a socialist style of union politics that embraced the Saul Alinsky radicalism of the 1950s and 1960s. Today, Obama is succeeding in advancing far-left goals the radical New Left of the 1960s had no hope of implementing without him. The irony is that Reagan managed to advance true conservative goals despite having to emerge from the midst of liberal-dominated politics. If Reagan achieved that in the 1970s and 1980s, a Republican conservative with charisma could do so once again.

Reagan knew the Republican coalition he inherited from Richard Nixon would have reelected him a third time, almost as certainly as Obama must know the Democratic coalition he inherited from Bill Clinton would reelect him a third time. Absent the ability to run Obama a third time, however, the Democratic Party faces a less certain lock on the presidency, unless a celebrity of Hillary Clinton's magnitude manages despite her age to endure a two-year or longer grueling presidential primary and general election campaign.

But there is another, more important point: Reagan conservatives and Tea Party activists have a hope, not only of remaining relevant, but also of controlling the Republican Party, provided one or more of the advancing stars from among the growing number of Republican governors and new generation of Republican leaders in Congress emerges from the ranks as a sufficiently charismatic candidate to run for president. Even kingmaker Karl Rove, determined to advance himself by exerting a self-derived prerogative to say who should and should not get the GOP-establishment seal of approval to run for office, must step aside if confronted directly by a new Reagan who emerges from truly conservative ranks to challenge Rove's big-government and internationalist ambitions to create a modern-era Big Tent Republican Party.

Within the next four years, however, politics should not be expected to be pretty in either the Democratic or Republican party. Within both parties, infighting is required for a new leader to emerge. It took Reagan a decade and a half of struggle, dating back to the mid-1960s, to emerge first as governor in California and then as presidential candidate. Every step of the way, Reagan had to fight the same GOP establishment that was happy to undermine Goldwater in 1964. Similarly, if Hillary is to emerge as the Democratic Party candidate in 2016, she will have to push back contenders who see her as a centrist, despite her youthful years in which she was a true Saul Alinsky acolyte.

Despite presidential victories in 2008 and 2012, the next four years be not be entirely pleasant for Democrats. In the midterm 2014 elections, Democrats will have to hope a tanking economy does not destroy their ambitions to retake the House and expand the Democratic majority in the Senate. Given the nature of the coalition Obama has twice successfully courted for victory, Democratic Party success now depends on being able to continue bribing with ever-increasing government spending the modern-day New Deal coalition Obama has ridden to power. Failure to deliver economic gains promised could well lead to a credibility gap for a less charismatic Democrat seeking to overcome a record number of "Hope and Change" promises on which Obama failed to deliver.

What the nation will not tolerate easily is a return to the civil violence and race riots of the late 1960s or the gasoline lines of Jimmy Carter's presidency. African Americans and Hispanics fighting over housing and jobs will not be a picture that facilitates Obama passing through Congress an Obama administration plan of comprehensive immigration reform that amounts to amnesty. Nor will youths of the Millennial generation be happy to wait until well into middle age before they feel sufficiently economically secure to buy homes, get married, and start families.

By campaigning on themes of class conflict, Obama divided further an already divided nation in which nearly half pay no income tax, yet receive ample government-funded social welfare from a complex of entitlement programs even FDR and LBJ would have found dazzling.

Since the Civil War, this nation has never been as close to a class war amplified by a race war as it is today. The divide between "red" counties that voted Republican for president in 2012 and "blue" counties that voted Democratic makes it clear Democrats are in control of the nation's urban areas, with Republicans still dominating the South and much of the West.

With northeastern cities increasingly being abandoned to an unemployed and increasingly unemployable minority poor, the nation is on the verge of creating a generational underclass for which education is minimal and a "gangsta" drug culture predominates.

If Garry Wills was correct that the Republican majority coalition under Nixon was held together by resentment, the Democratic majority coalition under Obama is defined by a different kind of resentment—namely the resentment the "have-nots" feel for the economic advantages the "haves" enjoy. The obverse of the economic resentment felt by the "have-nots" is the fear of having to live without government-funded social welfare. Ever-increasing government spending on entitlement programs is the glue that holds the Obama coalition together.

In this divided nation, the fear the "haves" feel is fear of the confiscatory taxes and redistribution of income required to satisfy the "have-nots," who are taught by radical leftist Saul Alinsky to always demand more. The glue that holds the Reagan conservatives and Tea Party patriots together is the fear that a federal government expanded to the level demanded by the far left currently controlling the Democratic Party will leave the

United States an economically bankrupt nation, stripped of the liberty this nation was created to protect. What Reagan conservatives and Tea Party patriots fear is that an America weakened by repeated, trillion-dollar budget deficits and a national debt exceeding the nation's GDP under Obama is going to be a much crueler and more dangerous nation in which to live. A middle class squeezed to extinction and facing prolonged unemployment and never-ending home foreclosures is a certain formula for the type of discontent and protest in the streets witnessed in Europe as various EU nations like Greece have spent themselves into bankruptcy, much as the United States is doing right now. We are not yet at the point where the red states are seceding from the Union. But those states currently suing the federal government to opt out of the expanded social welfare state are already exerting the prerogative to declare what the Supreme Court by one vote has refused to declare, namely that under the Tenth Amendment, programs like Obamacare are by their very nature unconstitutional in ambition, intent, and implementation. Obama won reelection in 2012 by intensifying these conflicts, not by providing solutions to the fundamental social and economic problems the United States faces today. Rather than show any sign of willingness to compromise with his political opponents, Obama has chosen a message that energizes a political base that feels economically disenfranchised, while demonizing Republican candidate Mitt Romney as a "vulture capitalist" who cared nothing for the African Americans, Hispanics, single women, union workers, or the youths of the Millennial generation the Democrats are courting.

Given the economic problems on the horizon, the stability of the Obama majority coalition is by no means certain, especially after he is constitutionally forced to step down in 2016.

What happens then will depend on how well we understand what happened in 2012.

3

WHAT YOU DON'T KNOW *WILL* HURT YOU

We started with our supporters on the ground and they led us to victory.
—David Plouffe, *The Audacity to Win* (2009)[1]

MERELY APPEALING TO WIDE SWATHS of the culture and various special-interest groups isn't enough to get a candidate elected president, not even for the charismatic Obama. To make the strategy really pay off, the candidate has to also get those supporters to vote.

GOP postmortem analyses of the 2012 presidential election agreed that Obama's victory was fueled precisely by his use of technology and sophisticated behavioral science in understanding voting behavior to get voters to the polls.

As a result, the prognosis for all future elections is relatively simple: Here come the geeks!

Smoke-filled rooms that in bygone days were the domain of ward bosses are about to be replaced with "computer caves," where the denizens are likely to be academics who have never actually had an in-person conversation with a voter.

"OBAMA-METRICS"

Obama beat Romney the minute the Chicago-based bosses who managed his campaign, including Jim Messina and David Plouffe, brought ward politics to the Internet age.

In every political campaign there are two questions professional politicians ask regarding each voter: (1) Will this person vote? and (2) Who will the person vote for? The key to winning most elections reduces to getting the voters most likely to vote for your candidate to turn out on Election Day.

Beginning in 2008, the Obama presidential campaign resolved to apply advanced computer and Internet capabilities to answer these questions. What the Obama geeks accomplished working out of an enclosed facility within Obama's Chicago campaign headquarters, designated as "the Cave," will transform all future presidential campaigns.

"What [the Obama campaign analytics] gave us was the ability to run a national presidential campaign the way you'd do a local ward campaign," claimed David Simas, the director of opinion research for Obama's 2012 presidential campaign. "You know the people on your block. People have relationships with one another, and you leverage them so you know the way they talk about issues, what they're discussing at the coffee shop."[2]

In writing his 2012 bestseller, titled *The Victory Lab: The Secret Science of Winning Campaigns*,[3] a book Politico has dubbed "*Moneyball* for politics,"[4] journalist Sasha Issenberg explained how Obama's analytics team used behavioral science, psychological research, and randomized field experiments to construct a voter-intelligence system that would permit them to know how particular voters might vote or change their candidate preferences, even before the voters know themselves.

Just as the "Moneyball" tactics of computer geek Bill James revolutionized professional baseball by devising a set of unconventional statistics known as "sabermetrics" that permitted general managers to produce championship teams by hiring the right players, not the most expensive players,[5] the goal of the geeks working in Obama's campaign "Cave" was similar—to devise a set of equations that permitted them to identify, communicate with, and get to the polls not just any voters, but voters committed to voting for Obama.

After Oakland Athletics General Manager Billy Beane began applying sabermetrics to craft cost-effective teams capable of winning, the game of baseball was so transformed that general managers who refused to apply James's methods risked their jobs, choosing instead to put on the field costly baseball players capable only of producing disappointing results.

The geeks in Obama's 2012 campaign "Cave" accomplished the same. Future presidential campaigns might choose to ignore "Obama-metrics," but they would do so at the risk of losing.

Methodologies that had dominated the art of political consultation since the 1960s, including polls, focus groups, direct-mail campaigns, telephone banks, door-knocking, voter canvassing, and all forms of advertising, would never be the same after the Obama presidential campaigns of 2008 and 2012. Obama's team transformed the art of electioneering with methodologies borrowed from economics, political science, and psychology. Obama's geeks ran social science randomized field experiments to test outcomes in fundraising campaigns. They achieved breakthrough insights in sociology and political science in understanding voting behavior by utilizing empirically derived algorithms drawn from econometric methods. And they utilized the methodology of association maps obtained from burgeoning social networking technologies available only on the Internet, working with websites such as Facebook and Twitter that no one had imagined existing only a few years ago.

In the late 1980s, Democratic media consultants like Bob Shrum could brag that a campaign rally is "three people around a television set."[6] But now, in the age of smartphones, television-focused media consultants are about to become as obsolete as television sets and landline telephones—technologies ubiquitous in the post–World War II world that those approaching voting age today increasingly consider clumsy, redundant, and unnecessary.

Like a dinosaur that doesn't know it's a dying breed, Romney's campaign stressed traditional campaign methodologies, relying on messaging to frame the candidate, television and radio advertising to communicate the candidate's message to voters, and polling to measure the effect. A large part of the embarrassment GOP party professionals felt over losing to Obama a second time involved the realization that Mitt Romney, a candidate who predicated much of his election hopes on touting a successful business career, was outdone by Barack Obama, who at most brags of being a "community organizer." But where Obama applied what he had learned as a community organizer into techniques that brought his presidential campaign down to the grassroots level, Romney failed to apply his business management acumen to run a campaign that functioned like a successful Fortune 500 company.

Romney had more than a billion dollars to spend on his presidential campaign in 2012, yet the resources the Romney campaign devoted to developing computer-based "get out the vote," or GOTV, technology paled in comparison to the investment the Obama campaign made. Romney's campaign wrongly believed the candidate's message itself, properly communicated via traditional media with an emphasis on television and measured through polling, was sufficient to get out enough Republican voters to win.

Even in hindsight, despite an undisputed defeat, Romney campaign chief strategist Stuart Stevens continued after the election to insist messaging, not computer technology, wins elections. Stevens, in an opinion piece published in the *Washington Post* after the election, rejected the proposition that Obama defeated Romney because of superior voter-intelligence technology, describing Obama as "a charismatic African American president with a billion dollars, no primary and media that often felt morally conflicted about being critical."[7]

Stevens insisted that despite Obama's technological advantage, the Romney campaign generated an important message that came within reach of capturing the White House.

"But having been involved in three presidential races, two of which we won closely and one that we lost closely, I know enough to know that we weren't brilliant because Florida went our way in 2000 or enough Ohioans stuck with us in 2004," Stevens wrote in the editorial. "Losing is just losing. It's not a mandate to throw out every idea that the candidate championed, and I would hope it's not seen as an excuse to show disrespect for a good man who fought hard for values we admire."[8]

In an interview on the CBS "This Morning" show given one day after Stevens's editorial appeared in the *Washington Post,* he was even more direct in rejecting the contention that the computer-generated GOTV scheme devised by Obama consultants Jim Messina and David Plouffe was responsible for Obama's successful reelection campaign, pointing out that Obama received 3.5 million fewer votes in 2012 than in 2008. "I'm a bit baffled that people look at the Obama campaign and say they won because of their ground game," Stevens told the CBS audience. "At face value, when they turned out more voters four years ago than they did this time, I would give them more credit for their message in those states rather than just their ground game. I think it's somewhat underselling what the Obama campaign did in their messaging capability to say it was just a ground game."[9]

Stevens insisted messaging, not the ground game, was the critical variable in winning elections.

Stevens, however, was wrong.

THE BATTLE OF THE WHALES

The battle of GOTV computer technology in the 2012 presidential campaign boiled down to a contest between two whales: Narwhal versus ORCA.

Obama's tech team code-named its GOTV software "Narwhal," after a medium-sized whale that *National Geographic* describes as "the unicorn of the sea, a pale-colored porpoise found in Arctic coastal waters and rivers," a two-toothed animal with a prominent tooth that in males grows into a swordlike spiral tusk up to 8.8 feet long.[10]

Not to be outdone, the Romney tech team code-named their GOTV software "ORCA," after a killer whale that *National Geographic* describes as "the largest of the dolphins and one of the world's most powerful predators," which feeds on marine mammals such as seals, sea lions, and even whales, employing teeth that can be four inches long.[11]

The GOP point was that orcas eat narwhals, a natural science fact that appealed to GOP techies who wanted to imply that the Romney GOTV computer software would eat the Obama GOTV computer software for lunch.

Senior editor Alexis Madrigal, writing in the *Atlantic* ten days after the election, noted that on October 21, the Obama campaign shock-tested Narwhal, putting the technology through what geeks call "live action role playing," or "LARPing," to determine how the computer/Internet system would perform under every possible disaster situation.[12] What the Obama team realized was that on Election Day, the Narwhal GOTV data platform could be expected to experience an exponential surge in volume, requiring sufficient bandwidth for the Cave in the Obama headquarters in Chicago to receive data from campaign workers and volunteers in the field, and to issue directives back to the field. Without sufficient bandwidth, Narwhal would crash on Election Day, leaving campaign workers and volunteers in the field without the information and instructions needed from headquarters to coordinate efforts to transport voters to the polls so no prospective Obama voter would be left stranded without the communication or assistance needed to go vote.

Harper Reed, Obama's tech director, told the magazine, "I know we had the best technology team I've ever worked with, but we didn't know if it would work. I was incredibly confident it would work. I was betting a lot on it. We had time. We had resources. We had done what we thought would work, and it still could have broken. Something could have happened."[13]

So, on October 21, more than two full weeks before Election Day, Reed put Narwhal through "every possible disaster situation." He described the testing to the *Atlantic* as "three actual all-day sessions of destroying everything we had built."[14]

When Amazon, a key facility on which Narwhal had been built, experienced a shutdown in services, the Obama tech team experienced no downtime, because the tech team had already game-played that scenario. When Hurricane Sandy hit on October 29, Narwhal's East Coast infrastructure continued functioning because the tech team had backed up all their computer applications to West Coast facilities in the possibility that East Coast facilities might go down.

On Election Day, however, Romney's ORCA crashed, leaving thousands of Republican volunteers standing around. Unable to communicate with headquarters in Boston, they couldn't know who had voted and who had not, and were powerless to get instructions to Romney supporters who had not yet voted.

Writing in the *Boston Globe,* reporter Michael Kranish reported the Romney team had endeavored to keep ORCA secret until just before the election in order to prevent hacking of the system. "It was then trumpeted by Romney's aides as an unrivaled high-tech means of communicating with more than 30,000 fieldworkers who were stationed at polling places on Election Day," Kranish wrote. "These volunteers were supposed to track who voted and to alert Boston headquarters if turnout was lower than expected at key precincts."[15]

Yet, up until Election Day, the Romney team believed incorrectly its tech team had bettered Obama's tech team.

In a video released to campaign workers and volunteers in the field on October 31, Romney bragged about ORCA, saying on camera:

> Hello. The team in Boston has been updating me on the progress of our special Election Day project, and I'm encouraged to hear how well it's coming along. As part of this task force, you'll be the key link in providing critical real-time information to me and to the staff, so that we can ensure that every last supporter makes it to the polls. With state-of-the-art technology and an extremely dedicated group of volunteers, our campaign will have an unprecedented advantage on Election Day. It means a great deal to me to have such dedicated volunteers, and that's why I wanted to take a moment to personally thank you for your willingness to help. I know it's not an easy thing to volunteer for an entire day in the middle of the week. I know many of you have taken off from work and made other sacrifices to be a part of our team on such an important day for our country. I can't thank you enough for your help, and I'm so grateful to have you on our team. Together, we can restore the American dream.[16]

When ORCA crashed on Election Day, America knew Romney, as the chairman of his own presidential campaign, had failed to put in place a chief executive officer who could get the job done.

"We know ORCA was not tested properly because it failed," John Ekdahl, a thirty-four-year-old Romney campaign worker and computer expert from Jacksonville, Florida, told WND in an exclusive interview. "The Romney campaign did not properly train the volunteers how to use the ORCA system. Remarkably, the program was not made operative until Election Day."[17]

Ekdahl was particularly critical that the Romney campaign assumed the computerized GOTV system would work flawlessly on Election Day, even though no one had bothered to proof out fundamental practical realities.

"Sure, the Romney campaign held training sessions and there were conference calls, but that's not enough," he explained. "You need to have people in the field play with the system in advance, so they and you know technically the system works. The Romney campaign did no checking into how technically advanced the volunteer users were. The campaign didn't even bother to find out if the volunteers had iPads or smart phones."[18]

Writing on a computer blog immediately after the election, Ekdahl detailed that the entire purpose of ORCA was to digitize the decades-old practice of what in campaign methodology are known as "strike lists," paper-and-pen lists of people who had voted that were marked off hourly by campaign workers in the precincts and walked back to headquarters. Headquarters workers could then assign volunteers to go round up the people who had not yet voted, to encourage them to get to the polls.

"From the very start there were warning signs," Ekdahl noted on the Internet blog. "After signing up, you were invited to take part in nightly conference calls. The calls were more of the slick marketing speech type than helpful training sessions. There was a lot of 'rah-rahs' and lofty talk about how this would change the ballgame."[19]

But, Ekdahl noted, nobody at Romney headquarters in Boston bothered to stress test ORCA to see how it would actually perform under the volume of traffic that could be expected on Election Day.

Reporting in the *Boston Globe,* Kranish interviewed Ekdahl as well. Ekdahl told the newspaper the Romney campaign finally sent field volunteers a sixty-page document the day before the election that included instructions on how to use the ORCA program, which turned out to be a web page, not a typical smartphone application. When Ekdahl went to his assigned polling place, he was told he needed a certificate to work there, a requirement the Romney instruction document had not mentioned.

"[Ekdahl] spent several hours trying to tell the campaign about the problem but got nowhere," Kranish reported. "He gave up at 2 p.m., depriving the campaign of data at his station. He said he heard from a number of other volunteers across the country who had the same problem."[20]

Kranish reported that Romney campaign workers nationwide found on Election Day their usernames and passwords were wrong, reissued PINs failed to work, and the application would not be available in the iTunes or the Android store. At Boston's TD Garden, where eight hundred Romney workers were staffing phones and computers to direct fieldworkers overseeing the turnout, ORCA crashed for some ninety minutes, leaving the Romney campaign no effective means to communicate with some thirty thousand fieldworkers who were supposedly positioned at polling places on Election Day to report if turnout was lower than expected in precincts.

"The Garden definitely kind of buckled under the strain," Zac Moffatt, the Romney campaign digital director, told the *Boston Globe* in an interview. "The system wasn't ready for the amount of information incoming."[21]

Had ORCA worked on Election Day, Romney might have swung the election by getting out enough supporters who would not vote without assistance from a paid campaign fieldworker or a volunteer. The extra effort may have involved a ride to the polls or a couple of hours of arranged child care, but when thirty thousand Romney volunteers stood around on Election Day awaiting instructions, the opportunity was lost.

That ORCA was never beta-tested prior to Election Day is an unforgivable error that only technological rookies would be expected to make. Either that or the campaign assigned little importance to the technological GOTV data platform after being repeatedly encouraged by chief strategist Stuart Stevens that all Romney needed to bring out voters was a compelling message.

What would have been wrong with the Romney campaign seeking to supplement a compelling message with a certain-to-work GOTV effort? Perhaps Harper Reed was right when he told *Atlantic* magazine that the GOP messed up "in the hubris department."[22] But then, perhaps the *National Review* was also correct in observing that no GOP presidential campaign was likely to hire the computer geeks the Obama campaign hired, oddballs with facial hair like Harper Reed's, who fancied themselves as renegades living a fringe lifestyle outside polite society, computer hackers with a mission more comfortable in a computer start-up than a corporate management position.[23]

The ORCA disaster was so catastrophic that in the aftermath of the November 6 election, reporters investigating why the computer system failed had a hard time getting anyone in the Romney camp to take responsibility for having created the system in the first place.

The Daily Caller reported ten days after Election Day, "The makers of the campaign's over-hyped and extremely secretive Project ORCA election reporting tool are still nowhere to be found."[24]

According to the Daily Caller report, Romney senior campaign staff members were either hiding in silence or claiming they were not involved with ORCA at all. In the end, the Romney campaign paid $17 million to Moffatt's consulting firm, Targeted Victory, not including Moffatt's own salary and bonuses paid to Moffatt-hired digital staffers.[25]

Overestimating their more traditional GOTV methods and unaware their computer-driven technology was going to amount to a beached whale on Election Day, Romney-paid campaign workers in the field actually bragged that their ground game was going to be the margin of victory.

"In 2008, Obama won independents, but today we are winning independent voters overwhelmingly in Ohio," Scott Jennings, the Romney-Ryan campaign manager told me at an October rally in Ohio. "There's no way we can win independents by ten points and lose Ohio."

Jennings quantified what he considered the Romney ground-game advantage: "Sometime this week we are going to have knocked on two million doors since May, and we're going to make the six millionth voter contact. We are knocking on doors in all eighty-eight counties. We think absolutely this face-to-face contact is what's going to cut through all the clutter."

I asked Jennings if Obama didn't have an advantage with the number of offices and campaign workers in Ohio.

"Yes," Jennings admitted, "but the Obama offices are rented and the staff are paid. They've collected a lot of rent payments and a lot of leases. We've collected a lot of volunteers."

What about early voting?

"In 2008, Obama won the early voting by about 20 percent. We think today—with their erosion and our surge—the Democrats are winning the early voting by about 6 percent," Jennings conceded. "I'm not going to tell you we are going to win early voting, but we're keeping it close, we are going to blow them out on Election Day, and that's how we're going to win this race."

Upon further investigation, however, the door knocks Jennings cited did not require an in-person discussion with the occupants. Leaving printed campaign material in the mailbox was considered a "door knock," even when no one was home. Furthermore, there was no attempt to record in detail conversations with prospective voters. Romney fieldworkers canvassing voters on foot lacked handheld technology that would have permitted them to record important demographic data about interviewees or answers to opinion questions, including whether or not the people being interviewed intended to vote, and if so, whether they intended to vote for Romney.

"Door knocks" to Scott Jennings meant just that—not that data on individual voters were being collected for integration into a master database, nor that lists of likely supporters were being maintained for analysis by the campaign headquarters data managers. Where the Obama campaign geeks were harvesting information with handheld electronic devices that could be translated by headquarters computer analytics into operational plans that could be electronically transmitted to the field to get out the vote on Election Day, Romney's campaign workers were using a campaign methodology that was worn out decades ago, amounting to little more than expending shoe leather to leave behind some campaign literature when no one was home.

OBAMA'S ADVANCED ANALYTICS

GOTV technologies, however, only scratched the surface of what was going on inside Obama's "Cave" in Chicago campaign headquarters. Within the Obama campaign's complex digital and technology organization chart, a management box at the top of the chart was reserved for twenty-nine-year-old Dan Wagner, who oversaw a separate department broadly termed "Analytics," an area to which some fifty people reported. Wagner came to politics after studying econometrics at the University of Chicago and working at a Chicago economic consultancy firm.

Econometrics is a relatively arcane statistical specialty within economics that attempts to apply mathematical and statistical equations to available economic data to predict trends and outcomes in a wide range of dependent variables, ranging from the price of gold tomorrow to interest rate future values a year from today. Econometricians are typically more comfortable with multiple regression analyses, simultaneous equations models, and time series analysis than talking with people. Yet Wagner and other quantitatively trained scientists have learned that they don't have to talk to people when the science of econometrics can be used to identify variables that predict voting behavior precisely enough to forecast election outcomes.

Wagner first joined Obama's campaign team in 2008, when he agreed to serve as deputy manager of Obama's voter file, for a salary of $2,500 a month. Journalist Sasha Issenberg noted that in 2008, Obama's computers "were collecting a staggering volume of information on 100 million Americans and sifting through it to discern patterns and relationships."[26] This is the type of work in which econometricians like Dan Wagner were specifically trained to excel.

For the 2008 Iowa Caucus, Wagner ended up creating what was known as the "Caucus Math Tool," a computer program that could be loaded onto laptops that Obama campaign workers could carry into the field. Fieldworkers entered caucus tallies into the Caucus Math Tool after each round of voting and in turn were instructed on how to adjust for the next round of voting, so as to best position Obama to win or advance in that caucus round.

Econometricians are scientifically trained to create a "black box" into which various items of data are entered—the independent variables—such that the black box emits a prediction or instruction—the dependent variables—that, as with Wagner's Caucus Math Tool, tells campaign workers in the field what to do next.

The Obama Analytics Team took the computer science of political campaigns to a new dimension. What the Obama team aspired to do had never before been done: namely, to assemble a group of scientifically trained data analysts who could work miracles collecting information about individual voters that would permit accurate predictions of how a particular person would respond to a particular television advertisement or to a version of an e-mailed fund solicitation versus a differently worded version. Obama's geeks aspired to know how a particular person would respond to any given campaign message or policy issue, and ultimately whether a particular voter favored Obama or not, and whether that voter was likely to vote.

The mathematical modeling capabilities of Dan Wagner's analytics team proved so reliable the campaign was able to raise hundreds of millions of dollars on the Internet. In the process, Wagner's geeks were able to pinpoint individual voters, otherwise largely undetectable, living outside Democratic strongholds, who could be persuaded to vote for Obama despite who their neighbors, peers, coworkers and bosses, or even other members of their families were planning to vote for. Adding these outlying Obama supporters to Obama supporters Wagner's geeks knew lived in "blue state" strongholds gave team Obama a decided advantage when it came to cutting into the other side's margins.

Obama's campaign analytics introduced into political campaign science three arcane concepts that before 2012 had never before been applied to a presidential election: microtargeting, predictive algorithms, and randomized field experiments. A brief description of each follows, preceded by an admonition that anyone who wants to understand how to win elections from 2012 going forward has no alternative but to master these concepts:

- **Microtargeting** is the application of mass data collected in huge databases to individual people. The easiest way to understand microtargeting is to realize that commercial vendors, such as credit card companies, routinely collect massive amounts of data on individual cardholders, including where each purchase was made and how much the purchase cost. Data include payment history information, such as whether or not each month's minimum credit payment was made on time, average credit balances over time, and total interest charges attributed to each cardholder. The databases combine all the information gathered when the individual applied for the credit card, including any employment or annual income information that may have been in the credit report obtained after the credit card applicant gave approval to conduct a background check by providing a Social Security number and signing a form authorizing the credit card company to obtain, examine, and collect background information of all types—financial or otherwise. The Obama campaign in 2012 purchased many different commercially available databases to combine the data into the personal files the Obama geeks were assembling on millions of individual voters across the nation, and especially in the battleground states.

- **Predictive algorithms** are equations in which the independent variables on the left side of the equal sign are weighted and evaluated in relationship with one another to predict the value of the dependent variable that appears on the right side of the equation. Econometrics is a science, the predictive algorithms of which are typically regression equations taught in every beginning-level college statistics class. An example of a predictive algorithm applicable to voting could combine variables drawn from demographic information (age, sex, race, etc.), variables drawn from economic data (income, credit card balances, outstanding bank loans, telephone bills, etc.), and voting data (answers to survey questions on attitudes toward government or public policy issues) to predict whether a particular voter supported Obama or not and the probability that voter would actually go to vote. Predictive algorithms, once developed, can be applied to map likely outcomes (e.g., voter preference and/or probability of voting) onto voters who share similar characteristics (i.e., mapped onto voters with identical or similar configurations of independent variables).

- **Randomized field experiments** involve taking various treatments, for instance whether or not a prospective voter receives a particular direct mail piece or views a particular television commercial, and applying these treatments randomly, such that some prospective voters are chosen randomly to get the direct mail piece and some are not, or some prospective voters are chosen randomly to view the television commercial and some are not. The scientist then measures outcome, whether a person is likely to support and/or vote for a candidate or not, based on the impact of getting the direct mail piece or viewing the television commercial. If the only difference between the test group and the control group randomly selected was the "treatment" (getting the mail piece or not, watching the television commercial or not), and the test group has a statistically significant difference in outcome (is more or less likely to support or vote for a particular candidate), then the effect can be assumed to be due to the treatment, such that the direct mail piece or television commercial is judged to have been successful or not in influencing voting.

Two Yale political scientists revolutionized political campaigns when they conducted randomized field experiments that showed voting turnout could be increased by mailing to prospective voters summaries of how they and their neighbors had voted in previous elections, with the suggestion that the voting turnout in the current year's election would also be published. In other words, the political scientists demonstrated people could be shamed into voting, a conclusion proven valid by randomized field testing.[27]

Interestingly, these same Yale political scientists ran field experiments that showed that phone calls, especially robo-calls made by machine, had almost no effect on getting out the vote. What proved most effective in a GOTV effort was to have knowledgeable canvassers meet in person with prospective voters to interview them, asking questions and recording the prospective voters' opinions on a series of public policy questions. The Obama analytics team appreciated the impact of these academic voting studies from the start, while the Romney tech team was relying on old campaign adages advising that a message well crafted by "experts" in public relations and advertising was sufficient to win the presidency. Obama's team knew from the beginning that much of what the Romney team was doing in the field was a waste of time. Even more important, the Obama team came to those conclusions scientifically. It was not simply a matter of knowing their voters by name; Obama's geeks could profile Obama's voter segments to tell campaign managers what supporters felt, thought, and aspired to achieve by voting.

The goal of these analytic methods—microtargeting, developing predictive algorithms, and conducting randomized field experiments—was to permit the Obama campaign to assign *to every voter in the country* two scores that would measure first the likelihood the person supported Obama and second the likelihood the person would go vote for Obama. In each battleground state, Obama's campaign call centers conducted between 5,000 and 10,000 short-form interviews and 1,000 long-form interviews to make sure they were on target measuring voter attitudes and preferences. But here, the polling was used primarily to supplement and validate data gained through other methodologies. In other words, even the polling data was used not as a stand-alone methodology but to validate voter profiles being derived from microtargeting, voter preferences being predicted through algorithms, and voter behavior being tested through randomized field tests.

"To derive individual-level predictions, algorithms trawled for patterns between these opinions and the data points the campaign had assembled for every voter—as many as one thousand variables each, drawn from voter registration records, consumer data warehouses and past campaign contacts," reporter Sasha Issenberg wrote in the MIT *Technology Review*. "The innovation was most valued in the field. There, an almost perfect cycle of microtargeting models directed volunteers to scripted conversations with specific voters at the door or over the phone. Each of those interactions produced data that streamed back into Obama's servers to refine the models pointing volunteers toward the next door worth a knock."[28]

Compare the Obama methodology just described with the "door knocks" done by the Romney campaign that may well have ended up putting a piece of campaign literature on the door handle with a rubber band because nobody was home at the time the campaign worker visited the home. Compare the Obama team's ability to predict and measure how voters would respond to a particularly worded fundraising e-mail or a media campaign targeted to deliver a message pretested by randomized field testing with the Romney campaign's media wizards who used 1950s Madison Avenue "focus group" methodologies to judge which fundraising letters should be bulk mailed or what television/radio messages should be aired.

The Obama campaign analytics staff saw staffing and resources in 2012 jump 500 percent over the level of similar technical resources in 2008.[29] This alone should attest to the importance Obama and his key advisors gave to computer-driven voter-intelligence analytic systems.

Microtargeting is at the core of the intelligence efforts to monitor the US citizen population undertaken by the Obama administration through the National Security Agency, with little or no advance explanation to the American people and with little or no regard for the infringements of fundamental freedoms—especially Fourth Amendment freedoms.

Ultimately, the NSA has the technology to not only access the commercially available databases on consumer demographics and buying habits, but also to analyze telephone conversations, including mobile phone communications, text messages, e-mails, and Internet postings on social networking sites. Relationship analysis of this data would enable the NSA to determine the exact names of the most important personal contacts of every person in America, allowing econometricians within the NSA to make microtargeting databases that map whole networks of associations. Content analysis further would enable the NSA to determine precisely what a person thinks and says on a wide variety of topics ranging from family matters to job-related concerns to public policy issues.

Today, political operatives do not have free and open access to NSA information for use in political campaigns, even if the political party controlling the White House and/or Congress should ask for it.

Yet computer-oriented scientific analysts and database experts are on the verge of identifying less expensive methods to access and retain the type of information the NSA has at its fingertips. The beginning step will be for political campaigns to acquire the scientific expertise capable of capturing similar data on a sample basis, with the ability to extrapolate the sampled data to the population-microtargeted database through probability estimates based on matching characteristics from the sampled subjects to the total file.

To many readers, this may sound like science fiction, yet what the Obama campaign analytics accomplished in 2012 was reality, even if that reality was unimaginable until very recently.

INTERNET FUNDRAISING: ADVANTAGE OBAMA

The "Cave" of techno-savvy campaign workers also proved its worth by using newly developed technology and methodology to boost Obama's fundraising.

In 2012, the Obama campaign raised $690 million online from 4.4 million donors, an average contribution per donor of $156. This bettered the Obama 2008 total of raising $500 million from 3.95 million donors, an average contribution of $126 per donor.[30]

Yet as late as June 2012, the Obama campaign was registering dramatically less voter enthusiasm for the candidate than in 2008. Unless Obama beat his 2008 fundraising numbers, the campaign would never come close to raising its $1 billion goal, matching what Obama insiders expected the Romney campaign to raise from the GOP faithful by utilizing traditional, non-Internet fundraising methodologies that rely largely on big-dollar donors.

So on June 26, the Obama campaign sent an e-mail to potential donors, with Obama's signature, saying: "I will be the first president in modern history to be outspent in his re-election campaign, if things continue as they have so far. I'm not just talking about the super PACs and anonymous outside groups—I'm talking about the Romney campaign itself. Those outside groups just add even more to the underlying problem."[31]

The e-mail concluded with the admission that Obama could win even if outspent by Romney, but not by a margin of 10 to 1.

That single e-mail brought in $2,673,278. Why? Because randomized field-testing of the message proved it would be one of the most effective approaches the campaign could use to raise money. Armed with scientific methods, the Obama geeks realized brilliantly that their disadvantage—being seriously behind Romney in fundraising—could be turned into their distinct advantage, provided the message were crafted so as to achieve maximum return potential.

So, the Obama analytics department under Tim Wagner conducted randomized testing of various letter drafts prior to the e-mail launch, determining which version sent was the most effective. At the end of the campaign, the analytics department reported that if the least effective e-mail version of the campaign had been sent, the Obama campaign would have raised $2.2 million less.[32]

The Obama e-mail fundraising strategy in 2012 revolved around three points: (1) send considerably more fundraising e-mails in 2012 than in 2008, with at least four hundred national fundraising e-mails targeted; (2) submit all versions of e-mail campaign communication to rigorous randomized field testing before being implemented; (3) make recipients of Obama fundraising e-mails think Obama would lose the election unless the supporter contributed.[33]

The campaign regularly tested as many as eighteen variations on the subject line and the e-mail copy for each effort. The campaign could see as much as an 80 percent difference in results between different versions, with campaign management agreeing not to interfere in which version the analytics team ultimately decided to e-mail. By the end of the campaign, the Obama fundraising team had designed and implemented a system that stored donor credit card information on BarackObama.com, the campaign website, so that a person wanting to make a campaign contribution could do so with one click, using an application downloaded onto a mobile phone. The one-click mobile phone application raised $115 million from more than 1.5 million users. Obama supporters tweeted that the "Quick Donate" app became so addictive that some Obama supporters donated every time they saw a close poll reported in the media.[34]

Clearly, fundraising by e-mail is much cheaper than traditional direct-mail methods in which solicitations must be printed and postage paid even when the package is sent as bulk mail to the prospective donor. The cost-efficiency advantage of e-mails threatens to replace direct-response mail solicitations as yet another outmoded political campaign methodology that is rapidly headed for the history books, every bit as e-mail threatens the economic viability of a post office not predicated on the express delivery of high-priority print packages. Understanding political psychology also permitted the Obama campaign to realize that getting a supporter to contribute to the campaign, even with as little as $5, was important both for the funds raised by the method and because the act of making the contribution increased the commitment of the donor to the campaign. A contributor who gave $5 was likely to give more. The act of making a contribution increased the likelihood the person would vote, if only to preserve his or her investment. Furthermore, a percentage of donors could be converted to volunteer their time working for the campaign, perhaps as neighborhood canvassers.

Realizing the importance of getting a person to make that first contribution, the Obama campaign devised attractive opportunities for those able to give as little as $5.00, including a raffle to have dinner with Obama. "We rely on everyday Americans giving whatever they can afford—and I want to spend time with a few of you," the Obama e-mail solicitation read. "So if you can make a donation today, you'll be automatically entered for a chance to be one of the four supporters to sit down with me for dinner. Please donate $5 or more today."[35]

The letter continued with its populist appeal: "Most campaigns fill their dinner guest lists primarily with Washington lobbyists and special interests. We didn't get here doing that, and we're not going to start now. We're running a different kind of campaign. We don't take money from Washington lobbyists or special-interest PACs—we never have, and we never will."

Winners also received free airfare and hotel accommodations: "We'll pay for your flight and the dinner—all you need to bring is your story and your ideas about how we can continue to make this a better country for all Americans."

The Obama tech team tested variations on the e-mail sent, as well as variations the Obama surrogates offered for similar celebrity opportunities, such as two seats with actor George Clooney at the fundraiser Clooney was planning to hold at his Los Angeles home.[36] Then too, the campaign tech team tested the upscale version of the idea—dinner in New York City with rap star Jay-Z and his wife, Beyonce, to be held in the swanky 40/40 Club in downtown Manhattan, priced at $40,000 a ticket and limited to one hundred guests.[37] In the e-mail accompanying the offer, Beyonce said she was a huge Obama fan and that she would do whatever it takes to help him win a close race.

Or, if Jay-Z and Beyonce didn't appeal, the Obama campaign offered a similar $40,000-a-seat chance to have dinner with Anna Wintour and *Sex in the City* star Sarah Jessica Parker at Parker's New York City home.[38]

THE END OF POLLING?

The 2012 Obama campaign recognized traditional campaign methods are rapidly becoming as obsolete as landline telephones and transistor radios.

In most modern campaigns, for example, polling is considered indispensible, and it is hard to imagine a successful electoral campaign of any state or national importance in which public opinion polls did not play an important role. Obama's campaign, however, pictured a future in which polls will be considered but crude estimators of voter preferences and enthusiasm. That vision, furthermore, gave Obama a significant advantage over his challenger.

Deciding which of the dozens of polls taken regularly during a presidential campaign are reliable is not an easy analytic exercise. In the 2012 presidential campaign, approval rates for President Obama were consistently polled at under 50 percent, with most polls around 45 percent. Consequently, it became difficult to believe polls showing Obama with a substantial lead over Romney. How could that be? Approval/disapproval ratings typically predict how well a presidential candidate will do in a head-to-head challenge.

In 2012, however, America learned how polls have changed.

Romney supporters—still clinging to a paradigm that may soon be obsolete—charged that polls showing Obama with a substantial lead must be skewed in favor of Democratic voters. Scientifically conducted polls, after all, involve more than contacting random samples of eligible voters. The pollster must estimate the mix of voters likely to show up and vote on Election Day. In 2008, for instance, the enthusiasm over Obama running as the first serious US presidential candidate of African descent caused the number of Democratic voters showing up at the polls to exceed the number of Republican voters showing up at the polls by approximately 7 percent. This was an atypical year, however, given that rarely do Democrats or Republicans have more than a 3 percent advantage in presidential election turnout.

Therefore, Romney backers often argued, some 2012 polls were probably biased by oversampling Democrats based on a voter model that assumed Democrats in 2012 would outvote Republicans in 2012 by the same margins as in 2008. Thus, a poll showing Obama as much as 7 percent ahead of Romney may simply reflect oversampling Democrats by 7 percent when the poll was taken. An unskewed poll that removed the Democratic Party oversampling, theoretically, would then reflect a dead-heat campaign, instead of a 7 percent advantage for Obama.

"Republicans and Democrats alike have honed in on the fact that recent media polls are oversampling Democrats," political analyst Douglas Schoen wrote on FoxNews.com on September 27, 2012.[39] "There was the Washington Post/ABC poll that had a +9 Democratic skew in late August. There was the Marquette poll for Wisconsin from two weeks ago with a

D+8 sample. And the newest swing state poll from Quinnipiac gave Obama a spread between Democrats and Republicans that was even greater than the historic Democratic advantage in 2008, a seven point spread between voters identifying themselves as Democrats or Republicans at 39 percent to 32 percent, in each state they polled."

The question was important: Should 2008 turnout be used as the predictor for 2012 turnout?

If skewed polls manage to convince the electorate as a whole that one candidate or the other is ahead with a distinct advantage, that alone could impact the election, perhaps by convincing partisans of the underdog candidate to give up because the race looks hopeless. This line was echoed by many Romney backers.

"The liberal mainstream media and blogosphere are desperately trying to write Romney's funeral using polls that oversample Democrats by as much a[s] D+10, D+11 and D+13," wrote Chicago-based political operative John Giokaris on Townhall.com on September 26, 2012. "In 2008, an historic election wave for Democrats, the electorate was D+7. In 2004, when George W. Bush won re-election, the electorate was evenly split. In other words, D+0. So was the 2010 midterm election: evenly split."[40]

The expectation in September and October 2012 was that Democratic Party voter enthusiasm for Obama was down considerably, while voter enthusiasm in general gave the edge to Republicans.[41] This would suggest the proper sample for 2012 would be closer to the 2004 and 2010 models than 2008. Analysts like Giokaris concluded, "Any poll trying to replicate 2008 is going to artificially inflate Obama support."

This is exactly what many Republican pundits believed the mainstream media and the majority of polling organizations were doing: namely, allowing their partisan bias to justify skewing the poll in favor of Obama by oversampling Democrats, with the intent to influence the electorate as a whole.

Romney was banking on an increase in GOP voter enthusiasm, a belief that made the 2012 result all the more startling. A Quinnipiac poll of Colorado, Virginia, and Wisconsin, for example, showed in September 2012 that in all three states a majority of Republicans said they were more enthusiastic about voting this time around, compared to about a third of Democrats who expressed the same opinion.[42]

Political polling is further complicated by the fact that not all adults eligible to vote are registered voters. Moreover, not all registered voters actually vote. So, professional political pollsters are faced with the difficulty of determining who will be the likely voter. As seen above, more likely Democrat voters in 2008 does not predict more likely voters in 2012 would be Democrats as well.

"You can conduct the best poll in the world in terms of accurately ascertaining the views of a population that mirrors your sample—but if your sample doesn't mirror that season's electorate, your poll will mislead its readers," wrote Dan McLaughlin in RedState.com on October 31, 2012.[43]

Democrats countered that census data show minorities make up a greater share of the population, driven by the surging Hispanic population, and there was no reason to expect African Americans would be less enthusiastic about Obama in 2012 than African Americans had been in 2008.[44]

Nate Silver, a statistician who gained fame first for developing a sabermetrics-based system for forecasting the performance of major-league baseball players, advanced his reputation as a political forecaster by accurately predicting the winner of forty-nine of the fifty states in the 2008 presidential election. Following the 2012 campaign, Silver attempted to analyze which of the many polls taken that year were the best and which were the worst.[45] Silver based his analysis on ranking the two dozen polling firms that issued at least five surveys in the final three weeks of the campaign, comparing the poll results against the actual results. He determined that TIPP, a firm that conducted national polls for *Investor's Business Daily*, was the most accurate in 2012.

Interesting as this is, while TIPP may have been the most accurate in 2012, there is no assurance it will also end up being the most accurate in 2016. Determining which polling service is the most accurate is a calculation that can be made only at the conclusion of a race, not while a race is in progress. Moreover, a poll shown to be most accurate at the end of a race was not necessarily the most accurate during the race. Since there is no actual voting until the end of a race, there is no objective yardstick against which to measure the accuracy of polls taken while the race is in progress.

The Obama campaign in 2012, however, obviated the need to pay attention to the polls at all. It had something smarter—and more accurate—up its sleeve.

By constantly calling small samples of voters in the Obama campaign's microtargeted voter database, the Obama analytics team could accurately measure and predict changes in voter preferences far more sensitively than could the polls. This evolved into a system where every week, the Obama campaign call centers would conduct between 1,000 and 2,000 long-form calls to already profiled voters in each battleground state, while at the same time conducting as many as 5,000 to 10,000 quick calls that would ask as few as two questions to gauge a voter's candidate preference and likelihood of voting. By getting polling data on specific voters already profiled in the Obama database, as opposed to the traditional methodology of getting polling data on a random sample of voters, the Obama campaign could use its predictive algorithms to apply poll data from the specific voters questioned to other voters like them in the Obama voter database. This permitted the campaign to create models of "shifters," voters changing preferences between Obama and Romney, while allowing the campaign to refine the category of "undecideds" to specific voter segments with known voter profiles.

Political scientists and psychologists, meanwhile, have struggled with defining "undecideds" because the term applies not only to voters who have legitimately not yet made a choice between candidates, but also to voters who were not yet paying attention to the election and voters who hesitated to tell a stranger their preference. The Obama campaign could tell more precisely which undecideds were which in the category of undecided voter.

"Using algorithms to find other undecided votes who looked like shifters (and determine which direction they were likely to go) would help the Obama campaign know which were worth targeting and when to do so," journalist Sasha Issenberg wrote about the 2004 Obama campaign.[46]

This method allowed the Obama campaign to observe voter shifts before the shifts showed up in the polls. The sensitivity of the analysis and the ability to map the results on econometrically constructed microtargeted profiles of the voter base as a whole meant the Obama campaign had a constantly more sensitive measure against which to assess voter preferences and voter turnout rates than could be provided by any traditionally conducted poll. Traditional polls merely report this or that particular sample of voters who were questioned for the particular poll being reported. Professional polling organizations do not build complex mathematical models to understand who their respondents are, nor is there any attempt made to sample the same voters longitudinally over time. Each poll is typically its own snapshot of the particular voter sample that happened to be selected and to respond for that particular poll.

Ken Strasma, an Obama analyst in 2012 who made major contributions to creating the campaign's "black box" model of voter behavior, believed his predictive modeling gave Obama's staff the tools of the fortuneteller.

"We knew who these people were going to vote for before they decided," Strasma told Issenberg.[47]

In contrast, the Romney campaign relied on internal polls to make campaign decisions. These polls suffered from the same difficulties publicly disclosed professional polls experience.

From conversations conducted during the 2012 campaign with top Romney campaign advisors, I discovered Romney's internal polls were using a statistical voting model that favored Republican turnout by approximately 3 percent over Democratic turnout, an assumption in hindsight likely incorrect, given the extraordinary capabilities the Obama campaign's voter intelligence gave it in getting supporters to the polls. The bias built into Romney's internal polls led the Romney campaign to believe on Election Day that Romney was ahead by one or two points in Ohio and by as many as five points in Florida, assumptions that turned out to be disastrously inaccurate.

Ultimately, the Obama campaign never even bothered to conduct a nationwide survey. Instead, Joel Benenson, the campaign's lead pollster, conducted voter surveys at regular intervals across eleven battleground states: Colorado, Florida, Iowa, Michigan, Nevada, New Hampshire, North Carolina, Ohio, Pennsylvania, Virginia, and Wisconsin.[48] During September and October, the Obama campaign was completing as many as eight thousand to nine thousand calls per night to conduct short-form interviews to assess voter preference and strength of support, with the data fed back to the complete microtargeted database to refine predictions on a continuous, rolling basis.[49]

"We ran the election 66,000 times every night," explained Obama campaign manager Jim Messina, describing how the campaign calculated on an ongoing basis the Obama odds of winning each swing state. "And every morning we got the spit-out—here are your chances of winning these states. And that is how we allocated resources."[50]

As a result of the campaign's sophisticated methodology, Obama's top advisors were able to provide estimates fantastically more reliable than the Romney campaign had available. Obama campaign internal estimates showed that from April through the conventions in August and September, the race was "fixed" in the battleground states, with a 3- to 4-point advantage to Obama, with 50 percent of voters going for Obama and 46 to 47 percent for Romney. There was a rise right after the Democratic Convention, with the Obama advantage swinging to approximately 6 points in September, with 50 percent of voters going for Obama and 44 percent for Romney. But within forty-eight hours after the first debate in October, voters returned to Romney, with Obama settling back to the 3 to 4 percent advantage across the eleven battleground states.

"Our final projection was for a 51-48 battleground-state margin for the president, which is approximately where the race ended up," explained David Simas, the Obama campaign's director of opinion research.[51]

THE SCIENCE OF TV BUYS

Obama's campaign further found a way to outsmart Romney's in television buys.

What sense does it make to spend hundreds of millions of dollars on television advertising, when television viewers can watch on-demand programming on the Internet that shows no commercials, and cable television services offer hundreds of specialty channels that carry no political content?

On the surface, Obama's campaign outspent Romney's campaign on advertising by as much as $200 million. But when spending by pro-Obama and pro-Romney PACs was added to the calculation, Romney had the edge in overall television advertising dollars. Still, the results were not commensurate with the spending in that Obama's campaign also applied quantitative methodologies to transform the process of buying television advertisements into a science.

"In market after market, the Obama campaign ended up putting more ads on target than the Romney campaign did," said Ken Goldstein, president of Kantar Media's Campaign Media Analysis Group, a nonpartisan media consulting firm that worked for both campaigns.[52]

How? Simple: Obama's team approached television media buys with a scientific rigor. Obama's team built a technology known as "Optimizer" to buy television time by focusing on audiences, not channels. Mining the campaign's database to determine their supporters' television viewing habits, the Obama campaign projected how many targeted voters were likely to be watching any given television program at a specific time, on both network and cable channels. Then the Obama team negotiated to find the shows that were most cost-effective, seeking to make their television buys 10 to 20 percent more efficient.

This meant the Obama team bought micro-audiences that the Romney campaign did not seek to buy, spending less per ad. The Obama campaign targeted women on channels such as the Food Network and Lifetime and men on networks such as ESPN. While the Romney media team focused on mass saturation of broadcast television, the Obama camp focused on maximizing exposure across the options. At one point the Obama campaign was up on sixty different channels, compared with the Romney campaign on eighteen channels,[53] and not necessarily because it was buying more, but because it was buying *smarter* and more efficiently. While the Obama campaign was targeting specific voters in the niches where they watched TV, for two of the last seven days of the campaign, the Romney camp was entirely dark on cable television.[54]

For every five commercials Romney ran in the swing state of Colorado in the last two weeks of September, Obama ran seven, the *New York Times* reported. In Florida, the number of pro-Obama ads outnumbered Romney's by 50 percent, some thirteen thousand of them accusing Romney of outsourcing jobs to China, gutting Medicare, and hiding his tax returns from the public. The same was true for other battleground states the newspaper surveyed, including Ohio, Iowa, Virginia, and New Hampshire. "Mr. Obama's continued advantage on the airwaves, which counters Democratic predictions that he would be far outgunned by Mr. Romney and his allied 'super PACs' by now, may help explain why polls in most of the competitive states have shifted in his direction over the last month," wrote *New York Times* reporters Jim Rutenberg and Jeremy Peters.[55]

The reporters also noted that Obama ran television campaigns virtually unopposed throughout much of 2012, while Republicans were still locking horns in the primaries.

One of the big losers in the Romney camp was Karl Rove, whose American Crossroads Super PAC spent $104,746,715 supporting GOP candidates in the 2012 election. In total, Rove's two organizations—American Crossroads and Crossroads Policy Strategies—spent a total of $175 million, primarily investing in high-cost television advertising. Of this, Rove spent $127 million on more than eighty-two thousand television spots for Romney. Yet every single candidate supported by Rove, including every single candidate for the US House and Senate, lost. Rove's only claim to success was that American Crossroads opposed two candidates who lost, representing only 1.29 percent of the total funds the Super PAC spent in the 2012 election cycle.[56]

For these dismal results, Rove was roundly criticized: first, for slighting conservatives by diverting money from campaign operatives that might have produced more impressive results, including blocking operatives looking for funding to bolster the GOP Election Day ground game; and second, by placing ads without concern for reducing the fees, Rove's organization could receive maximum compensation. "Right now there is stunned disbelief that Republicans fared so poorly after all the money they invested," said Brent Bozell, president of For America, a nonprofit organization based in Alexandria, Virginia, that advocates for Christian values in politics. "If I had 1/100th of Karl Rove's money, I would have been more productive than he was."[57]

"[There] were people who gave [Rove's] Super PAC $10 million," said GOP strategist Susan Del Percio, "and what do they have to show for it?"[58]

In the end, all the GOP had to show for their billion dollars was an outdated, outsmarted, out-scienced campaign and another four years of watching Obama in the White House.

4

THE NEW DEAL COALITION RIDES AGAIN

The 1936 election marked the birth of the Roosevelt coalition—a unique alliance of big-city bosses, the white South, farmers and workers, Jews and Irish Catholics, ethnic minorities, and African Americans that would dominate American politics for the next generation.

—Jean Edward Smith, *FDR* (2007)[1]

LIKE FRANKLIN D. ROOSEVELT IN 1936, Barack Obama faced reelection to his second term in office amidst a severe economic downturn he had been unable to reverse in his first four years in office.

Both FDR and Obama had no choice but to argue the economic policies launched in their first four years needed more time to succeed. Interestingly, both FDR and Obama found themselves abandoned by establishment interests in big business and Wall Street, only to be embraced by a coalition of the downtrodden. Neither would have succeeded without the active involvement of labor unions, although there are differences in that the labor movement that supported FDR was struggling to get established in the United States and the labor movement that supported Obama was struggling to remain relevant. Neither president would have succeeded unless he had been able to appeal successfully to those who felt some combination of disadvantage by their minority status, economic vulnerability, and need for a champion.

Obama's "New Deal" coalition differed from FDR's in that the South after the realignment of the Nixon era voted solidly Republican against Obama, and the remaining family farmers still operating in 2012 voted with the GOP, as did the majority of voters in rural America. In FDR's era, single women did not show up in sufficient numbers or with the needed economic agenda to be a viable voter bloc capable of influencing the outcome of the presidential election. During World War II, however, women were enlisted for the first time in US history in large numbers into the workforce, setting the stage for the feminist movement of the 1960s that encouraged women to be wage earners on a basis competitive with men. By 2012, Obama and the Democratic Party had found that single women, including those with children, supported him in their continuing aspirations to advance in the workforce, even as traditional family structures in America were undergoing dramatic changes. So, too, Obama's core advisors derived much of their adult experience from Chicago politics, a big-city environment in which bosses, ward politics, class differences defined by economics, and well-organized minority interests remained alive and well.

In the broad outline, Obama won by pursuing identity politics, recruiting as his core coalition African Americans, minorities, a growing number of Hispanics, those remaining labor union members, and single women, while continuing to draw majority support from both Jews and Catholics.

Once the geeks in Obama's "Cave" determined there were sufficient numbers pursuing these targeted groups to the exclusion of all others, the political operatives directing Obama's campaign could set a partisan strategy designed to appeal to the narrow interests of Obama's reengineered New Deal coalition, even at the risk of antagonizing the rest of the electorate. Voters outside these targeted groups, the number crunchers realized, simply weren't needed to complete a winning equation.

Obama's political gurus, including David Axelrod, Jim Messina, and David Plouffe, knew exactly what they were doing in crafting a campaign in which Obama would deliver divisive messages, including the Saul Alinsky mantra to "tax the rich." At the same time, the Obama campaign risked nothing by demonizing Mitt Romney as a "vampire capitalist" who got rich by preying on Obama supporters, including the left-behind minorities in central cities, the Hispanics branded as illegal immigrants, and women neglected by men in general. The attacks demonizing Romney only served to rally the Obama voter coalition base. Though Obama would deny it, the campaign his numbers geeks and Chicago "pols" crafted for him was necessarily a "divide and conquer" strategy, precisely because that is how Axelrod, Messina, and Plouffe, as advised by the numbers geeks, calculated they would win.

AFRICAN-AMERICAN VOTERS

At the end of the Civil War, the Republican Party held the voting allegiance of African-American voters after Republican president Abraham Lincoln signed the Emancipation Proclamation and pushed through a reluctant Congress the Fourteenth Amendment, abolishing slavery.

Biographer Jean Edward Smith noted, "African Americans deserted the party of Lincoln" in the 1936 election, when "for the first time since Emancipation, blacks voted Democratic."[2]

Smith commented that this shift was not because FDR was in the forefront of the fight for civil rights, but because "no segment of American society had suffered more severely from the Depression, and the New Deal provided relief."[3]

Over 70 percent of the African-American vote went to FDR in the presidential election of 1936.[4] The previous year, the Roosevelt administration had conducted "an impressive outreach" to the black community, with Interior Secretary Harold Ickes able to produce a rise in black voter registration by making sure African Americans were given a greater share of government-funded construction work than ever before allotted.[5]

In his 2008 book, *New Deal or Raw Deal? How FDR's Economic Legacy Has Damaged America*, historian Burton Folsom Jr. argues that FDR actually did little for African Americans. Burton points out that FDR refused to endorse laws before Congress to make lynching a federal crime, despite a 40 percent increase in African-American lynching to a rate of almost 1.4 a month during his first term.[6] Yet the black vote was nonetheless key to FDR's winning coalition.

Similarly, David Plouffe, in his book on the 2008 presidential campaign, acknowledged the importance of the African-American vote to Obama's electoral success. In the run-up to the 2008 Iowa Caucuses, Obama expressed discomfort to Plouffe over the African-American endorsements Hillary was receiving. "I told him I would try to do better with the African-American community and would make sure we picked up our game in this regard," Plouffe wrote. "And we did. Valerie Jarrett began holding a daily call with our staff and key supporters involved in outreach, which helped to instill more discipline and allowed us to track progress more closely. Each day, Valerie had people on the call report on their conversations with various African-American political targets and what their next steps would be."[7]

Even immediately after Obama beat Hillary in the January 3, 2008, Iowa caucuses, the Congressional Black Caucus was still divided, with more than one-third of the African-American members of Congress determined to support either Hillary Clinton or John Edwards.[8]

Exit polls showed that in the 2008 general election, however, Obama won 96 percent of the African-American vote, with blacks constituting 13 percent of the electorate, reflecting a 2 percent rise in African-American voter turnout over 2004.[9]

In 2012, between 3 and 4 million new African-American voters joined the electorate.[10] Again, African-American turnout was 13 percent of the electorate. Although the black vote for Obama slipped marginally in 2012 compared with 2008, Obama still got an overwhelming 93 percent of African-American votes, despite unemployment in the African-American community registering 14.3 percent, nearly double that for the nation as a whole.[11]

"This week, after years of a down economy, months of a dispiriting campaign, and long-running rumblings about whether Obama has neglected the black community, distanced himself from it, or taken it for granted, they were still at 13 percent of the electorate," wrote Jill Lawrence of the Joint Center for Political and Economic Studies.[12]

Even though a disproportionate number of African Americans live in Southern states that voted for Romney, the African-American vote was pivotal to Obama's victory in several swing states, including Ohio, Florida, and Virginia.

"Black voters were absolutely not going to let Obama lose if they could help it," Lawrence's colleague David Bositis, a senior political analyst at the Joint Center for Political and Economic Studies, said immediately after the 2012 election.

The effectiveness of the Obama campaign's GOTV effort was credited with keeping the percentage of the African-American vote virtually as high in 2012 as it was in 2008. "The Obama campaign moved heaven and earth to locate those voters and make sure they turned out," Lawrence concluded. "Republicans not only underestimated the depth of Obama's potential voting pool and the reach of his turnout effort, they disregarded signs of its success."

That over 90 percent of African Americans voted for Obama in 2008 and 2012 leaves no doubt the vote was racially motivated, despite Obama's claim in 2008 that he intended to establish a new dialogue that would assist the United States in transcending racial prejudice.

When Obama finally repudiated his race-baiting former pastor of twenty years, Rev. Jeremiah Wright, in April 2008, a *New York Times* editorial crowed: "This country needs a healthy and open discussion of race. Mr. Obama's repudiation of Mr. Wright is part of that. His opponents also have a responsibility—to repudiate the race-baiting and make sure it stops."[13]

Still Obama supporters even today routinely castigate as "racists" anyone who dares criticize Obama's public policy positions. In 2000, George W. Bush got 8 percent of the African-American vote and in 2004, 11 percent. Historically, Democratic Party presidential candidates since World War II could count on getting no less than 60 percent of the African-American and typically more than the 70 percent African-American vote FDR got in 1936.

"Blacks get insulted when people say we all think alike," wrote John H. McWhorter, an African-American contributing editor to the Manhattan Institute's *City Journal*. "But then why don't we take our individuality to the voting booth? For one thing, a great many black people associate the Republican Party with racism. This means that voting Democratic is often less about making a personal choice than voting on the basis of a group concern. This is understandable. But it's also obsolete. It's time for the black community to start spreading its vote across the two main parties. The Democrats have no reason to address our concerns in any real way, because we're a slam-dunk."[14]

But with the control the leftist mainstream media still have on political correctness in the United States, any political commentator daring to observe African Americans voted for Obama in nearly lock-step percentages risks being ostracized for a double whammy of pursuing a "racist conspiracy theory," despite the obvious statistics.

In 2012, African-American Bishop E. W. Jackson Sr. launched a campaign to wake up African-American voters to the reality of Democratic Party politics in the Obama era. "[African Americans] have been used, manipulated, deceived, insulted and generally taken for granted," he wrote in an e-mail broadly sent across the Internet. "Black Church goers have in the past overwhelmingly voted for Democrats, but we are on the cusp of an historic shift. [African Americans] are waking up, but they need courageous leaders willing to speak the truth."[15]

Bishop Jackson also criticized the Democratic Party for rejecting what he considered fundamental Christian principles. "A radical Democrat Party . . . has completely rejected the historic Judeo-Christian values of America," the e-mail reads. "At their Convention, they took God out of the platform, removed acknowledgement of Jerusalem as the capital of Israel. They affirmed abortion on demand, glorified homosexuality and made same-sex marriage an official plank in their platform." He further argued that since the Democratic Party has "turned their back on all those fundamental Judeo-Christian principles," then it is time "for us to turn our backs on them."[16] Still, Bishop Jackson received little support from the African-American community in 2012.

Better received was the rhetoric of Gerry Hudson, an African-American international executive vice president of Service Employees International Union, or SEIU, the union of choice for public service workers that has moved to center stage of the union movement in the United States with Obama's expansion of the federal government bureaucracy.

"In Mitt Romney, we have a candidate lacking substance who hasn't put forth a real plan to build the nation's middle class because he doesn't have one," Hudson wrote on Huffington Post, the day before the presidential election in 2012. "In the final stretch of this campaign, Mitt Romney has verbally scampered to a more moderate position and professed concern for the middle class. But the crux of his plan for America remains the same failed economic policy approach of George W. Bush's Administration (tax cuts for the rich and sort everything else out later), which pushed our country into a deep recession that further weakened the already fragile middle class and wiped out decades of economic gains for black families."[17]

Continuing to echo Democratic Party talking points, Hudson attacked Republican vice presidential candidate Paul Ryan's budget proposal, characterizing Ryan's plan as "a how-to guide on concentrating wealth at the top and disassembling education, healthcare, Social Security and other programs for working people."[18]

HISPANICS

Hispanics voted for Obama over Romney by 71 percent to 27 percent, according to the Pew Research Hispanic Center. This represented a gain in Hispanic supporters for Obama since 2004, when Hispanics voted 67 percent for Obama, compared to 31 percent for McCain. George W. Bush registered the strongest Republican share of the Hispanic vote since 1980, when in 2004 he drew 40 percent of the Hispanic vote, versus 58 percent for John Kerry. Clearly, the support George W. Bush showed as president for US relations with Mexico and the support Bush and McCain gave to passing comprehensive immigration reform legislation during Bush's second term cut into the historic affinity Hispanics have felt for the Democratic Party.[19]

The Pew Research data also supported the contention that Obama's national vote share among Hispanic voters was the highest seen by a Democratic candidate since 1996, when President Bill Clinton won 72 percent of the Hispanic vote. Moreover, the Hispanic vote represented 10 percent of the electorate in 2012, up from 9 percent in 2008 and 8 percent in 2004. The data also showed Hispanic support for Obama was key to victory in several swing states: In Florida, Obama carried the Hispanic vote 60 percent to 39 percent, an improvement over 2008, when Obama won 57 percent of the Hispanic vote in Florida, compared to 42 percent for McCain; in Colorado, Obama carried the Hispanic vote by a wide margin, 75 percent to 23 percent, again bettering his performance in 2008, when Obama won the Hispanic vote in Colorado by 61 percent to 38 percent; and in Nevada, despite a drop from 76 percent in 2008, Obama still won the Hispanic vote 70 percent to 25 percent. In 2012, Hispanics made up 17 percent of the vote in Florida, 14 percent in Colorado and 18 percent in Nevada. Obama also won 68 percent of the Hispanic vote in North Carolina, 65 percent in Wisconsin, 64 percent in Virginia, and 53 percent in Ohio.

Combining African Americans at approximately 13 percent of the electorate in 2012 and Hispanics at 10 percent of the electorate, Obama had a solid advantage on 23 percent of the electorate, virtually 1 out of every 4 voters. So, in the 2012 presidential election, where roughly 110 million votes were likely to be cast, Obama ended up gaining from African-American voters 95 percent of the 14.3 million votes cast, for a total of 13,585,000 votes. From Hispanics, Obama ended up gaining 71 percent of the 11 million votes cast, for a total of 7,810,000. Thus, from African-American and Hispanic voters combined, Obama got in 2012 a total of more than 21 million votes. In other words, Obama got one-fifth of the total votes cast for both candidates from those two ethnicities alone. The impact is even greater when measured in terms of Obama voters. In 2012, Obama received a total of 65 million votes, meaning that approximately one-third of the votes Obama needed for victory came from a combination of African-American and Hispanic voters alone. Put another way, Mitt Romney could well have begun the presidential election campaign against Obama calculating he would get very little support from one-fifth of the electorate, almost regardless of what "message" he attempted to deliver.

Obama solidified the Democratic Party hold on Hispanic voters when he gave a speech in the White House Rose Garden on June 15, 2012, endorsing the key principles of what is known as the "DREAM Act." In this speech, Obama implemented by executive fiat a new Department of Homeland Security policy in which eligible Hispanic youths born in the United States to immigrant parents would be able to request temporary relief from deportation proceedings so they could apply for work authorization and pursue opportunities to go to college in the United States. "That's what gave rise to the DREAM Act," Obama said. "It says that if your parents brought you here as a child, if you've been here for five years, and you're willing to go to college or serve in our military, you can one day earn your citizenship. And I have said time and time and time again to Congress that, send me the DREAM Act, put it on my desk, and I will sign it right away."[20]

Two days later, on June 17, 2012, John Morton, director of US Immigration and Customs Enforcement in the Department of Homeland Security, issued a memorandum authorizing the use of prosecutorial discretion to grant a reprieve from deportation orders for aliens who came to the United States as young children or were born in the United States to parents who were not US citizens, provided they had graduated from a US high school or were pursuing a college or advanced degree at a legitimate institution of higher education in the United States.[21] With these actions, the Obama administration effectively bypassed Congress to implement the key provisions of the DREAM Act, relying only on the executive authority of the office of the presidency and the ability of ICE and DHS to issue memoranda.

The policy went into effect in mid-August, just as the Democrats were preparing for the Democratic National Convention to be held the following month in Charlotte, North Carolina. Beginning in mid-August, some eight hundred thousand illegal immigrants who believed themselves eligible under this new policy could start applying to ICE to be covered on the new policy.[22]

DHS Secretary Janet Napolitano carefully distinguished that this policy shift did not amount to amnesty. "The grant of deferred action is not immunity," she told reporters. "It is not amnesty. It is an exercise of discretion so that these young people are not in the removal system. It will help us to continue to streamline immigration enforcement and ensure that resources are not spent pursuing the removal of low-priority cases that involve productive young people." She added, "More important, I believe this action is the right thing to do."[23]

Never mind that Obama's action not only circumvented Congress in that the administration submitted no new legislation to accomplish the goal. Moreover, by using executive action to implement the policy, Obama defied Congress, which passed a version of the DREAM Act through the House of Representatives in 2010, but could not get similar legislation through the Senate.[24] In other words, Obama pursued executive action to implement the DREAM Act both because he did not have time for another showdown over the issue in Congress and because he was not sure Congress was ready to pass the DREAM Act.

As was the case with African Americans, Obama's favorable rating with Hispanics going into the reelection campaign was by no means certain. In a town hall–style appearance on Spanish-language television network Univision on September 20, 2012, Obama was grilled on why he had failed to pass comprehensive immigration reform in his first term as he had promised he would do when campaigning for office.

"There's the thinking that the president is somebody who is all-powerful and can get everything done," Obama responded defensively. "In our branch, in our system of government, I am the head of the executive branch. I'm not the head of the legislature. I'm not the head of the judiciary. We have to have cooperation from all these sources in order to get something done. So I am happy to take responsibility for the fact that we didn't get it done, but I did not make a promise that we would get everything done, 100 percent when I was elected as president."[25]

Later in the forum, Obama was asked what his biggest failure as president was.

"As you remind me, my biggest failure so far is we haven't gotten comprehensive immigration reform done," Obama answered, "so we're going to be continuing to work on that. But it's not for lack of trying or desire."[26]

Asked whether the executive actions taken to implement DREAM Act provisions were politically motivated, Obama again answered defensively. "I think if you take a look at the polls, I was winning the Latino vote before we took that action," he argued, charging that Republicans "had completely abandoned their commitment to things like comprehensive immigration reform."[27]

Throughout the 2012 campaign, Obama attacked the Republicans and Romney in particular over Hispanic issues. "The only reason we do not have a law right now that has provided a citizenship not just for DREAM Act kids but for folks who are here, are law-abiding citizens, is because the Republicans have consistently demagogued the issue and have blocked action in Congress," Obama said in an interview on Spanish-language television network Telemundo in April 2012.[28]

The Obama campaign further hammered Romney over a statement Romney made in a Republican debate in Florida in January 2012 during the primaries that he favored "self-deportation" as a solution to illegal immigration.[29] The idea, circulated in conservative circles, involves passing state laws that make it difficult for the estimated 11 million illegal immigrants in the United States to live and work here comfortably. This is achieved simply by states denying illegal immigrants the right to apply for jobs and work, not permitting illegal immigrants to apply for driver's licenses, and clamping down on public welfare benefits received by illegal immigrants and their families.

Romney proposed issuing legal immigrants a card under a national verification system at the time of hiring that would allow legal immigrants to find work. In the Republican debate in Florida, Romney maintained that those unable to obtain such cards verifying their right to work would effectively self-deport.

Obama's team also hammered Romney for statements he made in June, after the Supreme Court ruled on Arizona's tough immigration law, saying Romney would like to see the states given more latitude to establish state-specific immigration laws. Romney repeatedly said he would drop federal lawsuits against Arizona and other states with similar legislation "on day one" of his presidency.[30]

UNION WORKERS

According to Fox News exit polls, Obama got approximately 60 percent of the votes of union workers, compared to 40 percent for Romney.[31] This represented an increase over 2008, when 56 percent of union workers supported Obama and 43 percent McCain.[32]

In a 2011 report, the Progressive Policy Institute found 21 percent of the electorate came from union households, a percentage that had dropped since 2000, when it was closer to 26 percent.[33]

While union membership has declined in the United States as a percentage of all workers, union membership continues to grow among government workers. Moreover, unions still represent a large and important bloc of voters in states no presidential candidate can afford to ignore. The Bureau of Labor Statistics of the US Department of Labor estimated on January 27, 2012, that 11.8 percent of all wage and salary workers in the United States were union workers, for a total of 14.8 million workers, down from 1983, the first year for which comparable union data are available, when the union membership rate was 20.1 percent and there were 17.7 million union workers.[34] The BLS study found that public-sector workers had a union membership rate of 37 percent, five times higher than that of private-sector workers. Over half the union members lived in just seven states: California, 2.4 million union workers; New York, 1.9 million; Illinois, 0.9 million; Pennsylvania, 0.8 million; Michigan, 0.7 million; and New Jersey and Ohio, 0.6 million each.

Immediately after the election, labor unions claimed credit for Obama's victory. Richard Trumka, the president of the AFL-CIO, claimed that without the huge push by the labor unions, Obama would never have won Ohio, Wisconsin, and Nevada. "We did deliver those states," Trumka said.

"Without organized labor, none of those states would have been in the president's column."[35]

In assessing the impact of unions on the 2012 presidential election, Steven Greenhouse, reporting for the *New York Times*, noted the AFL-CIO claim that during the last four days of the campaign, union workers and their community partners contacted eight hundred thousand voters in Ohio alone, as part of the 10.7 million door knocks and phone calls made by the federation's fifty-six unions. The SEIU, the largest union representing government employees, said that its members knocked on 5 million doors, including 3.7 million in battleground states. "We had 100,000 volunteers across the country in the final days," Mary Kay Henry, SEIU president, told the *Times*.[36]

Greenhouse concluded that 60 percent of voters from union households in Ohio voted for Obama, with union households accounting for 22 percent of the electorate. In Wisconsin, Greenhouse concluded union households made up 21 percent of the electorate, and they voted for Obama over Romney by 66 percent to 33 percent. Greenhouse further reported the possibility that white working-class voters in the battleground states leaned toward Obama because of the auto industry bailout and because of Obama campaign advertisements attacking Romney for Bain Capital closing plants and outsourcing jobs.[37]

The numbers-savvy Mike Podhorzer, political director for the AFL-CIO, argued that an important impact of union support was to increase Obama's relatively weak numbers among white working-class workers. Podhorzer told Dave Jamieson, writing in the Huffington Post, that while Obama polled in the range of 30 percent support among white working-class men nationally, his numbers among this demographic in states where the AFL-CIO had aggressive campaigns tended to be 10 points higher, in the range of 40 percent support.

"For the first time, those blue collar workers who didn't have a union were hearing about Romney's plan to cut Social Security, to cut Medicare, to continue tax cuts for the rich," Podhorzer explained. "So it wasn't so much that we were out there talking. What was special was that they were hearing for the fist [*sic*] time what union members were hearing for decades. And so they responded just like union members."[38]

Jamieson noted that Ohio's Republican Governor John Kasich had signed a bill in Ohio known as SB 5 that stripped many of the state's public workers from their collective bargaining rights. Voters overturned the bill after union political volunteers were mobilized in a statewide effort to fight Kasich on the measure. Jamieson reported more than 60 percent of union voters polled for the AFL-CIO said Romney's backing of SB 5 made them less likely to vote for him.[39]

That unions support Democrats is clear, especially when we examine the teachers' unions—the National Education Association, or NEA, and the American Federation of Teachers, or AFT, both of which went all out in 2012 to elect Obama. The teachers' unions were particularly active in the swing states of Ohio and Florida.

"The arguments have been made," AFT President Randi Weingarten told fellow union members in Cincinnati, as they prepared to launch a bus trip in Ohio during October to support Obama's reelection. "This trip is about mobilizing and getting out the vote."[40]

Weingarten and NEA President Dennis Van Roekel portrayed Obama as someone who genuinely cares about education, compared to Romney, whom they characterized as someone who would gut the public education system in favor of privatization. The Ohio Education Association, the NEA affiliate, asked its 124,000 members to volunteer for Obama, while all twenty-six NEA offices throughout Ohio created phone banks to call voters to urge them to vote for Obama. The AFT and NEA combined have 4.5 million members nationwide, with both unions committed in 2012 to making campaign contributions and urging their teachers to campaign for Obama.[41]

Combining African Americans at approximately 13 percent of the electorate in 2012 with Hispanics at 10 percent of the electorate and union members at 20 percent of the electorate becomes a more complex process, because the groups overlap in that union members include some African Americans and Hispanics. If we assume union members included 10 percent of the electorate not included in the independent counting of African Americans and Hispanics, we can assume the category "union members" adds to the total such that Obama held a comfortable majority of around 33 percent of the electorate, one of three voters, before the presidential election campaign even started.

SINGLE WOMEN

Exit polls showed a sharp divide between married women and unmarried women, with married women voting 53 percent for Romney, while unmarried women favored Obama in a better than 2-for-1 ratio, at 68 percent for Obama to 30 percent to Romney.[42] Unmarried women were estimated to constitute approximately 24 percent of the electorate in 2012.[43]

Author Dante Chinni, director of the Pathwork Nation project, pointed out in the *Atlantic* that Obama's advantage was not a "gender gap"—in that women favored Obama and men Romney—but more specifically a gap between unmarried and married women.

"The 'marriage gap' was also more important than gender in determining votes in 2012," Chinni pointed out. "Obama won voters who were not married by 20 percentage points. There was a gender gap here—Obama won 67 percent of unmarried women and 56 percent of unmarried men—but he won single women and men."[44]

The Obama campaign specifically focused on single women voters, declaring that the GOP had decided to wage "a war on women."[45]

Phoenix-based AP writer Pauline Arrillaga, commenting on the catchphrase "war on women" that arose as a charge against the GOP in the presidential election of 2012, wrote: "Whether seen as real or manufactured, something about the so-called 'war' is resonating among American women, who could well make the difference on Election Day. Many are acting out and speaking up. Many are, in fact, girding for battle, in one way or another."[46]

Fuel was added at the Democratic National Convention, where speakers such as attorney activist Sandra Fluke emphasized "reproductive rights," another catchphrase standing for access to government-funded contraceptives and abortions.[47]

"Despite an electorate that is overwhelmingly pro-choice, there is no doubt that the GOP's first goal is to deprive women of their reproductive rights and to frame that argument not as one of health but religion," PoliticusUSA.com wrote, publishing a comprehensive list of legislative initiatives on the federal and state level.[48]

"By almost any measure, issues related to reproductive health and rights at the state level received unprecedented attention in 2011," the Guttmacher Institute, a nonprofit group advocating abortion rights, noted in a report issued in January 2012. "In the 50 states combined, legislators introduced more than 1,100 reproductive health and rights-related provisions, a sharp increase from the 950 introduced in 2010."[49]

"In an election focused on the economy, single women present a complicated case," noted Shaila Dewan, reporting in the *New York Times*. "They already earn less than married people and single men, and they have not fared well during the Obama administration. They have had a harder time than married women paying rent, getting medical care and finding jobs. While the jobless rate for married women has stayed relatively low, at 5.6 percent compared with 2.6 percent before the recession, the rate for unmarried women has risen to 11 percent, from a prerecession level of 6 percent."

Still, she noted, single women were reluctant to blame the Obama administration for their economic woes, especially since their reliance on programs like welfare, food stamps and Medicaid has grown significantly since 2007. Dewan pointed out that 55 percent of households headed by single women got some form of government assistance, not counting school lunches, compared with 18 percent of married women's households.[50]

Evidence suggests the political left has benefited from the negative impact an increasingly secular US society has made on traditional marriage. Today, compared with generations past, fewer adult women are married, while an increasing number of children are born to unmarried women, a growing percentage of whom are yet in their teenage years. Sociologists have long recognized that among the formulas that predict economic disadvantage are bearing and raising children out of wedlock, for the simple reason that a single mother must both devise a means of providing an economic living, typically involving getting a job, and providing child care, to allow the child to be watched and assisted while the mother is working.[51]

Writing in 1995, leftist sociologists Frances Fox Piven and Richard A. Cloward predicted that women in the future were likely to become an increasingly important factor in identity politics, in large part because of economic concerns, including equal pay for equal work.[52]

Again, combining single women at 24 percent of the electorate, African Americans at approximately 13 percent of the electorate in 2012, Hispanics at 10 percent of the electorate, and union members at 20 percent of the electorate, becomes a more complex process because the groups overlap in that the groups of African Americans, Hispanics and union workers include many single women. If we assume the category "single women" included 10 percent of the electorate not included in the independent counting of African Americans, Hispanics, and union members, we can assume the category "single women" added to the Obama voter total such that Obama could be assumed to have had a comfortable majority hold on over 40 percent of the electorate before the presidential election campaign even started. Again, this is an important calculation, because nearly half of all voters had their minds made up to vote for Obama, regardless how attractive a candidate Romney was or what policy issues Romney decided to make the focus of his candidacy.

LIFESTYLE POLITICS

Obama pushes even closer to securing half the electorate when lifestyle politics are added into the equation. While the LGBT—lesbian, gay, bisexual, and transgender— population probably accounts for no more than 2 percent of the electorate, exit polls showed 76 percent of voters who identified as gay voted for Obama in 2012, compared to 22 percent for Romney.[53] Obama also derived support for those seeking to legalize marijuana, as evidenced in swing-state Colorado, where 53,281 more voters voted for Amendment 64 to legalize and regulate the recreational use of marijuana than voted for Obama.[54] Obama won Colorado by just over 110,000 votes.

YOUTH

According to Fox News exit polls, Obama won 60 percent of the youth vote, ages eighteen to twenty-nine, with Romney taking 37 percent; the youth vote was approximately 19 percent of the electorate.[55] This was reduced from the height of Obama mania, when in the 2008 presidential election, Obama won 66 percent of the youth vote, compared to 32 percent, a huge, 34-point advantage for Obama.

"Obama promised the obligatory liberal smorgasbord of programs and free goodies that would help his loyal subjects overcome their 'struggles,'" Jason Mattera wrote in his 2010 book, *Obama Zombies: How the Liberal Machine Brainwashed My Generation.* "Young people, in their heart of hearts, actually believed that a scrawny street-agitator-turned-presidential-candidate could save mankind, renew our faith in American politics, and restore faith in government. It was a message that hoodwinked my generation."[56]

The youth vote in 2012 shows the Obama charm from 2008 was tarnished for this group as well, as Obama failed on promises to create jobs for college graduates, find a solution for mounting student loan debts, and create a future in which young people could look forward assuredly to a middle-class lifestyle of marriage, home ownership, and family. A report by Generation-Opportunity.org noted the unemployment rate for eighteen-to-twenty-nine-year-olds was 11.5 percent in December 2012, considerably above the national unemployment rate of 7.8 percent in that month. Including young people who have given up looking for work, the unemployment rate for December 2012 was calculated at 16.3 percent.

"Our leaders in Washington can continue to make it seem like things are getting better, but the fact remains that way too many young people are scraping by, falling further behind on their student loan payments, still living at home with their Mom and Dad, sending out hundreds of resumes, and filling out numerous job applications, all with no result," wrote Terence Grado of Generation Opportunity, discussing the December 2012 youth unemployment rate.[57]

The youth vote was argued to be decisive in several swing states. The Center for Information & Research on Civic Learning and Engagement at Tufts University reported that without the youth vote, Ohio, Florida, Virginia, and Pennsylvania would have flipped from Obama states to Romney states.

"In those states, if Governor Romney had won half of the youth vote, or if young voters had stayed home entirely, then Romney would have won instead of Obama," the Tufts research center reported. "Those states represent 80 electoral votes, sufficient to have made Romney the next president."[58]

Again, combining single women, African Americans, Hispanics, union members, and youth gave Obama an edge on demographically identifiable subgroups that reasonably accounted for 50 percent of the electorate, after adjusting for group overlap so as not to double-count individuals falling in one or more subgroups.

While the coalition differs from the FDR coalition in that during FDR's era the voting age was twenty-one, youth voters remain a force as Generation X is supplanted by Millennials, who are now the new cutting edge in young voters. The youth vote fits with the other subgroups identified as target voters by Democrats, largely because youth voters typically have not established the economic foundation for their middle-aged years. A common thread through all the Democratic Party-targeted subgroups since FDR and the New Deal is that the subgroups voting Democratic could be argued to be economically disadvantaged in that these groups are currently aspiring to achieve and solidify future economic success.

Democrats derisively have characterized the Romney campaign as the last hurrah of white male dominance in an American society where the US Census Bureau projects whites will be a demographic minority in America by 2050.[59]

"For Romney, the support of white male voters offers the likeliest path to the presidency, even as betting on white men is proving an increasingly risky proposition for Republicans," wrote Samuel P. Jacobs, reporting for Reuters in October 2011. "His reliance on that voter group becomes more acute as polls show him far behind with African Americans, lagging badly among Hispanics and at a disadvantage with women in many polls, despite overall poll numbers showing him essentially tied with Obama in recent days."[60]

Reuters noted 90 percent of Republican voters were white in 2008 according to exit polls.

ROMNEY'S "47 PERCENT" GAFFE

That Romney was aware Obama and the Democratic Party had a substantial advantage from key support groups, harking back to FDR's ability to establish a New Deal coalition by appealing to economically disadvantaged subgroups, was suggested by his comment regarding what became known during the 2012 presidential campaign as "the 47 percent."

The controversy developed in September 2012, when *Mother Jones* published a surreptitiously made video of remarks Governor Romney made to a small group of wealthy donors at the home of private equity manager Marc Leder in Boca Raton, Florida. Romney said:

> "There are 47 percent of the people who will vote for the president no matter what. All right, there are 47 percent who are with him, who are dependent upon government, who believe that they are victims, who believe the government has a responsibility to care for them, who believe that they are entitled to health care, to food, to housing, to you-name-it.

> That that's an entitlement. And the government should give it to them. And they will vote for this president no matter what . . . These are people who pay no income tax."[61]

The basis for this claim appears to have come from data published by the Tax Policy Center in 2009, as initially reported by CNN, estimating that roughly 47 percent of all US households, roughly 71 million households in total, do not pay any federal income tax whatsoever.[62] Even though 1.5 percent of the households paying no income tax fall into the income group making more than $1 million a year, the vast majority of these households, 63.5 million, fall into the category of making under $50,000 a year. The Tax Foundation further reported that almost 20 percent of all US households could expect to get income tax "refunds," in the form of earned income tax credits, even though they have paid no income tax.

Immediately, the Obama-supporting media pounced on Romney, pointing out that within the ranks of the 47 percent who paid no income tax were obvious Romney voters, including middle-class white workers who lost jobs due to no fault of their own and were temporarily on unemployment insurance while searching actively for new employment, as well as seniors who were living on some combination of Social Security income, whatever pensions they may have accumulated, and any fixed income investments they might own.

Furthermore, a survey conducted by the Pew Research Center documented that approximately 55 percent of respondents reported they had personally received benefits from one or more federal programs—including Social Security, Medicare, Medicaid, food stamps, and/or welfare or unemployment benefits. An additional 16 percent said they themselves had not received any benefits, but a member of their family had, with the result that 71 percent of all adults are part of a household that has benefited from at least one of these programs. And if you add veteran benefits and federal college loans and grants to the mix, the percent of Americans who have personally received entitlement benefits rises to 70 percent, and the share of households in which at least one recipient has received entitlement benefits rises to 86 percent.[63]

Romney meant to state a strategic reality about the left's built-in political advantage, but ended up delivering a perceived insult to some 86 percent of Americans. "It's shocking that a candidate for president of the United States would go behind closed doors and declare to a group of wealthy donors that half the American people view themselves as 'victims,' entitled to handouts, and are unwilling to take 'personal responsibility' for their lives," Obama campaign manager Jim Messina said in a statement.[64]

Messina, of course, saw no hypocrisy in the free ride the mainstream media gave Obama for being caught in 2008 on a similar hidden camera at a private fundraiser in San Francisco, making his famous "cling to their guns or religion" comments about small-town voters in Pennsylvania.[65]

Liberal pundits, who were generally forgiving of Obama misstatements during both the 2008 and 2012 campaigns, were quick to place Romney's "47 percent" comment at the head of a list of the "Top 10 Public Relations Blunders of 2012,"[66] apparently determined to make sure Romney misstatements were much noticed and never forgotten.

Truthfully, the Pew Research Center study shows how extensively the social welfare state has penetrated US society, such that virtually every family in America is touched one way or another by a federal payment program. Romney was correct to charge that the Democratic Party has expanded the welfare state, and he was also correct to understand that those who become dependent upon government-funding payments are more likely to vote Democratic. The mistake Romney made was to paint the picture with too broad a brush. Many millions receiving various kinds of government-funded payments would be happy to give up these payments or supplement them with a combination of employment opportunities, personal savings, and private pensions.

FRAMING ROMNEY

To successfully pull the Obama coalition together, however, Obama campaign strategists realized they needed more than a candidate to unite behind. What the Obama campaign needed was an enemy, a force the Obama voting coalition could be united against—in this case, an enemy named Mitt Romney.

The Obama team decided from the moment Romney emerged as the likely Republican nominee in April 2012 to beat the GOP to the punch in defining Romney's image. By running triple the number of television commercials Romney ran all the way through mid-September, the Obama campaign risked running out of money to purchase television time when it counted most—in the last days of the race, when the Romney campaign had decided to spend the bulk of its money, calculating that undecided voters in the final days of the presidential campaign would swing disproportionately to Romney, the challenger.

But to the scientifically oriented gurus directing the Obama campaign, the gamble Obama took would be worth every penny if Obama could succeed in "framing" Romney as an old, white, rich guy who made millions as a "vulture capitalist" destroying businesses by firing middle-class US workers and outsourcing their jobs to China and India.

"Framing" is a highly effective psychological technique that involves crafting a mental image so strong that the image once created cannot be easily dismissed, regardless how untrue or inaccurate it happens to be.[67]

According to political advertising monitoring firm Kantar Media, from the moment Romney emerged as the likely Republican candidate, the Obama campaign ran about 347,000 television commercials from April through most of September, with some 270,000 of them negative. In the same period, Romney ran only 121,000 television commercials, with approximately 99,000 of them negative.[68] But once again, the Obama campaign applied the investment scientifically. Drawing from research in behavioral psychology, the Obama campaign realized that after four years in office, voters already had a well-formed image of Obama. As a result, Romney would have a tough time "reframing" the positive image Obama held in the demographic subgroups forming the core constituency of his political base, what is described here as the modern-day reconstitution of the 1936 FDR coalition.

A particularly effective television advertisement run by the Obama campaign in May 2012 told the story of an investment Bain Capital made in 1993—under Romney's leadership—in CS Industries, a steel company in Kansas City, Missouri. The advertisement accused Bain Capital of taking millions of dollars of dividends out of CS Industries by piling debt on the corporation. Romney was portrayed as a "vampire capitalist" who destroyed people's lives to make as much money as possible.[69]

"If he is going to run the country the way he ran our business, I wouldn't want him there," one worker said on camera. "He would be so out of touch with the average person in this country."

The ad showed worker after worker explaining how CS Industries had helped them build families, buy homes, and put children through school, only to be shut down in a bankruptcy filing engineered by Bain—but only after first terminating the company's pension, life insurance, and health insurance.

"Those guys were all rich," another worker said on camera, "yet they did not have the money to take care of the very people who made the money for them."

The Obama commercial hammered home the conclusion Romney was a callous business executive who cared only about his personal profits, not the lives of the middle-class workers who made those profits possible.

The *Wall Street Journal* refuted many of the accusations made by the Obama television spot. The newspaper documented that Bain Capital was highly successful when Romney was in charge. During his tenure there, the venture capital firm produced approximately $2.5 billion in gains for its investors in seventy-seven deals, recording between 50 and 80 percent annual gains in his period. Experts agreed Bain Capital's performance record while Romney was with the firm was among the best track records for buyout firms in that era.[70]

Still, the Bain success story was not without its failures. While Romney led the firm, from its start in 1984 until early 1999, some 22 percent of the companies in which Bain invested filed for bankruptcy, reorganized, or closed doors. An additional 8 percent had such difficulties operating that Bain Capital lost all the money invested. The *Wall Street Journal* concluded that ten deals produced more than 70 percent of the Bain Capital dollar gains during Romney's tenure. But even here, success was not without problems. Of the ten businesses producing the biggest gains, four later landed in bankruptcy court. The *Wall Street Journal* story stressed what should have been obvious: the investment banking business has never been a place for the fainthearted.

Knowing this, Obama sought to undermine Romney's message by emphasizing the negative. The point of the Obama advertising blitz was to argue that Romney's private-sector experience did not make him the best candidate to turn around the ailing US economy. Instead of seeing a caring investor working hard to build businesses, the Obama campaign's early advertising painted Romney as wealthy and aloof, out of touch with the demographic groups Obama courted—African Americans, Hispanics, union workers, single women, and youth. The goal of Obama's advertising was to make Obama's core supporters imagine themselves as the victims in a Bain

Capital get-rich-quick scheme for Republican fat cats.

By stirring among his core supporters Saul Alinsky-like economic resentment, Obama and his team successfully framed Romney as the villain. In doing so, his campaign united Obama's modern-day, New Deal coalition against a common enemy—Republican "fat cats" in general, and Romney in particular—"the rich." Obama characterized them as unwilling to pay their fair share in taxes aimed at providing social justice by helping the downtrodden poor, the disadvantaged minorities, single women facing discrimination, and the struggling youth afraid they would not find jobs equal to the challenge of their educations.

5

THE BATTLEGROUND STATES TIP THE BALANCE

Ohio was the next nail-biter. The rule of thumb was that if a Democrat carried Cuyahoga County, the area around Cleveland, by 150,000 votes, he won the state.
—Karl Rove, *Courage and Consequence* (2010)[1]

IN 2000 AND 2004, Rove was right. The key to winning Ohio was to surpass in Republican areas of the state the turnout of inner-city African Americans who were the majority in Cuyahoga County—Ohio's largest county, dominated by the state's largest city, Cleveland. In 2004, Rove knew Democratic Party presidential hopeful Senator John Kerry was on the way to a nearly 227,000-vote margin in Cuyahoga County. But Rove was not despondent, because he knew George W. Bush was over-performing in virtually every other Ohio county, and especially well in the rural counties that constituted the majority of Ohio's counties.

"In sparsely populated counties in the southeast of the state, such as Belmont, Gallia, Harrison, and Monroe, we beat our targets by nearly double digits," Rove wrote. "And in the Northwest and Southwest, we were burying Kerry. Democrats had boosted turnout in Cleveland and Columbus, but we had more than countered their efforts."[2]

In 2012, Rove miscalculated.

On Election Night, having spent millions of dollars in an embarrassing Super PAC effort to elect Romney and Republicans around the nation, Rove was facing the worst defeat of his career, as Fox was preparing to call Ohio for Obama.

"We have 4.5 million votes in, roughly, and we have a difference of 991 votes between the two candidates, according to the secretary of state's website," Rove argued with Bret Baier and Megyn Kelly on air, at 11:40 p.m. on Election Night, saying it was too early to call Ohio for Obama. "There were 5.7 million votes cast last time around. If we had just simply the same number of people to cast votes, that would be about 1.2 million people out. If you look at Cuyahoga County, 414,000 votes have already been cast. Last time around 668,000 votes were cast, so somewhere around 260,000 votes would still come out of Cuyahoga County."[3]

Rove proceeded to inventory the Ohio counties, arguing there were many Republican counties to come in, including the counties around Cincinnati in Hamilton County in the southwestern part of the state. What Rove had miscalculated was the turnout in Cuyahoga County was stronger than expected this time around, while the Republican turnout statewide remained largely disappointing.

Obama's strategists, armed with data from microtargeting scores, created voter goals for each state, but the estimates were informed with human intelligence, including interviews with county party chairmen and local pollsters. In each battleground state, Team Obama asked three questions:

- "How many votes do we need in this state to win?"
- "How are we going to get them?"
- "Where are we going to get them?"

Answering these three questions boiled down to tactics: "What percentage of this victory is going to be boosting turnout and what percentage of it is going to be convincing independents or other people to come our way?"[4]

Depending on the answers, goals were developed for each state according to three different strategies—registering new voters, persuading target voters not initially inclined to vote for Obama, and developing turnout targets to make sure all possible Obama supporters, wherever they could be found, voted on Election Day. Spreadsheets developed for each battleground state refined these strategies into numerical targets according to demographic subgroups residing in targeted geographical areas of the state.

By comparison, all Rove had working for him on Election Night were his "rules of thumb" regarding how Ohio counties had voted in the past.

Obama could win in 2012 simply by denying Romney victory in Ohio and Florida, with 18 electoral votes and 29 electoral votes, respectively. Analyzing these two states in detail makes clear how the Obama strategists applied their demographic analysis of Obama's reconstituted New Deal coalition to efficiently design a geographically based area-by-area ground game capable of winning each state. For the Obama campaign, victory in the battleground states reduced to a carefully calculated and meticulously implemented numbers game.

OHIO BY THE NUMBERS

Twice now, Obama has been elected president, both times taking Ohio. The state has picked the winner of every presidential election since 1964. If there was one state the Obama campaign felt it was necessary to win in 2012, it was Ohio.

In 2008 and 2012, Obama won Ohio the same way, by getting exceptionally high turnout in Cuyahoga County and by winning nearly every African-American vote cast there. Cuyahoga County dominates state voting in Ohio because Cleveland is in the county, and as a consequence, the county is packed with African-American voters. In Ohio, Democratic Party strongholds include the cities and the precincts around the cities: Cleveland, Youngstown, the Akron-Canton-Dayton cluster of cities in the Southwest, Cincinnati at the state's extreme southwestern corner, and the state capital, Columbus, in the center of the state. In Democrat-dominated precincts,

Obama-paid campaign workers and volunteers, assisted by union-member ground troops, collected votes from African Americans, Hispanics, single women, youth voters, and liberal white supporters, crafting a majority.

Republican precincts, which dominate the state geographically, give the visual appearance that Ohio is a "red" state. The problem is that Ohio's "red counties" are predominately rural and sparsely populated. McCain and Romney were compelled to seek voters virtually one by one across miles and miles of open land, while Democrats had the advantage of transporting the minority residents in their core voter base to the polls, often bused in groups, within densely populated inner cities.

Consider the following voting totals in the 2008 presidential election in Ohio:

- In 2008, Obama won Ohio with 2,940,044 votes, 51.38 percent of the total, compared to 2,677,820 votes for McCain, 46.80 percent of the votes—giving Obama a 262,224-vote advantage.
- In Cuyahoga County, Obama more than doubled McCain's vote total by getting 458,422 votes, 68.70 percent of the total 667,299 votes cast in the county, compared to 199,880 votes for McCain, 29.95 percent.
- This means that of the 262,224 votes he needed to beat McCain, Obama received 258,542 from his advantage in Cuyahoga County *alone*. Obama got virtually the entire edge he needed to beat McCain simply by focusing on one county.[5]

As noted earlier, Cuyahoga County, encompassing Cleveland, Ohio's largest city, dominates Ohio's eighty-eight total counties. The US Bureau of Census estimated the 2011 population of Cuyahoga County was 1,270,294, constituting approximately 11 percent of Ohio's 11,544,225 total population. Approximately 30 percent of the residents of Cuyahoga County were African-American in 2011, compared to only 12.4 percent of the state as a whole.[6] Cleveland remains a highly segregated city, with the majority of the city's African-American population concentrated on the east side of the city, while Cleveland's rapidly growing Hispanic population remains concentrated with the city's remaining white population on the west side (separated by the Cuyahoga River). The City of Cleveland Planning Commission estimates that in 1990, half of Cleveland's residents were nonwhite, with the proportion of nonwhites growing to 61.5 percent during the following decade, largely because of increases in the African-American and Hispanic populations, a population trend that has continued until today.[7]

Given Cuyahoga County's fairly stable rate of 65 percent turnout in presidential elections since 1980, more than 600,000 votes were likely to be cast in Cuyahoga County in the 2012 presidential election, approximately 11.3 percent of Ohio's total vote count.

Consider the following voting totals in the 2012 presidential election in Ohio:

- In 2012, Obama got 2,827,709 votes in Ohio, 50.58 percent of the total, compared to 2,661,437 votes for Romney, 47.6 percent. Obama won Ohio in 2012 by 166,272 votes.
- In Cuyahoga County, of the 645,262 votes cast in 2012, Obama again more than doubled up his Republican opponent, getting 447,273 votes, 69.32 percent, compared to 190,660 votes for Romney, 29.55 percent—giving Obama a margin of victory in Cuyahoga County of 256,613 votes.
- Once again, Obama won Ohio thanks to Cuyahoga County, this time getting more than twice his statewide advantage—166,272—in Cuyahoga County alone: 256,613.

A county analysis of Ohio voting in the 2012 presidential election makes clear the Democratic Party controls voter strongholds associated with Ohio's urban areas.

Cleveland and Cuyahoga County dominate Northern Ohio, creating a sprawling metropolitan area that stretches east to include Youngstown, a greater metropolitan area that overlaps Trumbull and Mahoning Counties, two of Ohio's three most northern counties bordering Pennsylvania. Columbus, the state capital, is in the center of the state. Athens County in southeastern Ohio is a blue county, largely attributable to the presence of Ohio University. Cincinnati is located in Hamilton County in the extreme southwestern corner of the state. Dayton dominates Montgomery County to the northeast of Hamilton County.

Even though Ohio geographically looks like a red state, given that the majority of Ohio's counties are rural and Republican controlled. But, in both 2008 and 2012, Obama carried Ohio by winning a smaller number of Ohio's larger counties containing the state's largest cities, while McCain and Romney lost by carrying the state's rural areas. Ohio's ten largest counties typically account for more than half the state's vote.[8]

BARNSTORMING OHIO

"President Obama today is making his 24th visit to Ohio as president—the second trip in under a month—an openly political gesture that is costly to taxpayers but potentially of huge benefit to Ohio's reelection prospects," wrote veteran White House reporter Keith Koffler on August 1, 2012, just over a month prior to the Democratic National Convention in Charlotte, North Carolina.[9]

Koffler noted that even White House Press Secretary Jay Carney "for a moment dropped the pretense that Obama's Ohio sojourns are for official business, sardonically referencing Obama's political motivation to travel to the state."

Responding to questions from reporters in the White House pressroom, Carney responded, "There's not an inch of Ohio that the president does not love to visit. It's a great state."

Koffler concluded that Obama in his first term as president traveled repeatedly to Ohio "because winning the state would make his reelection almost a certainty."

Obama's campaign to capture Ohio in the 2012 election can be traced back to his 2009 decision to authorize a $80 billion government bailout to keep Chrysler and General Motors in business.

"The bailout is a very big deal in Ohio, especially in the northern tier of the state," John B. Russo, a labor studies professor at Youngstown State University and codirector of Ohio's Center for Working Class Studies, told reporters for the *Boston Globe*. "It's one of the things a lot of working people are going to hold against Romney."[10]

According to exit polling released by the Associated Press, 60 percent of Ohio voters backed the auto bailout, and three-quarters of these voted for Obama.[11] Peter Brown, assistant director of Quinnipiac University Polling Institute, credited the auto bailout as the reason Obama led in Ohio polls.[12]

The Obama campaign hammered Romney on a 2008 editorial he wrote in the *New York Times* in which he called for letting Detroit go bankrupt.

"Without that bailout, Detroit will need to drastically restructure itself," Romney wrote, identifying the course he as a businessman with venture capital expertise favored. "With it, the automakers will stay the course—the suicidal course of declining market shares, insurmountable labor and retiree burdens, technological atrophy, product inferiority and never-ending job losses. Detroit needs a turnaround, not a check."[13]

Romney, born in Detroit, should have had an advantage in both Michigan and Ohio, given that his father, George Romney, was a former president of American Motors Corporation who served as a very popular Republican governor of Michigan from 1963 to 1969. Ultimately, Obama let GM and Chrysler file for bankruptcy, much as Romney had suggested, but only after the Obama administration arranged deals in which the United Auto Workers received preferential treatment over secured lenders, violating a cornerstone of bankruptcy policy in that traditionally bankruptcy courts preserve creditors' priorities by favoring secured creditors over unsecured creditors.[14]

Then, at a Romney campaign rally at the football stadium at Defiance High School in Defiance, Ohio, on an unseasonably cold night that still brought out some twenty thousand Romney supporters, Romney commented: "I saw a story today that one of the great manufacturers in this state, Jeep—now owned by the Italians—is thinking of moving all production to China. I will fight for every good job in America. I'm going to fight to make sure trade is fair, and if it's fair, America will win."[15]

Romney's statement appeared to be an incorrect interpretation of a story run a few days earlier by Bloomberg, reporting Chrysler was considering the manufacture of Jeeps in China, but only those Jeeps scheduled to be sold in China.[16] The confusion came from the first sentence of the Bloomberg article, which explained that Chrysler-owned Fiat "plans to return Jeep output to China and may eventually make all its models in the country."

Before the Romney rally in Defiance, Chrysler issued a press release designed to set the record straight by insisting, "Jeep has *no intention of shifting production* of its Jeep models out of North America to China."[17]

A line added to the Bloomberg story after it was published stated that Mike Manley, chief operating officer of Fiat and Chrysler, was referring to "adding Jeep production sites rather than shifting output from North American to China," making it clear Fiat and Chrysler had no plans to close plants in Michigan, Illinois, and Ohio that manufacture Jeep for sales scheduled for North America.[18]

The Romney campaign fueled the controversy by running a television ad, initially aired in Toledo, Ohio, claiming that Obama took GM and Chrysler into bankruptcy, and that Obama "sold Chrysler to Italians who are going to build Jeeps in China."[19]

The Obama campaign immediately counterattacked, claiming the ad was false and misleading, given Chrysler's clarification of the Bloomberg story.

"What's in there that's false? Are they building Jeeps in China or not?" an unnamed Romney aide reportedly asked. "I think a lot of Ohioans are wondering why we can't make Jeeps here and ship them to China, just like they are wondering why we can't make—insert product here—in this country and export them to China."[20]

The Obama campaign retaliated with a television ad featuring Romney's 2008 "Let Detroit Go Bankrupt" editorial and maintaining that "Chrysler had refuted Romney's lie," proclaiming that the truth was Jeep planned to add eleven hundred jobs in Ohio. The Obama ad ended with a narrator proclaiming that Romney was "wrong then," when he wrote the editorial, and "dishonest now," on the Jeeps being built in China controversy.

"It appears the Obama campaign is less concerned with engaging in a meaningful conversation about President Obama's failed policies and more concerned with arguing against facts about their record they dislike," Amanda Henneberg, a spokeswoman for the Romney campaign, responded. "The American people will see their desperate arguments for what they are."[21]

Then, on January 14, 2013, at the North American Auto Show in Detroit after the 2012 presidential election was over, Chrysler CEO Sergio Marchionne told reporters that as part of a global expansion of the Jeep brand, Chrysler does plan to build Jeeps in China, first for the market in China, to be followed later by export to Russia.[22]

While Romney was incorrect to assert that Chrysler planned to move all Jeep production to China, he was not incorrect in asserting that Chrysler had plans in the works to outsource to China some of the Jeep production that is now done completely in the United States.

Still, despite the auto bailout and Jeep controversies, Romney took Defiance County, the home of a General Motors foundry, by 56 percent of the vote, compared to 42 percent for Obama.[23]

Even on the political left, commentators were hesitant to embrace the auto controversy as a reason Obama won Ohio.

"One of the most dangerous narratives to come out of the campaign was the idea that the unpopular-at-the-time auto bailout had given President Obama a valuable electoral boost in the midwest that played a role in his re-election," wrote Matthew Yglesias, economic correspondent for Slate.com. "You don't want future presidents thinking that any time a major employer in a swing state gets into trouble that a bailout is going to be electoral gold."[24]

Another election analyst who questioned whether the auto bailout cost Romney the election was Nate Cohn, a supporter of Obama. Writing in the *New Republic,* Cohn attributed Obama's win in Ohio not to the auto-related issues or even to the economic recovery for which Ohio's Republican governor John Kasich took credit for engineering, but to one factor alone—"historic black turnout."

Black voters, Cohn argued, were the main reason Obama has done better in Ohio than Kerry. In 2004, African Americans represented 11 percent of the Ohio electorate and voted 84 percent for Kerry. In 2012, African Americans constituted 15 percent of Ohio's electorate and voted 96 percent for Obama.

"In 2004, Kerry won the four counties corresponding to Ohio's largest black population centers—Cleveland, Toledo, Columbus, and Cincinnati—by 16 points while losing the rest of the state by 11," Cohn wrote after the election. "In 2012, Obama won the four large, urban counties by 25 points while losing the rest of the state by 9.1 points."

Cohn concluded that Obama did not improve his showing among "the predominantly white working class stretches of Ohio," with exit polls showing Obama did worse among Ohio's white voters in 2012 than Kerry did in 2004.[25]

Cohn disclosed that the Obama campaign escalated its advertising spending in Ohio from $4.3 million to "what is probably an unprecedented $9.5 million to lock-down the state."[26] Over the final four days of the campaign, Obama made six stops in Ohio.

Yet, in the final analysis, what won for Obama in Ohio was the ground game. Beginning in 2008, Obama opened more than a hundred offices around Ohio. Hundreds more "staging locations" were based in living rooms, office basements, and garages, where team captains responsible for polling places were ready to do whatever was necessary to get people to vote.

"The Obama operation established itself here by 2008, winning Ohio and, to the shock of local leaders in the county that surrounds this city [Cincinnati], Hamilton [County], which had long favored Republican candidates," Monica Davey and Michael Wines reported from Cincinnati for the *New York Times*. "Then [the Obama operation] never left."[27]

By October 2011, some among the 2008 Obama "neighborhood team leaders" began holding monthly meetings preparing for Obama's reelection campaign.

"The technology has grown elaborate," Davey and Wines added. "Rather than using only old-fashioned printouts of addresses and maps in manila folders, some volunteers use smart phones to be directed to homes the campaign wishes to target and then send back results of their stops electronically."

The *New York Times* reporters acknowledged that Obama campaign officials refused to disclose how many paid staff members were working in Ohio, but "they seem to be everywhere, and volunteers in Ohio number in the thousands—some from other states, but mostly, volunteers here say, locals."[28]

In Ohio's cities, the Obama team poured people and money, mobilizing a small army of cars and buses to transport African-American voters to the polls from wherever they could be found, including inner-city poverty areas, low-income housing projects, and even senior-citizen communities.

If Kerry had gotten Obama's 2012 turnout and voting percentage from Ohio's African-American population, Kerry would have been president in 2004.

Even in the final days, however, the Obama campaign realized victory was by no means certain. In the last three weeks of the campaign, Romney peppered Ohio with rallies. He ventured into Obama strongholds in Cleveland, Toledo, Columbus, and Cincinnati. He held rallies in Akron, Canton, and Dayton in the center of the state. Romney took time to travel to rallies in small communities, including Avon Lake, Kettering, and Findlay. Ohio Governor Kasich and Senator Rob Portman were constant warm-up speakers at Romney rallies. A star lineup of Republican notables turned up to campaign for Romney in Ohio, including John McCain and House Speaker John Boehner.

In the final analysis, despite all the time and resources Obama spent on Ohio, Romney lost Ohio by only 166,000 votes—a margin that might have been surmounted if only ORCA, the Romney campaign GOTV computer system, had worked as planned on Election Day.

FLORIDA BY THE NUMBERS

Florida differs from Ohio only in that Obama's victory depended more on gaining record turnout from the rapidly growing Hispanic population of a state in which Hispanics have overcome African Americans as the state's largest minority group. Florida has not yet reached the demographic tipping point where politicians can win elections by ignoring the interests of African Americans, but as long as Hispanics turn out and vote, Florida is headed in that direction.

In 2008 and 2012, Obama won Florida the same way, by focusing on Miami-Dade and Broward counties in South Florida and getting Hispanic and African-American supporters statewide to turn out and vote for him.

The US Census Bureau estimates that of the 19,317,568 people constituting the population of Florida in 2012, approximately 16.5 percent were African-American, while 22.9 percent were Hispanic or Latino in origin. The population of Florida grew 2.7 percent over the 2011 population of 19,082,262, largely because of the continuing immigration of Hispanics into the state.[29]

The Census Bureau estimated that in 2011, the population of Miami-Dade County was 2,554,766, approximately 13 percent of the state population, of which 19.3 percent were African-American and 64.5 percent were Hispanic or Latino in origin. The Census Bureau estimated that in 2011, the population of Broward County, north of Miami-Dade, was 1,780,172, approximately 9 percent of the state population, of which 27.4 percent were African-American and 25.8 percent were Hispanic or Latino in origin.

The second largest stronghold of Hispanic/Latino voters in Florida is in the center of the state: Orange County, which includes Orlando, the home of various popular theme parks, and Osceola County, adjoining Orange County to the immediate south. According to the Census Bureau, Orange County had a population of 1,169,107 people in 2011, approximately 6 percent of the total state population, of which 21.7 percent were African-American and 27.5 percent were Hispanic or Latino in origin. The adjoining Osceola County had a much smaller population of 276,163 in 2011, of which 12.8 percent were African-American, while 46.3 percent were Hispanic or Latino in origin.

The northern part of Florida is largely Republican, with the exception of Alachua County, which is home to the University of Florida, and a cluster of three counties—Gadsden County, Leon County, and Jefferson County—that include the city of Tallahassee, the state capital. These small northern counties typically vote Democratic because of a disproportionate African-American population.

The only other concentration of Democratic voters in Florida is in Hillsborough County on the Gulf Coast side, encompassing Tampa and St. Petersburg, Florida's largest Gulf Coast cities.

Duval County, encompassing Jacksonville on the Atlantic Ocean side of Florida, just south of the border with Georgia, typically votes Republican, even though the county has a sizable minority of African Americans. In 2011, the Census Bureau estimated the population of Duval County was 870,709, of which 29.8 percent were African-American and 7.9 percent were Hispanic/Latino. Despite an African-American population that is nearly double the state average, Duval County has been one of Florida's most solidly Republican-voting counties for two decades.[30]

"We have to drive up the score here so that we can make sure that we make up ground in other areas," Republican national chairman Reince Priebus said in Jacksonville in August 2012. "We're going to have a plan in this county [Duval] to not just win, but to try to win as big as possible. Winning here isn't enough. You have to do great in places you're strong."[31]

In 2004, Bush carried Duval County by 61,000 votes. In 2008, after a major effort by the Obama campaign to get out the African-American vote, McCain won Duval County by only 8,000 votes. In 2012, the GOP placed additional resources in Duval County, with the result that Romney beat Obama by almost 15,000 votes of the more than 400,000 votes cast. Jacksonville and Duval County support the argument that a substantial African-American minority is not enough without an even more substantial Hispanic/Latino minority to tip the vote Democratic in Florida.

Consider the following voting totals in the 2008 presidential election in Florida:

- In 2008, Obama won Florida with 4,282,367 votes, 50.91 percent of the total votes cast, compared to 4,046,219 votes for McCain, 48.10 percent—giving Obama an advantage of 236,148 votes.

- In Miami-Dade County, Obama won 499,831 votes, 57.8 percent of the total votes cast in the county, compared to 360,551, 41.7 percent, for McCain, for an advantage of 139,280 votes.

- In Broward County, Obama won 492,640 votes, 67.0 percent of the total votes cast in the county, compared to 237,729 votes, 32.3 percent of the total, for McCain—giving Obama a 254,911-vote advantage.

- This gave Obama an advantage of 394,191 votes over McCain in Miami-Dade County and Broward County combined, well more than his statewide total advantage of 236,148 votes. Once again, in 2008 Obama was able to win by focusing on winning big in an urban center, in this case the Miami metropolitan area.[32]

Broward County was the home to the infamous "hanging chad" controversy that dominated the Florida recount controversy in the 2000 election between George W. Bush and then-Vice President Al Gore. In 2012, voting in Miami-Dade and Broward Counties was hampered by long lines, with voters waiting as long as eight hours to vote. In part, the long lines were inevitable after Florida's GOP-controlled legislature cut the number of early voting days from fourteen to eight, worried about Democratic voting fraud. The problem was partly resolved when Democrats successfully sued on Sunday, November 4, attempting to extend voting hours, knowing that getting every possible vote in South Florida was key to the party's electoral success.[33]

That the GOP held the Republican National Convention in Tampa in 2012 was a testament to the importance of winning Florida if the Republicans were to have any chance to recapture the White House. While Obama's 2012 victory was narrower in Florida than his win in 2008, Obama still won the state convincingly, largely by the effort his campaign expended to identify and mobilize African-American and Hispanic voters to the polls.

Consider the following totals in the 2012 election in Florida:

- In 2012, Obama got 4,237,756 votes, 49.9 percent of the total, compared to 4,163,447 for Romney, 49.0 percent. Obama won Florida in 2012 by 74,309 votes.

- Compared to 2008, Obama received fewer votes than in 2012, and Romney bettered McCain's 2008. Clearly, the enthusiasm for Obama reduced noticeably among Democratic voters in the four years he was president. Yet even with an enthusiasm bump for Romney over McCain, the difference was not enough to outweigh the strong favorable margins Obama held among African-American and Hispanic voters in the state.
- In 2012, Obama got 541,440 votes, or 61.6 percent, of the votes cast in Miami-Dade County, compared to 332,981 votes for Romney, 37.9 percent, giving Obama a margin of victory of 208,459 votes.
- In Broward County, Obama got 508,312 votes, 67.1 percent of the votes cast in the county, compared to 244,101 votes for Romney, 32.2 percent, giving Obama a margin of victory of 264,211 votes.
- So in 2012, Obama had a margin of victory in Miami-Dade and Broward Counties combined of 472,670 votes, more than six times the 74,309 votes by which he beat Romney statewide.

A red county/blue county geographic map of Florida based on voting in the 2012 election makes clear the Democratic Party controls a voter stronghold associated with Florida's urban areas.

Like Ohio, Florida geographically looks like a red state. In 2008 and 2012, Obama carried Florida much as he carried Ohio, by winning the big counties containing the state's largest cities, while McCain and Romney lost by carrying virtually all the state's smaller, rural counties. Obama won in 2012 by carrying only twelve of the state's sixty-seven counties, but he won the most populous counties containing the state's largest cities.

"The numbers in Florida show this was winnable," Brett Doster, Florida advisor for Romney, told the *Miami Herald*. "We thought based on our polling and range of organization that we had done what we needed to win. Obviously, we didn't, and for that I and every other operative in Florida has [*sic*] a sick feeling that we left something on the table. I can assure you this won't happen again."[34]

Exit polls show why Romney lost Florida: Obama won 60 percent of the Hispanic vote and approximately 95 percent of the African-American vote, bettering how he did in 2008.

"Obama's Hispanic-vote margin came despite a massive Hispanic-outreach effort by Romney, who struggled at times in the general election because of the hardline policies he espoused during the Republican primary," wrote Mark Caputo and Scott Hiaasen in the *Miami Herald*. "Obama won big in Osceola and Orange counties, home to a burgeoning Democratic-leaning Puerto Rican population that's starting to counterbalance Cuban-American Republicans in Southeast Florida."

The Miami newspaper noted that Obama's Hispanic effort in Florida was so robust that he planted one of the more than one hundred Obama field offices in Florida in the once-Republican stronghold of Miami's Little Havana neighborhood.[35]

ROMNEY'S HARD LINE ON IMMIGRATION

To gain the Republican nomination for president in 2012, Romney had to compete in a series of primary battles that involved numerous nationally televised debates showcasing the various GOP contenders. The political perils of a prolonged primary fight were magnified in a media environment where policy positions the candidates took were aired before a critical, generally very liberal press sympathetic to the Democratic Party, with reporters happy to explain policy nuances in favor of the Democrats to a national audience evaluating the candidates for office generally. The nationally televised GOP debates in 2012 were by their nature not confined to the scrutiny of a state-specific press or a media audience limited to the geography of the state in which the primary was being held.

Another dynamic is that only the most committed voters tend to vote in primaries. This means that primary voters in the GOP tend to be conservatives. Thus, if Romney intended to run as the GOP presidential candidate in the general election on a centrist policy platform, he faced a dilemma: to win a particular primary contest, he might be forced to articulate more conservative policies than he would otherwise advocate.

Once articulated in a primary contest, policy positions stuck, to be debated over again as various GOP primaries were held throughout the nation. Centrist candidates like Romney appear to be flip-flopping on issues if conservative policy positions advocated to win primary elections are abandoned in favor of more centrist issues favored by general election voters. In Florida, given the importance of Hispanic voters, the various conservative positions Romney took to help him win the primaries, especially on issues regarding immigration and open borders, inevitably came back to haunt him when the time came to court Hispanic voters in the Florida general election.

The Obama campaign, assisted by its friends in the liberal press, remembered in particular several of the policy statements Romney made during the primary campaign that could be used to hurt his chances in the election.[36]

For instance, during a nationally televised GOP primary debate broadcast from the Orlando Convention Center in Orlando, Florida, on September 11, 2011, the third GOP presidential debate in three weeks, Texas Governor Rick Perry explained his support for allowing the children of illegal immigrants to be eligible for in-state tuition rates at Texas colleges and universities.

Romney responded as follows: "It's an argument I just can't follow. I've got to be honest with you. I don't see how it is that a state like Texas—to go to the University of Texas, if you're an illegal alien, you get an in-state tuition discount. You know how much that is? That's $22,000 a year.

"Four years of college, almost $100,000 discount if you are an illegal alien go[ing] to the University of Texas," Romney continued. "If you are a United States citizen from any one of the other 49 states, you have to pay $100,000 more. That doesn't make sense to me. And that kind of magnet draws people to this country to get that education, to get the $100,000 break. It makes no sense. We have to have—just as Speaker Gingrich said, and as Michele Bachmann said as well, Congresswoman Bachmann, and that is we have to have a fence, we have to have enough Border Patrol agents to secure the fence, we have to have a system like E-Verify that employers can use to identify who is here legally and illegally.

"We have to crack down on employers that hire people that are here illegally," he concluded. "And we have to turn off the magnet of extraordinary government benefits like a $100,000 tax credit—or, excuse me, discount, for going to the University of Texas. That shouldn't be allowed. It makes no sense at all."[37]

Perry drew boos from the largely conservative audience of five thousand GOP faithful in the Convention Center in Orlando to hear the debate when he defended the Texas law in response to Romney, saying: "If you say that we should not educate the children who have come into our state for no other reason than they've been brought there by no fault of their own, I don't think you have a heart."

USA Today in reporting on the debate called it "a Sunshine State smack-down."[38]

Then, on December 31, 2011, in response to a voter's question in Le Mars, Iowa, Romney was asked if he would veto the DREAM Act if he became president and Congress passed the legislation. Again, the context was the Iowa caucus meetings.

"The answer is yes," Romney said, in what ended up a video clip posted on YouTube. "I'm delighted with the idea that people who come to this country and wish to serve in the military can be given a path to become permanent residents in this country. Those who serve in our military and fulfill those requirements, I respect and acknowledge that path. For those that come here illegally, the idea of giving them in-state tuition credits or other special benefits I find to be contrary to the idea of a nation of laws. If I'm the president of the United States I want to end illegal immigration so that we can protect legal immigration. I like legal immigration."[39]

In an interview with the Huffington Post on December 29, 2011, with the Iowa caucus only days away, liberal reporters raised with Romney the concern of GOP strategist Ed Gillespie that "a hard line against immigration is bad for the party and even dangerous for the party's prospects in the future with Hispanics."

Romney responded by sticking firm on his immigration position: "I think we have to be very clear with the American people that we will enforce our laws and secure our border, at the same time we welcome legal immigration, and we want to prevent illegal immigration in part to protect and, in my view, expand the benefits of legal immigration."

The line of questioning continued: "But you've been very strong about people needing to go home no matter how long they've been here. Is that kind of thing going to hurt the Republican Party's standing with Hispanics?"

"What I indicate is that there should be a transition period where people are able to transition to ultimately returning home and being in line and applying for the right to come to this country," Romney said. "But I don't think people who come here illegally should get a special privilege relative to those who have been waiting in line legally."

"But what about the party's relationship with Hispanics?" the Huffington

Post persisted. "I mean, that's important. They're a big part of this country and growing."

"No question," Romney replied. "And I believe that Hispanic voters, like other voters in this country, are in America because it's the land of opportunity. And I believe that my party and my positions on issues will demonstrate that I'll keep America the land of opportunity, and the president is turning it into something they wouldn't recognize."[40]

Virtually all Romney's statements would make perfect sense to the conservative base of GOP voters participating disproportionately in primary elections. But when seen through the lens of general election politics, Romney was easily portrayed as unsympathetic to Hispanics simply because he did not want to turn a blind eye to the violation of US law that is an intrinsic part of illegal immigration. So, by taking a conservative position on immigration, Romney improved his chances of navigating the GOP primaries with enough victories to win the GOP presidential nomination—even though policy positions he took to get there would backfire in the general election campaign.

Finally, when Romney dared suggest in a Republican primary debate that the lack of jobs in the United States, given the economic downturn under Obama's presidency, might cause some illegal immigrants to self-deport, the narrative was set to depict Romney as hostile to Hispanics. Now, even other GOP primary contenders saw an opportunity to attack.

In a day of outreach to Florida's Hispanic voters, former House Speaker Newt Gingrich on January 25, 2012, in an extensive interview on Spanish-language television and in a speech at Florida International University, mocked Romney's plan to deal with illegal immigration by encouraging self-deportation. "You have to live in a world of Swiss bank accounts and Cayman Island accounts and automatic $20-million income for no work to have some fantasy this far from reality," Gingrich told Univision interviewer Jorge Ramos. "For Romney to believe that somebody's grandmother is going to be so cut off that she is going to self-deport, I mean this is an Obama-level fantasy."[41]

In the final weeks of the presidential campaign, an immigration-rights advocacy group called on Romney to take down a Spanish-language television advertisement the campaign was airing, claiming Romney had worked with Democrats on immigration reform while he was Massachusetts governor and promising that he would do the same as president. The ad attacked Obama for failing to introduce comprehensive immigration reform legislation during his first term, a promise Obama made when running for president in 2008.

"Romney's ad is a fraud," Frank Sharry, executive director of pro-immigration reform group America's Voice, explained in an e-mail to Elise Foley of the Huffington Post. "The only permanent solution we know Romney will advocate is 'self-deportation,' which is code for a purge of millions of hardworking Latino immigrant families."[42]

NORTH CAROLINA, THE ONLY SWING STATE TO VOTE FOR ROMNEY

The only swing state Romney won was North Carolina. So what happened differently in the Tar Heel State?

On the surface, the demographics in North Carolina appear to favor the Democrats. With an estimated 2012 population of 9,752,073, North Carolina's population is 22 percent African-American and 8.6 percent Hispanic.[43]

Mecklenburg County, which includes Charlotte, the state's largest city, contains nearly 10 percent of the state's population and voted for Obama at over 60 percent. Charlotte is considered the banking and business center of the state and home to one of the nation's largest black middle-class populations.

Mecklenburg County includes a disproportionate number of African Americans, 31.5 percent in 2011, with Hispanics at 12.4 percent. Another Democratic stronghold clusters around Wake County in north central North Carolina, encompassing Raleigh, the state capital, with approximately 10 percent of the state's population. Wake County voted 55 percent for Obama in 2012. The Research Triangle area of Raleigh–Durham–Chapel Hill holds three of the nation's most prestigious universities: North Carolina State University, Duke University, and the University of North Carolina at Chapel Hill. Many left-leaning high-tech workers have flocked to the region's technologically oriented industries located within the Research Triangle to take advantage of the abundant high-tech talent employed on the region's university faculties.

Yet difficulties for the Democrats in North Carolina began surfacing once the DNC announced a decision to hold the party's nominating convention in Charlotte, scheduled for September 4–6, 2012.

In May, North Carolina voters approved a ballot referendum to ban same-sex marriage. This did not sit well with the lifestyle coalition supporting the Democratic Party. In response to the voter referendum banning same-sex marriage, Gay Marriage USA, an advocacy based in New York, launched an Internet-based protest asking the Democratic National Convention to move the nominating convention out of the state.[44]

Union leaders objected to holding the DNC in North Carolina because the state is a right-to-work state, and Republican pressure caused the North Carolina House to pass a nonbinding resolution asking the Democratic National Convention to change any rules that require contractors to be union shops.[45] In 2011, North Carolina had the lowest rate of union membership in the nation, with only 2.9 percent of the state's workers belonging to unions.[46]

The Obama campaign put significant resources into the voter-intelligence GOTV effort in North Carolina in 2012, only to lose the state by fewer than 100,000 votes out of more than 4.45 million votes cast, giving Romney a narrow 50.4 percent advantage. In 2008, Obama won North Carolina by fewer than 15,000 votes, with a 0.32 percent margin of victory.

In 2012, Romney's base of support came from the state's 70 percent white, strongly evangelical, and traditionally conservative population, still dominating the state's majority of rural, low-density-population counties.[47] With unemployment in North Carolina remaining above 9 percent throughout 2012, many white, middle- and working-class workers in the state blamed Obama for a failed economic recovery, adding to Obama's reelection difficulties.

Perhaps a clear sign Obama would have trouble with North Carolina should have been realized when the DNC decided to move Obama's acceptance speech from the Bank of America football stadium, where the NFL's Carolina Panthers play, to the much smaller, twenty-thousand-seat Time Warner Cable Arena, where the convention took place. The DNC blamed the change on a weather forecast that threatened thunderstorms, but that decision was made only after first arranging and then abandoning as unrealistic a plan to bus supporters from all across North Carolina to fill the larger venue.

In North Carolina, Obama's coalition didn't quite have the gas to deliver the state. The convention controversy, combined with lower union participation and a higher percentage of African Americans living in the middle class, prevented the Obama team from garnering the 100,000 additional votes it needed to win.

THE SWING-STATE MASSACRE

The remaining swing states—two in the West, Colorado and Nevada, plus Iowa in the Midwest, and Virginia on the Atlantic Seaboard—all went for Obama.

Why did Romney lose all these states to Obama?

On Tuesday, October 23, Romney drew a crowd of 12,500—the maximum fire marshals would allow—at the Red Rocks Amphitheater in Morrison, Colorado, north of Denver. People of all ages began arriving at noon, ready to make the forbidding high-altitude climb from the facility's many parking lots to the tiered seats of Colorado's famed outdoor music venue, some to be sure they would get good seats and others to be sure they would not get turned away. Romney campaign workers handed out red, blue, yellow, and white T-shirts to those seated in the center of the audience, in a pattern designed to form the Colorado logo that appears on the state flag. The applause for Romney and Ryan in the amphitheater was thundering as supporters stood throughout, while Romney, on the stage at the bottom of the scenic outdoor amphitheater with his running mate, Paul Ryan, promised supporters that this year the Republican ticket would beat Obama in Colorado, something John McCain failed to do in 2004.

"We're going to make it happen," Romney said in conclusion, to rousing and sustained applause. "I love this country. I believe in America. I believe in you. We can do it together."

By comparison, crowds for Obama in Colorado were much smaller and less enthusiastic in 2012 than the "rock star" crowds he drew only four years earlier. Back then, in 2008, Obama drew a crowd of 100,000 to the parks in front of the state capitol in downtown Denver, a crowd that exceeded by 25,000 the capacity of the Denver Broncos' stadium, the venue for Obama's acceptance speech at the 2004 Democratic National Convention. But on Wednesday, October 23, 2012, Denver's fire chief generously estimated at 16,000 the crowd Obama drew at the more modest venue of Denver City Park.

At Red Rocks, the Republican enthusiasts heard candidate Romney proclaim "What a place this is!" to loud shouts and wild applause amplified by thundersticks the Romney supporters clapped together.

In Denver, Obama countered by claiming, "I love Red Rocks more than just about anybody, but it could never hold all of you guys."

In the final count, however, Romney lost Colorado by roughly 138,000 votes of the more than 2.36 million votes cast, with Obama taking 51.5 percent of the vote. Once again, a rapidly growing Hispanic population, measured by the Census Bureau at 20.9 percent of Colorado's total population in 2011, made the difference for Obama.[48]

Polls showed Romney holding a 53 percent to 34 percent lead in Colorado Springs, but in Denver, the state's largest city, polls showed Obama leading by approximately the same margin Romney held in Colorado Springs.[49]

Romney also lost Nevada narrowly, by 67,806 votes of the nearly 1 million votes cast in the state, with Obama winning 52.5 percent of the total. The only two counties Romney lost in Nevada were Washoe County in the Northwest of the state, where Reno is located, and Clark County, in the extreme Southeast of the state, where Las Vegas is located. Again, the main factor was the influx of Hispanic immigrants into the state's two major cities.

The Census Bureau estimates that in 2011, Hispanics constituted some 27 percent of the state's 2.7 million population.[50]

"Nevada should be a state Barack Obama has no chance of winning," wrote John Dickerson in *Slate* magazine the summer before the 2012 election. "The unemployment rate is 11.6 percent, the highest in the nation. Sixty-one percent of the homes are worth less than the mortgage on them, also the highest in the nation. Las Vegas is in the middle of the desert, but everyone there is underwater."

Yet Obama also won Nevada by 12 points in 2008. Why?

"The growing Hispanic population helps Obama in Nevada more than any other state," Dickerson continued. "In 2008, 15 percent of the electorate was Hispanic. Nearly 2 million Latinos have turned 18 since then. In national polls, Obama leads Romney by as much as 40 percent among Hispanics."[51]

Obama won Iowa's six electoral votes by capturing the majority of the counties in the eastern, Catholic part of the state, adjoining the blue states of Minnesota, Wisconsin, and Illinois, while losing the counties in the western, predominantly Protestant part of the state, adjoining the red states of South Dakota, Nebraska, and Missouri.

Iowa was not a story of minority voters, as the Census Bureau reported an African-American population constituting 3.1 percent and a Hispanic population constituting 5.2 percent in 2011.[52] Viewed simply, Iowa is a split state in which the east votes Democratic, while the western part of the state votes Republican.

With Des Moines, Iowa's capital and most populous city in virtually the center of the state, the Hawkeye State's other major cities, including Cedar Rapids, are in the eastern, Democratic part of the state.

Iowa was one of the few states where the economy was a plus for Barack Obama, with unemployment relatively low, holding at under 6 percent throughout 2012, and the farm economy booming. In Iowa, Obama had an advantage in the voter-intelligence GOTV ground game, while Romney was at a disadvantage, having to fight through the Iowa Caucus battle in which his narrow win[53] was later reversed, giving the win to social conservative candidate and former Senator Rick Santorum by a margin of 34 votes after recount.[54] Until late in the Iowa Caucus campaign, Romney had largely ignored the state, wary after spending $10 million in Iowa in 2008 only to finish a distant second to former Arkansas Governor Mike Huckabee, who captured the state's sizable, socially conservative evangelical community.[55]

Virginia, like Iowa, is a split state, in which the eastern, more urban part adjoining Maryland and Washington, DC, tends to vote Democrat, while the western, more rural part of the state tends to vote Republican. In 2012, Obama won Virginia narrowly by approximately 148,000 votes out of nearly 4 million votes cast, with Obama taking 51.2 percent. Virginia, with an estimated 8.1 million population in 2011, had a sizable, 19.8 percent African-American population and a growing 8.2 percent Hispanic population, both largely concentrated in the state's eastern urban areas, including Richmond, the state's capital.[56]

In 2008, Obama was the first Democratic presidential candidate to win Virginia in more than forty years, a win he secured a second time in 2012. Obama benefited from the expansion of federal employment in his first term, with many federal employees working in Washington making their homes in the suburban communities of northeastern Virginia. Exit polls showed Obama winning in Virginia by getting 53 percent of college graduates' votes, 54 percent of women's votes, and 93 percent of African Americans' votes. Romney won Virginia independent voters by 53 percent to Obama's 43 percent, while the two candidates tied 49 percent each among veterans and active military voting.[57]

6

THE ESTABLISHMENT CANDIDATE VERSUS THE CELEBRITY

Who are these guys? What are they like? I still did not know what kind of life would lead a man (in my lifetime, all have been men) to think he *ought* to be President. I could only guess at the habit of triumph that would make him conclude he *could* be President.

—Richard Ben Cramer[1]

IT IS HARD TO IMAGINE two more different men competing with each other to be president of the United States than Mitt Romney and Barack Hussein Obama.

Mitt Romney made virtually every campaign appearance wearing a dress shirt and tie, looking very "preppy," with nicely pressed dress pants, sweaters that would be at home on a college campus, and Windbreaker-type jackets that would meet dress code standards at a prestigious members-only yacht club. His meticulously groomed hair had just the right touch of gray at the temples, with a lock only occasionally slipping from place to dangle on his forehead.

At the Alf Landon Dinner in New York City on October 18, 2012, Romney quipped, "A campaign can require a lot of wardrobe changes—blue jeans in the morning perhaps, suits for a lunch fundraiser, sport coat for dinner—but it's nice to finally relax and to wear what Ann and I wear around the house."[2]

At the time, of course, Romney and Obama were on the dais as guests of honor, both wearing tuxedos at a white-tie dinner.

If Mitt Romney looked as though he belonged in a country club, Barack Obama, in contrast, looked as if he would be most comfortable on the streets of Chicago. Obama typically showed up at his campaign rallies wearing an open-collar shirt with the sleeves rolled up to his elbows, ready for action. In a contrast with four years ago, Obama's closely cut hair now showed sprinkles of gray throughout, suggesting the angst of four years' hard work doing the people's business in the nation's capital. Yet somehow, even when Obama visited a country club for a round of golf, as he frequently did during his first term in office, he typically wore Bermuda shorts, a polo shirt, and a White Sox baseball cap, not exactly the look members of the nation's most elite country clubs generally prescribe as dress code.

Truthfully, while Romney was an establishment candidate groomed to be as comfortable in the governor's office in Massachusetts as he was in the corner office at Bain Capital, Obama was by nature a celebrity candidate, more comfortable dancing on television with Ellen DeGeneres or trading quips with Jay Leno on late-night television than debating face-to-face with a presidential challenger.

In 2004, Obama was propelled into the political spotlight by charisma. That charisma allowed Obama to turn the opportunity for an unknown state legislator from Illinois to give a keynote speech to the 2004 Democratic National Convention into a launching pad for an unprecedented rise to the top of the Democratic Party's presidential ticket a short four years later.

In 2012, while George Clooney and Sarah Jessica Parker headlined a host of glamorous stars from Hollywood, television, and pop music to campaign for Obama, personalities such as Clint Eastwood and Kid Rock, celebrities with blue-collar appeal, campaigned for Romney.

The Romney campaign castigated Obama for the many appearances Obama made on popular television networks and shows, including MTV and David Letterman's late night show, or for giving interviews to *Rolling Stone* and entertainment magazines instead of to serious news outlets that might subject Obama to hard questions.

But Obama's pop-star appearances and interviews were not by accident.

David Axelrod, the public relations guru behind Obama's rise to national political stardom, knew precisely what he was doing, scheduling Obama to show up for interviews with the women hosts of ABC's morning chat show, *The View*.

Obama, Axelrod calculated correctly, would not win reelection by pressing issues of the economy or foreign policy, where first-term shortcomings and failures would be scrutinized. He would win by flashing his broad smile, certain to be liked by voters willing to think "Forward!" with a social welfare agenda so broadly defined that the candidate could dismiss as work yet undone a host of economic problems, including persistent high unemployment, rising taxes, and trillion-dollar federal budget deficits.

As the first US president of African descent, Barack Obama was a celebrity not only in the United States but also around the world.

Even charges of a failed first term could neither diminish nor tarnish Obama's place in history, nor his fundamental likability to Democratic voters.

In 2012, a loving mainstream media allowed Obama to borrow "Forward!" without commenting he was copying the hackneyed slogan European socialists have used for decades, much as the mainstream media in 2008 allowed Obama to campaign on the broadly promised "Hope and Change" without demanding precise definitions of what exactly that slogan meant.

Democratic voters, identified through techniques of interest group identity politics, were happy to vote for Obama, as long as he promised to keep the social welfare state working for their benefit.

If the candidate could avoid press scrutiny, Axelrod calculated, Obama's coalition would vote for him a second time, without asking whether Obama had done anything concrete in his first term in office to improve their economic condition.

The candidate as celebrity was exactly the positioning Jim Messina, David Plouffe, and David Axelrod wanted in running Obama's successful 2012 presidential campaign.

A celebrity like Obama was by personality and temperament "cool." This showed well on television. "No Drama Obama" was exactly the appeal

Axelrod had calculated would win the hearts and minds of voters a second time, propelling Obama into his second term as president.

Ironically, Obama's credentials could not have been more establishment: Occidental College in California, followed by Columbia University in New York City, and Harvard for law school. Yet, Axelrod cleverly positioned Obama, in running for president, as the community organizer from Chicago who was out to champion the downtrodden—much as FDR, equally well-groomed by high school at Groton, an undergraduate degree from Harvard, and two years law school at Columbia, hid his "blue blood" heritage when appealing to the minority downtrodden, the unemployed, and the working poor at the depth of the 1930s Depression.

In his day, FDR was every bit as much the celebrity as Obama is today, appealing to America through radio fireside chats that made middle-class voters feel at home with him, despite his Hyde Park pedigree. Even in the darkest hours of the Great Depression, the liberal press could always count on FDR for a cheerful smile and a confident wave of the hand, with softly curling smoke lofting high from the cigarette lit in an elegant cigarette holder perched upward in the corner of his mouth.

And in 2012, even as the Arab Spring turned into radical Islamic takeovers in North African countries and a US ambassador was murdered in a vicious terrorist attack, Obama could always be counted on to flash his famous smile and wave with confidence as he hopped off the stage at a campaign rally to shake hands with admiring supporters eager to touch him.

THE 2012 PRESIDENTIAL ELECTION: A REPEAT OF 1948?

In many ways, the 2012 presidential election was a repeat of the 1948 election, when Democrat Harry S. Truman, who became president in April 1945 with the death of FDR, defeated GOP challenger Thomas E. Dewey, who was then the forty-seventh governor of the state of New York.

In 1948, the presidential campaign pitted the establishment favorite, Dewey, against the people's choice, Truman, with Truman rolling up his sleeves to hop on a "whistle-stop" railroad campaign stopping at countless small Midwest towns to give speeches from the back of the caboose to ordinary folks, while Dewey campaigned in pin-striped suits to ballrooms of city slickers paying fundraiser prices to eat rubber chicken in New York hotels.

Eight years earlier, in 1940, corporate attorney Wendell Lewis Willkie lost to FDR, who was then running for an unprecedented fourth term as president. Willkie and Dewey were both considered members of the liberal wing of the GOP, contrasted with Robert Taft—son of the former president and Supreme Court chief justice William Howard Taft—who then led the conservative wing of the GOP.

Willkie so closely resembled a Democrat that FDR even had appointed him to be an ambassador-at-large after the 1940 election. After globetrotting in this position among the Allied nations during World War II, Willkie, very much sounding like a leftist utopian, wrote a book published in 1943, titled *One World*, which articulated an internationalist vision of a "one world government" that would unite nations against white colonialism, imperialism, and fascism.[3]

Dewey turned out to be a two-time loser, nominated for president by the GOP in 1944 and then again in 1948. The mainstream media, in those years sympathetic to the GOP's liberal Eastern establishment, championed Dewey's presidential candidacy in a determined effort to quash the more conservative Taft's presidential ambitions.

Elected to the US Senate in 1938, Taft was an outspoken critic of the New Deal, irritating the mainstream media every bit as much as his criticism of FDR rankled the big-government establishment GOP in Washington and New York.

The moment Dewey became the GOP presidential candidate in 1948, the mainstream media of the day proclaimed this time Dewey was the presumptive winner who would oust from the White House Truman, a president who had yet to be elected to the office.

In 1948, the press corps in Washington, the nation's political capital, and New York, the nation's financial capital, portrayed Truman as inept, an insignificant politician largely unqualified to be president, a leader who could never live up to FDR's standard. The liberal press, in their lingering adoration of FDR, castigated Truman as having ascended to the presidency only because he was lucky enough to have been selected by FDR to be his running mate in FDR's fourth and last campaign for the White House. The liberal press of the day portrayed Truman as if his only qualification for politics was that the Tom Pendergast, corrupt political machine had promoted him to be a local hack politician in Kansas City, Missouri. The press never tired of pointing out that Truman's haberdashery business in Kansas City, which he opened when he returned home after World War I, failed in bankruptcy. The mainstream media parroted with great delight the GOP's Eastern establishment talking point, that Dewey embodied the postwar path to prosperity.

To promote Dewey's candidacy in 1944 and 1948, the GOP establishment enlisted the assistance of George Gallup, the former head of the American Institute of Public Opinion in Princeton, New Jersey, who in 1935 founded the Gallup Organization to conduct public opinion polls. In 1944, a Gallup poll announcing Dewey had 68 percent of Republican voters supporting him virtually assured him the nomination. In 1948, the Republican National Committee met in the first-ever televised presidential nominating convention at the Municipal Auditorium in Pennsylvania from June 21 to 25, 1948, to nominate Dewey a second time, convinced he could beat Truman even though he had failed to beat FDR. The Gallup polls throughout the campaign season suggested public opinion was with Dewey, despite the undecided voters who were dismissed as unimportant. Still, large numbers of undecided voters persistently showed up in the polls, casting a shadow on the drum roll to victory the GOP establishment, with the willing complicity of the left-oriented mainstream media, was trying to orchestrate.

A CHOICE, NOT AN ECHO

Phyllis Schlafly's 1964 self-published book titled *A Choice, Not an Echo* contains a brilliant analysis of the 1948 presidential campaign between Truman and Dewey.[4] Schlafly charged that Dewey, to win the 1944 GOP presidential nomination, "abandoned his isolationist views, joined with the New York internationalists," and accepted the blessing of the small group of GOP "kingmakers" who then ran the party. Dewey's mission, according to Schlafly, was to exclude true conservatives like Senator Taft from setting the future direction of the GOP.

After characterizing Dewey's 1944 presidential effort as a "me-too" campaign, Schlafly wrote that Dewey's second, 1948 campaign would not be much different: "[The New York kingmakers] will not permit a candidate on the ticket—even in second place—unless he has a foreign policy acceptable to the New York financiers and banking interests who profit so greatly from the New Deal foreign policy."[5]

Schlafly charged that Dewey and "the kingmakers" chose then-California Governor Earl Warren as vice presidential candidate, after both promised that neither would mention "the hottest issue of the day—the one on which the Democrats were most vulnerable—the issue of communist infiltration in the federal government."[6]

Even in 1948, the left in the Democratic Party New Deal did their best to dictate what was considered politically correct, determined to exclude certain topics as unacceptable, not permitted in public policy discourse.

In 1948, Truman campaigned against the "do-nothing" Republican Congress, a congress dominated by Taft.

Schlafly berated Dewey for failing to defend conservative principles:

> Truman pitched his campaign against the Republican 80th Congress. Dewey made a fatal mistake when he did not defend it. The Republican 80th Congress, under the leadership of Robert Taft, had made the greatest record of any Congress in the 20th century. For the first time since the start of the New Deal, it reduced taxes, balanced the budget and reduced the national debt. It exposed Alger Hiss, Harry Dexter White and other communists in the New Deal. It launched the Greek-Turkish Military Aid Plan which under General Van Fleet crushed the communist guerillas in Greece. It enacted the Taft-Hartley Law over Truman's veto. It rejected Truman's plan to draft railroad strikers into the Army. It authorized the Hoover Commission to reorganize the government. It passed the 22nd Amendment to the Constitution limiting the president to two terms. By any standard, it was a constructive, responsible Congress and would have been a winning issue for Republicans.[7]

But by running yet another "me-too" campaign in 1948, refusing to criticize sharply Truman or the New Deal, Dewey "truly snatched defeat from the jaws of victory," Schlafly concluded.

Establishment Republicans woke up on November 3, 1948, the day after Election Day, surprised to discover that even favorable Gallup polls and a lapdog mainstream media were not enough to stampede American voters into electing Dewey over Truman. That day, Truman reveled in having confounded the pundits, famously holding up for the press to photograph the front page of the *Chicago Daily Tribune,* which proclaimed incorrectly, "Dewey Defeats Truman."

In *A Choice, Not an Echo*—a book that sold over 3 million copies—Schlafly argued the GOP should stop picking as presidential candidates establishment Republican politicians whose public policy positions were largely indistinguishable from those advanced by their liberal Democratic Party counterparts. In arguing for the GOP to select a truly conservative presidential candidate, Schlafly championed Senator Barry Goldwater's 1964 campaign, an effort that prefigured the rise of Ronald Reagan.

Schlafly's main point was that "me-too" GOP presidential candidates were almost certain to lose, precisely because they were closet leftists presenting themselves as centrists.

By echoing the Democratic Party, the GOP in 1948 failed to give the American public a true choice.

Ultimately, Schlafly argued, the GOP establishment was in agreement with the internationalist "one world government" ambitions of a leftist Democratic Party determined to expand the New Deal into the type of cradle-to-grave social welfare state modern Democrats led by Barack Obama are advancing. Establishment Republicans, she insisted, have a vested financial and business interest in a globalist foreign policy and a burgeoning federal government, while heavily regulating the economy to their elitist advantage.

Rather than evade the issues in a "me-too" campaign, Schlafly wanted GOP presidential candidates to take on liberal Democrats directly, arguing strong conservative public policy alternatives she felt would be well received by voters.

"America is best served when the two great political parties compete with one another to the fullest possible extent consistent with ethical conduct," Schlafly urged. "It was in the forum of vigorous political debate that the United States Constitution was hammered out by the Founding Fathers. Abraham Lincoln rose to greatness from the platform of hard-hitting partisan debates with Stephen A. Douglas over issues that were just as important to our country's survival as any issues today."

Schlafly argued that political campaigns should be "competitive and adversarial," advancing her argument that establishment GOP presidential candidates are doomed to lose precisely because they echo Democratic Party policies, presenting the American voter with no real choice between the two.

When the 1948 presidential election votes were tallied, Truman won twenty-eight of the nation's then forty-eight states, for a total of 303 electoral votes.

Dewey won only sixteen states in total, for 186 electoral votes.

ROMNEY, A MODERN-DAY DEWEY

In 2012, Romney was the choice of the establishment GOP, every bit as much as Willkie had been in 1940 and Dewey was in 1944 and 1948.

Given Romney's left-leaning record as governor of Massachusetts, he would have difficulty drawing sharp public policy disagreements with Obama. After all, "Romneycare" in Massachusetts preceded "Obamacare," arguably serving as the model for Obama's government-engineered takeover of the entire health-services sector of the US economy. In Massachusetts, Romney had supported abortion, stem-cell research, and same-sex marriage, making it difficult if not impossible to attract support from moral conservatives.

Conservative opponents of Romney's candidacy had compiled enough opposition research on Romney's tenure of office as governor in Massachusetts to fill more than one book discrediting Romney as a right-leaning Republican. With a huge quantity of opposition research on Romney readily available to conservatives, going back to 2005 when Romney first started making sounds that he intended to run for president, Obama's opposition research in 2012 was certain to have readily available numerous Romney speeches and press conferences from which sound bites could be hammered into television commercials making Romney as governor in Massachusetts appear to be in lockstep agreement with President Obama on virtually any policy issue under discussion.

"The road to the White House gets rocky when you're a Massachusetts flip-flopper," wrote Joan Vennochi in the *Boston Globe* in 2006.[8]

Vennochi was criticizing Romney for an appearance on *Fox News Sunday* when host Chris Wallace pressed him to reconcile a past pro-choice statement with his current anti-abortion stance. Vennochi dismissed Romney's attempt to say his position on abortion had "evolved," arguing instead that Romney's position on abortion revolved around where Romney was in his political career—in the Bay State or beyond.

"But thanks to Massachusetts, the man born Willard Romney has a Clintonesque 'Slick Willie' image problem to overcome," Vennochi concluded. "Romney said certain things to win election here. He will have to answer for them."

But to appreciate Schlafly's argument, realize that in 2012 Romney was the preferred choice of the establishment GOP precisely because he did not hold firmly any political beliefs fundamentally in conflict with Obama.

Regardless which candidate won—Romney or Obama—establishment Republicans on Wall Street in New York and on K Street in Washington, DC, could fully expect nothing much would change. Globalism would continue to dominate US domestic policy, with the International Monetary Fund and the World Bank playing a central role in US domestic economic policy dominated by the Federal Reserve and the Treasury, regardless of whether Romney or Obama won. Equally, in a Romney administration or a second Obama term, the United Nations and NATO would remain center stage in US foreign policy.

Under Romney, the federal government would continue to grow, if only at a slightly less accelerated rate of increase. Under Romney, entitlement programs would continue to grow, if only at a slightly less accelerated rate of increase. Under Romney, the United States would remain in NAFTA and the World Trade Organization.

In 2012, the presidential election once again proved Schlafly was right: establishment Republicans running "me-too" presidential campaigns tend to lose.

ROMNEY'S "DON'T-ROCK-THE-BOAT" ADVISORS

Much overlooked in the surreptitiously video-recorded fundraiser in which Romney made his infamous "47 percent" comment are the questions from supporters regarding why he was not attacking Obama more aggressively.

When pressed by the financial supporters in attendance to start trumpeting Obama's first-term failures, Romney responded he did not want to attack Obama directly.

"Those people I told you, the 5 to 6 or 7 percent that we have to bring onto our side, they all voted for Barack Obama four years ago," Romney reasoned. "So, and by the way, when you say to them, 'Do you think Barack Obama is a failure?' they overwhelmingly say no. They like him. But when you say, 'Are you disappointed that his policies haven't worked?' they say yes. And because they voted for him, they don't want to be told that they were wrong, that he's a bad guy, that he did bad things, that he's corrupt. Those people that we have to get, they want to think they did the right thing but he just wasn't up to the task. They love the phrase, 'He's in over his head.'"[9]

Romney continued to stress he needed to win over Obama voters who were disappointed, but not so disappointed that they agreed with the GOP. For this reason, Romney explained he did not want to vilify Obama, even though Romney conceded that Obama's attempt to vilify him as "an evil, bad guy" who succeeded in business by closing businesses and laying people off was succeeding.

When one donor attending the event expressed disappointment that Romney was not attacking Obama with sufficient intellectual firepower, Romney countered that the campaign trail was no place for detail-oriented arguments.

"Well, I wrote a book that lays out my view for what has to happen in the country, and people who are fascinated by policy will read the book," Romney answered. "We have a website that lays out white papers on a whole series of issues that I care about. I have to tell you, I don't think this will have a significant impact on my electability. I wish it did. I think our ads will have a much bigger impact. I think the debates will have a big impact . . . My dad used to say, 'Being right early is not good in politics.' And in a setting like this, a highly intellectual subject discussion on a whole series of important topics typically doesn't win elections. . . . For instance, this president won because of 'Hope and Change.'"

Romney supported his team of advisors, arguing his key people had won important races before, apparently in defense of his contention that not attacking Obama directly would be a successful strategy.

"I have a very good team of extraordinarily experienced, highly successful consultants, a couple of people in particular who have done races around the world," Romney said. "These guys in the US—the Karl Rove equivalents—they do races all over the world: in Armenia, in Africa, in Israel. I mean, they work for Bibi Netanyahu in his race. So they do these races, and they see which ads work, and which processes work best, and we have ideas about what we do over the course of the campaign. I'd tell them to you, but I'd have to shoot you."

He explained that the campaign was using his wife, Ann Romney, "sparingly . . . so that people don't get tired of her." He said he turned down an invitation to be on *Saturday Night Live* because he was concerned the appearance "has the potential of looking slapstick and not presidential."

In the final analysis, Romney was confident people would see his business experience as a promise that he would be more capable than Obama in creating jobs and restoring prosperity to America.

STAY POSITIVE, MAINSTREAM MEDIA ADVISES WHILE ATTACKING

What Romney had not fully anticipated was the desire of the mainstream media to shape the message.

Writing in November 2011, a full year before the 2012 presidential election, Michael Barbaro of the *New York Times* began investigating and writing about Romney's tenure at Bain Capital. One of the deals Barbaro reported was Dade International, a medical technologies firm that went bankrupt, but only after Bain Capital collected $242 million.

"At Bain Capital's direction, Dade quadrupled the money it owed creditors and vendors," Barbaro wrote. "It took steps that propelled the business toward bankruptcy. And in waves of layoffs, it cut loose 1,700 workers in the United States, including Brian and Christine Shoemaker, who lost their jobs at a plant in Westwood, Mass. Staggered, Mr. Shoemaker wondered, 'How can the bean counters just come in here and say, *Hey, it's over?*'"

Barbaro detailed how Bain and a small group of investors acquired Dade International in 1994, "with mostly borrowed money, limiting their risk." He then explained how Bain and the other investors "extracted cash from the company at almost every turn—paying themselves nearly $100 million in fees, first for buying the company and then for helping to run it."[10]

Barbaro laid the groundwork for accusations that Dade collapsed only because it was unable to pay the debt Bain added to the company, giving the company enough capital to acquire other companies in leveraged acquisitions, always with the result that Bain collected large fees. Romney and his fellow investors were depicted as only interested in their own profits, going so far as to close a Dade International plant in Puerto Rico. After Bain convinced the Puerto Rican workers to move to Miami, Bain close down the Miami plant as well.

To make the story even worse, critics charged that Bain refused to allow the workers to return to Puerto Rico from Miami until they first reimbursed Dade for the cost of moving them to Miami in the first place. The idea was that Romney and his investor buddies had "absolutely no concern for the employees."[11]

During the 2012 presidential campaign, Barbaro worked as "traveling press" with the Romney campaign, finding time between campaign flights to travel to Boston to locate and interview Romney's barber.

"Nobody has a more complicated and intimate relationship with Mr. Romney's hair than the man who has styled it for more than two decades, a barrel-chested, bald Italian immigrant named Leon de Magistris," Barbaro reported in the *New York Times*. "For years, Mr. de Magistris said in an interview, he has tried to persuade Mr. Romney, 64, to loosen up his look by tousling his meticulous mane. 'I will tell him to mess it up a little bit,' said Mr. de Magistris, 69. 'I said to him, 'Let it be more natural.' That suggestion has not gone over well. 'He wants a look that is very controlled.' Mr. de Magistris said. 'He is a very controlled man. The hair goes with the man.'"[12]

Barbaro described Romney's hairstyle as "a restrained, classic look: short at the neck, neat on the sides and swept back off the forehead." In Belmont, Massachusetts, "a well-heeled suburb of Boston," as Barbaro described the town, the style was so well-known in 2011 that patrons asked Mr. de Magistris for the cut by name: "The Mitt."

Barbaro reported that Romney paid seventy dollars for a trim and that the hair color was completely natural, including the white tints on the side of Romney's forehead. He added that Romney's hair held its shape under all but the most extreme conditions, completely gel- and mousse-free.

"I don't put any product in there," the barber told Barbaro.[13]

In reporting on Romney, Barbaro appeared to have multiple goals. Yes, he wanted to convey to voters an image of Romney as an impersonal, uncaring corporate type. But more than that, Barbaro also wanted to convince the Romney camp the best way to win was to lay off attacking Obama. Barbaro used the pages of the *New York Times* to send a message to the Romney camp that Obama could not have delivered better himself: Romney should conduct a positive campaign focused on his message, because that's what Republican voters wanted him to do. Forget the conventional wisdom that voters enjoy political contests much as they enjoy sports. A baseball or football game is best when two equally matched teams go all out to win. Besides, professional politicians know that while voters tell pollsters they do not like negative ads, the reason successful campaigns produce negative ads is because negative ads work.

"Prominent party leaders, unsettled by the frequently combative tone of Mr. Romney's presidential campaign, are pressing the presumptive Republican nominee to leaven his harsh criticism of President Obama with an optimistic conservative vision that can inspire the party faithful, appeal to swing voters and set out a governing agenda should he win in November," Barbaro wrote in April 2012, as Romney was still slugging it out with Republican contenders in the primaries. "In these interviews, these Republicans said that Mr. Romney should focus more on what he is for, not just what he is against."[14]

Barbaro reinforced his argument by suggesting conservative William Kristol was giving Romney the same advice.

Barbaro cited Kristol writing in the *Weekly Standard*, where he said, "If I had to put money down now, I'd bet that Mitt Romney will win an easy victory after a relatively predictable, issue-focused, and not-too-nasty campaign."[15]

Big themes and big challenges, not mean-spirited attacks on Obama's records, were also Kristol's advice, disdaining the "small and nasty stuff" that Kristol felt was the grist mill of campaigns where Democrats excelled.[16]

After four years in office, Obama and those who supported his reelection correctly suspected the most assured way to win four more years was to convince Romney he had a better chance of winning if the GOP avoided pressing Obama to defend his record in office.

Ultimately, Romney and his advisors took the bait.

OBAMA'S DEBATE WOES

Ironically—and perhaps predictably—the only time Romney's star rose noticeably in the 2012 presidential campaign was during the first debate, when Romney decided uncharacteristically to take the offensive, attacking Obama.

At the first presidential debate in Denver, Colorado, on October 3, 2012, dealing with domestic policy, Romney was aggressive, constantly pressing Obama on issues.

"You've been president for four years," Romney insisted. "You said you'd cut the deficit in half. It's now four years later. We still have trillion-dollar deficits."[17]

The reaction was immediate, strong, and very positive for Romney. A

CNN poll just after the debate showed 67 percent believed Romney won, with only 25 percent for Obama.[18]

Even the *New York Times* had to admit Romney scored points.

"If Mr. Romney's goal was to show that he could project equal stature to the president, he succeeded, perhaps offering his campaign the lift that Republicans have been seeking," wrote Jeff Zeleny and Jim Rutenberg. "The two quarreled aggressively over tax policy, the budget deficit and the role of government, with each man accusing the other of being evasive and misleading voters."[19]

But having gained an advantage being aggressive in the first debate, Romney suddenly shifted strategy, so as not to offend the Obama voters Romney felt must be induced to his side. Romney abandoned attacking Obama as he had in the first debate. By the third debate, Romney spent much of the time agreeing with Obama, even when Obama did not want to appear to be in agreement.

Consider, for instance, the following exchange in the third debate, regarding Iraq:

> MR. ROMNEY: Number two, with regards to Iraq, you and I agreed, I believe, that there should have been a status of forces agreement. Did you—
>
> PRESIDENT OBAMA: That's not true.
>
> MR. ROMNEY: Oh, you didn't—you didn't want a status of forces agreement?
>
> PRESIDENT OBAMA: No, but what I—what I would not have done is left 10,000 troops in Iraq that would tie us down. That certainly would not help us in the Middle East.
>
> MR. ROMNEY: I'm sorry, you actually—there was a--
>
> PRESIDENT OBAMA: Here—here is—here is--
>
> MR. ROMNEY: There was an effort on the part of the president to have a status of forces agreement. And I concurred in that and said we should have some number of troops that stayed on. That was something I concurred with.[20]

Not surprisingly, a *USA Today*/Gallup poll showed 56 percent of the viewers believed Obama won the third debate, while only one-third preferred Romney.[21]

ROMNEY, NOT OBAMA, LOSES GROUND ON BENGHAZI

In a press conference in Jacksonville, Florida, within hours after the attack in Benghazi, Libya, that killed US ambassador Christopher Stevens on the anniversary of 9/11, Romney criticized a statement released by the US embassy in Cairo some six hours prior to the attack in Benghazi.

"The embassy in Cairo put out a statement after their grounds had been breached, protestors were inside the grounds, they reiterated that statement after the breach," Romney told reporters. "I think it's a terrible course for America to stand in apology for our values; that instead when our grounds are being attacked and being breached that the first response of the United States must be outrage at the breach of the sovereignty of our nation. An apology for America's values is never the right choice."[22]

Basically, Romney was charging the Obama administration's response to the Benghazi attacks was "disgraceful" and amounted to apologizing to the militants.

Almost immediately, reporters peppered Romney with questions, suggesting his statement was inappropriate because events were still unfolding. Obama himself charged Romney with "shooting first and aiming later."[23]

Romney's position was compromised because the statement from the Cairo embassy was issued some six hours prior to the Benghazi attack and was addressing only the reaction of Egyptian Muslims to an anti-Islam film that moved to the center of the controversy, both over the embassy attack in Cairo and the Benghazi attack that cost Ambassador Stevens his life.

Romney's "gaffe" quickly became the focus of press attention, not the Benghazi attack itself.

"I can't avoid the feeling that this tragedy—four American diplomats killed—was just overshadowed by the intense focus on the Romney gaffe, if it was a gaffe," admitted CNN host Howard Kurtz.[24]

The liberal press used Romney's statement to turn the Benghazi attack not into a question of whether Obama policy in the Middle East had failed, but into an examination of whether Romney was trying to take advantage of the tragedy to score unfair political points in the presidential campaign.

The lesson the Romney campaign appeared to take from the incident was that it would be better for Romney to avoid making news during the remainder of the presidential campaign. Quickly, the Romney campaign changed gears and went back to the policy of focusing on Romney's positive economic message, making a conscious decision to avoid attacking Obama directly if and when such opportunities should arise.

After the first debate, the press narrative continued to pound that Romney's comments on Benghazi proved he was not prepared to be president, while dismissing Obama's debate debacle as proof only that Obama needed to take the campaign a little more seriously. The mainstream media traveling with the Romney campaign could not imagine Obama might lose to what they considered an obvious also-ran like Mitt Romney, a second-rate politician many if not most of the traveling press believed had peaked several years ago when serving as governor of Massachusetts.

Skillfully, the mainstream media managed to transform much of the 2012 presidential campaign into a referendum on Romney, not on Obama's first-term performance.

Romney's "47 percent" comment surfaced just days later, filling newspapers, radio talk shows, and twenty-four-hour television news broadcasts with endless opportunities for Republican and Democratic pundits to face off and debate. Both issues were identical in raising questions about Romney's qualifications to be president. Both issues were identical in deflecting attention from the struggling economy or a foreign policy marred by violence in the Middle East—issues the Obama campaign did not want to discuss or debate.

In retrospect, the only professionals to think Obama's debacle in the first debate was a watershed event in the campaign were Romney's top staff, and that conclusion ended up being to the detriment of the campaign's prospects for success.

ROMNEY'S DEBATE MISCALCULATION

"October 3, 2012, was an historic date," Romney long-term political consultant Beth Myers said on the campaign trail. "It's the day everything changed for the Romney campaign."

Myers was convinced that when Romney won the presidency, beating

Obama, history would show the tide had changed during the first debate. Following the first debate, Romney's crowds grew appreciably. From the moment the first debate ended, the Romney team believed they were winning.

Obama did poorly in the first debate because preparing for the debates demanded what Obama liked least: hours spent studying public policy challenges and even more hours spent practicing in mock debates against Romney stand-ins. To Obama, already a sitting president, the preparation required to run for president was a tedious if not unbearably boring chore. Besides, why debate at all? Debates predictably meant Obama's actions and decisions as president would be criticized, perhaps severely, in front of millions of voters—something Obama did not view as fun, certainly not nearly as fun as celebrity guest appearances on national television.

Put simply, Obama gave every appearance of resenting criticism. Rather than seeing criticism as an opportunity for self-improvement, Obama showed signs of being particularly thin-skinned, sensitive to being called on the carpet for allegedly falling short.

In the three days running up to the Denver debate, Obama watched football rather than cram. Next, he visited volunteers in a field office. Then finally, on the day before the debate, he visited the Hoover Dam.

"The power generated here, where's it going?" Obama asked Rob Skordas, the assistant dam manager in charge of history and operational logistics, as reported by Politico.

Obama expressed surprise that most of the power went to Southern California.

"I always assumed Vegas got its power from here," he said, being photographed smiling, wearing sunglasses but no hat, looking cool and relaxed in the Western sun, with the Hoover Dam squarely behind him, framed in the distant background.[25]

"In an extraordinary insight into the events leading up to the 90 minute showdown [that] changed the face of the election, a Democrat close to the Obama campaign today reveals that the President also did not take his debate preparation seriously, ignored the advice of senior aides and ignored one-liners that had been prepared to wound Romney," wrote Toby Harnden in the *Daily Mail* in the United Kingdom, on October 9, 2012, in the wake of the first 2012 presidential debate in Denver. "The Democrat said that Obama's inner circle was dismayed at the 'disaster' and that he believed the central problem was that the President was so disdainful of Romney that he didn't believe he needed to engage with him. 'President Obama made it clear he wanted to be doing anything else—anything—but debate prep,' the Democrat said. 'He kept breaking off whenever he got the opportunity and never really focused on the event.'"[26]

The second debate was a different story.

"The Oct. 3 debate sharply exposed Mr. Obama's vulnerabilities and focused the president and his advisers to work to reclaim the campaign over a grueling 30 days, ending with his triumph on Tuesday," wrote Adam Nagourney, Ashley Parker, Jim Rutenberg, and Jeff Zeleny in their *New York Times* summary of the election campaign, published in the newspaper the day after the election. "After a summer of growing confidence, Mr. Obama suddenly confronted the possibility of a loss that would diminish his legacy and threaten his signature achievement, the health-care law. He emerged newly combative, newly contrite and newly willing to recognize how his disdain for Mr. Romney had blinded him to his opponent's strengths and ability to inflict damage."[27]

The *Times* reporters chronicled how Obama's campaign began an all-out assault on Romney's credibility and conservative views following the first debate, determined to tip the balance back in their favor. The Obama campaign's internal polls showed Romney had scored points in the first debate, but the gain for Romney was not enough to put Romney in the lead.

The Romney campaign saw it differently. Immediately after the first debate, Romney's internal polls put him ahead in the presidential race—a position Romney's internal pollsters believed Romney held right through the campaign until Election Day.

After the third debate, Ron Fournier, writing in the *National Journal*, concluded that even though Obama won the third debate, Romney won the debate season.

"With an acceptable, though far from exceptional, performance in his third and final face-off with President Obama, the former Massachusetts governor became one of the few presidential candidates to make debates matter," Fournier wrote. "Bottom line: Obama won Monday night's debate on points, benefiting from the blessings of incumbency and hard-world experience. But the challenger held his own, and thus the state of the race is likely unchanged."[28]

Romney and his advisors incorrectly chose to believe the first debate had washed out everything that occurred before, including the mainstream media's ability to make his experience at Bain Capital and his unfortunate "47 percent" remarks impact the election. This miscalculation was one of the most severe made by the Romney campaign, and it was a miscalculation reinforced by the willingness of the campaign's top advisors to believe their internal polls.

Obama's campaign had the advantage in that the extensive expenditure in voter-intelligence computer metrics served to correct internal polls. Running thousands of simulations of voter preference and voter turnout through the millions of voter microdata records the campaign had collected on individual voters allowed Obama's top campaign advisors to realize Obama's New Deal coalition was holding together, largely unaffected by Romney's superior performance in the first debate.

Lacking a sophisticated computer-driven voter-intelligence system, Romney's top advisors had only their gut instincts to tell if their internal polls were correct or skewed.

Obama's team correctly calculated members of his New Deal coalition were so deeply into the grasp of identity politics that their support for Obama was virtually unshakable, immune to the gains and losses of a presidential campaign's daily gyrations. Put simply, African Americans, Hispanics, union workers, single women, and a large contingent of the nation's youth were so determined to vote for Obama that what happened in the campaign was basically irrelevant to their decision.

The contrast with the thinking of Romney's top campaign advisors could not have been sharper. Romney's advisors still saw the election in traditional terms, as if the election would be decided by which of the two candidates did the best convincing yet undecided voters.

To make matters worse, Romney's advisors felt their internal polls were correct because they showed an uptick for Romney after the first debate that mirrored a simultaneous turn in major national polls. The Gallup poll is particularly relevant in demonstrating this point. In the days up until the first debate in Denver, Gallup had been reporting Obama was beating Romney by 4 points, 49 percent to 45 percent. After the Denver debate, Romney shot to a lead over Obama of 49 percent to 47 percent.[29] By October 20, 2012, Gallup was reporting Romney's lead over Obama was as much as 6 points,

51 to 45 percent.[30] This major a turnaround, especially with the campaign's internal polls echoing it, convinced Romney's camp that the first debate was historic in that it marked the beginning of the end for Obama.

In retrospect, what the Denver debate may have really marked was the end of presidential campaigns relying on polling methodologies.

Romney's internal polls suffered from the same defect Romney's campaign insisted made unreliable previous polls showing Obama in the lead: oversampling. Romney's pollsters had factored in a lower Democratic Party turnout for 2012 than in 2008, anticipating Obama's economic record in the first term would dampen the enthusiasm of some 2008 Obama voters to return to the polls for him a second time. Romney's pollsters also overestimated the ability of Romney to attract Obama voters, failing to realize that the politics of personal interest was the driving force behind the identity groups forming Obama's 2012 voter coalition. In other words, Romney's top advisors failed to appreciate fully that Obama voters were going to vote for Obama because they believe Obama would do more for them than Romney would, regardless of what Romney promised. Debate points scored by Romney were irrelevant to the core group of identity voters that had already made up their minds Obama should be reelected. When Romney quit attacking Obama, no information was forthcoming that might force this core group of Obama identity voters to reconsider their prejudged conclusion.

The only time Romney was truly aggressive was in the first debate when his advisors felt he was behind and needed to score points. After the first debate, when Romney's advisors felt their candidate had turned the election around and Romney was headed to victory, the campaign made the fatal mistake of becoming cautious. By doing so, the Romney campaign abandoned the one tactic that might have given Romney a chance to beat Obama. If Romney had been as aggressive in the second and third debates as he had been in the first debate, it was possible to imagine the lead he had opened versus Obama in the polls might have continued widening. But with Romney dropping the offensive, Obama was given a chance to go on the offensive instead.

Clearly, the Romney campaign realized the mainstream media were only going to defend Obama if Romney had chosen to remain on the offensive. The way the media had pounced on Romney for daring to criticize Obama over Benghazi was proof of their intent. Skillfully, the mainstream media transformed the Benghazi attack into a Romney gaffe. Attacking Romney, the media traveling with the Romney campaign launched a narrative supported by the White House that Romney reacted before all the information was available. The press charged Romney for making a rookie error by not realizing the statement issued by the Cairo embassy blaming the anti-Islam film for Muslim violence was issued hours before, not after, the Benghazi attack.

The exchange over Benghazi in the second debate showed the Romney camp just how prepared the White House and the mainstream media were to defend Obama from criticism on the death of an ambassador, a scandal which probably would have tanked Obama's campaign had he been a Republican.

The key moment came in the second debate when moderator Candy Crowley of CNN, an obvious Obama proponent, interrupted Romney to insist Obama's Rose Garden statement the day after the Benghazi attack did mention "act of terror" late in the press conference.

Even the Obama-supporting Huffington Post acknowledged that Crowley's assertion allowed the president to dodge the real issue of why his administration had insisted for days the Benghazi attack was a reaction to the anti-Islam movie.[31] In the end, the Benghazi incident became much like the debate later in the campaign over whether or not GM was going to produce Jeeps in China: The Obama administration had indeed tried to mischaracterize the Benghazi attack as a reaction to the Islamic movie, and GM was going to produce Jeeps in China, but the truth was impotent to stop the perception once established. Romney ultimately had a claim to being right on both issues. But with a mainstream media determined to circle the wagons to protect Obama, Romney was ambushed on both issues the moment the press saw an opening to do so.

If the Romney campaign had decided to stay on the offensive after the Denver debate, the press most certainly would have redoubled efforts to undermine Romney's campaign, if only to assist Obama in slowing the momentum Romney would have gained from staying in attack mode.

The antagonism of the mainstream media was apparent to me as I rode the Romney campaign airplane for the last three weeks of the campaign, reporting for WND as a member of the traveling press. The moment a major spokesman for Romney walked to the back of the airplane, the mainstream media reporters riding along were ready to pounce. Their preferred questions inevitably moved to wedge issues, such as asking Romney to take a stand on abortion, especially after the mainstream media had induced Tea Party candidates to take compromising positions on the subject. Rather than ask what the Romney campaign's reaction was to UN ambassador Susan Rice's insistence on Sunday morning television shows after the Benghazi attack that the assault was caused by Muslim indignation over the film,[32] the mainstream media on the Romney airplane wanted to know if Romney agreed with Richard Mourdock, the Republican candidate running for the US Senate in Indiana, that rapes are "something God intended to happen."[33]

Clearly, any comment by Romney aides or surrogates on the subject of abortion would be twisted against Romney in the attempt to take his campaign off the economic issues where the campaign thought it could win, throwing public attention on issues of social morals where the Romney camp knew the campaign could only lose ground, regardless of what Romney said.

The point of bombarding Romney aides and surrogates with such questions was to get the Romney campaign off-message. Once off-message, the campaign was bound to make mistakes, venturing into territory where campaign strategists had not fully calculated the political impact of different answers. Besides, the mainstream media knew lifestyle issues like abortion were wedge issues that would only throw more single women voters into the Obama camp.

Rather than serving as objective reporters, the mainstream press on the Romney campaign plane acted as if they were secret agents that had somehow managed to infiltrate the enemy command post. Getting a Romney aide to say something about rape and God's intent became a coveted first prize these double agents posing as journalists coveted to win. The goal became not to report the truth, but to outdo for laughing rights a colleague competing for how much damage could be caused to the Romney camp from within.

LET THE GROUND GAME BEGIN

At the conclusion of the third presidential debate, held at Lynn University in Boca Raton, Florida, on October 22, 2012, a change occurred in the mood of Obama's top advisors, as noticeable as the change that took place in the mood of Romney's top advisors at the end of the first debate.

After the third debate, Obama's surrogates returned to the spin room to press the point that the debates were over and the campaign was about to enter the final postdebate phase—the ground game, where Obama's top advisors felt they would win. Obama top advisors declared correctly their candidate had weathered the debates, despite his initial irritation at being forced to appear toe-to-toe with a rival who was merely a challenger. If anything, October 22, 2012, marked the day when Obama, the celebrity, could return to what he did best—namely, giving campaign speeches—while the technocrats running his campaign could get serious about what they did best—the mind-numbing detail of the deadly serious mechanics involved in getting out the vote.

"What I care about is 15 more days to get 270 electoral votes, and I think we are on a pathway to do that," an Obama campaign manager said in the spin room after the third debate. "Our voters are excited, and we have the ground game to get there. We are leading in the early vote by 2-to-1. It says two things—it says our people are excited, and it says we have an organization that matters. We continue to feel good about our operation on the ground: person-to-person, having discussions supporter-to-supporter about why you're supporting the president. The next 15 days are about two things and two things only—persuading the undecided and turning out your supporters—and our ground game gives us the ability to do both things in a way that is verifiable. We are going with the president on a 48-hour trip around the country that is a big enthusiasm boost, and we are excited about it. This is about winning 270 electoral votes and watching battleground states that are very close. We feel good about our pathway."

Rather than focusing on the ground game after the third debate, Romney's team decided to expand the campaign into Obama territory, confident not only that the campaign's internal polls showed Romney remaining ahead, but also that the internal polls were so good for Romney that he had a chance to capture possibly two Obama-leaning blue states. On November 2, 2012, the Romney campaign headed into Wisconsin because Romney thought he could win the state that Barack Obama won by nearly 14 points in 2008, as explained by Romney campaign strategist Stuart Stevens.

"There's no bluffing in this game now," Stevens insisted.[34]

With Romney scheduling rallies in the final days of the 2012 presidential campaign in Pennsylvania as well as Wisconsin, top Romney strategists believed they were putting Obama on the defensive, forcing the Obama campaign to spend time and money in states once considered safely in Obama's column.

At the rally in Milwaukee on November 2, 2012, famed Green Bay Packers quarterback Bart Starr, Republican National Committee chairman Reince Priebus, and Wisconsin Governor Scott Walker introduced Romney. Romney spoke to a large crowd of twenty-five hundred supporters who gathered inside a window manufacturer's warehouse at the Wisconsin Products Pavilion at the State Fair Park, while another twenty-five hundred supporters who could not get in watched from a large, outdoor TV screen.

"What a great state, and what a great welcome. And by the way, this state is gonna help me become the next president of the United States," Romney told the enthusiastic crowd, a message similar to what he delivered in Ohio.

"Next to Ann Romney, Paul Ryan is the best choice I've ever made," he quipped, acknowledging to the Wisconsin audience that his vice presidential running mate was a native. "We are so very grateful to you and to people across the country, for all that you have given of yourselves to this campaign. This is not just about Paul and me—it is about America, and the future we will leave to our children. We thank you, and we ask you to stay at it all the way—all the way to victory on Tuesday night."[35]

At a gaggle held aboard Romney's campaign airplane in the first week of November 2012, Kevin Madden, Romney's campaign manager, stressed Romney intended to maintain a positive tone and planned to lay out a vision of what he would do in the first days of his presidency.

"For the remainder of the campaign until Election Day, the governor wants to talk about specifically what he would do on taking office to get the country back on track and fix the economy," he emphasized. "The theme 'Day One, Job One,' explains the theme Romney will take related to creating jobs, fixing schools, getting America energy independent—a whole number of these specifics, the governor is going to continue."

Madden stressed the Romney campaign had managed in the final weeks to capture the momentum.

"We can and we will win Ohio," Madden insisted. "If you take a number of these polls together, the trend line is in our favor. What I find very encouraging is that Governor Romney is leading with independents. But where we feel most confident is that we are playing offense with the map, while the Obama campaign has been forced to play defense."

This was the reason, Madden mentioned, that the Romney campaign planned to hold rallies in states like Wisconsin and Pennsylvania, states once considered safe for Obama. The Romney campaign's strategy was to give Obama no choice but to spend additional time and money in the final hours of the campaign visiting states like Minnesota, Wisconsin, and Pennsylvania and spending money with new advertising in the attempt to avoid erosion of his counted-upon Electoral College vote base.

"Obama is defending territory while we're playing offense," Madden argued. "As a result, we feel we are very well positioned right now."

7

OBAMA'S AMERICA VERSUS ROMNEY'S AMERICA

The commitments we make to each other—through Medicare and Medicaid and Social Security—these things do not sap our initiative; they strengthen us. They do not make us a nation of takers; they free us to take the risks that make this country great.

—Barack Obama, Second Inaugural Address, Washington, DC, March 21, 2013[1]

The president says he loves private enterprise, but he thinks government somehow has to get in there and pull all the strings. . . . The government needs to encourage free enterprise but then let the people to pursue their own dreams, pursue their own visions, pursue happiness as they know it.

—Mitt Romney, Campaign Rally at Chesapeake, Virginia, October 17, 2012

NO ANALYSIS OF THE 2012 ELECTION would be complete without examining the impact of the candidates' respective visions for America—their ideas, their philosophies, their platforms—as expressed during the campaign. But in 2012, the election didn't boil down to "Vision A" duking it out with "Vision B" for the title. Rather, it became a contest between one vision that reinforced the beliefs and fears of a coalition of voters and another that was drowned out or fell upon deaf ears. In fact, the two visions never had the opportunity to debate one another, to determine which might be the most beneficial for the nation—for in the end, 2012 wasn't so much a contest of ideas . . . as it was a contest in capturing voters.

Barack Obama and Mitt Romney presented contrasting visions of America that were almost diametrically opposed. Obama called for a continuation of the massive expansion of the federal government that began under his first term. Romney called for a rollback of government involvement in a cradle-to-grave social welfare state that promised no signs of curtailment under a second Obama term. Obama's core political principles derived from a leftist progressive agenda that can be traced back to his predecessors Teddy Roosevelt and Franklin Delano Roosevelt. In contrast, Romney argued for a reduction in the size and scope of government, with the intention of reviving private enterprise initiative to stimulate economic growth. If Obama drew policy inspiration from John Podesta's left-leaning Center for American Progress, Romney was closer to the conservative Heritage Institute.

In 2012, the question the two candidates put before the electorate was whether the United States would continue along the path of the European welfare states, with expanded government regulation and increased bureaucratic control of the economy, or whether the United States would return to an era of smaller government with restrictions on economic activity curtailed, so as to allow business in the United States to return to a more unregulated environment reminiscent of Ronald Reagan.

Under Obama, a new US government website, Regulations.gov, listed in November 2012 upwards of six thousand new regulations posted by US government agencies over the previous ninety days on a continuous basis, such that the Obama administration has averaged as many as sixty new regulations per day.[2] After the November 2012 election, US government agencies were ready to issue, should Obama win reelection, a "tsunami" of new regulations implementing Obamacare and favoring groups that supported the Democrats in the election, including environmentalists and labor unions.[3] The Environmental Protection Agency alone had held off implementing a series of restrictions on the use of coal that were anticipated to result in a wave of power-plant closings around the nation, with the result that tens of thousands of workers would be unemployed.[4]

"We know that to fix our economy, we've got to make sure: that we have the most competitive workforce in the world, that we have a better education system, that we are investing in research and development, that we've got world-class infrastructure, that we're reducing our health care costs, and that we're expanding our exports," Obama told Chris Hughes in an interview published in the *New Republic* shortly after the second inauguration.[5]

This statement confirms Obama's intention to reward teachers' unions, to continue government expenditures on infrastructure such as the $787 billion stimulus package Obama pushed through at the start of his first term, and to implement Obamacare with the anticipated result that at full implementation Obamacare would result in placing one-sixth of the US economy under government control.

"On climate change, it's a daunting task," Obama continued in the interview with the *New Republic*. "But we know what releases carbon into the atmosphere, and we have tools right now that would start scaling that back, although we'd still need some big technological breakthrough." Obama suggested that if he could not get new legislation through Congress, he might just decide to pursue implementing climate control measures by executive fiat.

Ideologically, Obama planned to give free reign to the EPA to restrict the use of hydrocarbon fuels and possibly angle toward implementing a carbon tax, again targeting an identity group—the environmentalists—who would support his reelection. The statement suggested Obama intended to advance an ideological concern over global warming even if the scientific basis for it had been discredited by the "Climategate" release of e-mails from the Climatic Research Unit at the University of East Anglia, beginning in November 2009.[6]

THE ROMNEY ECONOMIC PLAN

In Ames, Iowa, on Friday, October 26, 2012, in what was billed as a major economic policy address, Romney presented his vision for achieving genuine economic growth in the next four years, while charging Barack Obama with a record of failure in his stewardship of the economy.[7]

"The choice you make this November will shape great things, historic things, and those things will determine the most intimate and important aspects of every American life and every American family," Romney began, stressing that the electorate in 2012 stood at a crossroad. "We are at a turning point today. Our national debt and liabilities threaten to crush our future; our economy struggles under the weight of government and fails to create essential growth and employment. At the same time, emerging powers seek to shape the world in their image—China with its model of authoritarianism and, in a very different way, jihadists with Shariah, repression, and terror for the world."

Romney billed the election as an election of consequence: "Our campaign is about big things, because we happen to believe that America faces big challenges. We recognize this is a year with a big choice, and the American people want to see big changes. And together we can bring real change to this country.

"President Obama promised to bring us together, but at every turn, he has sought to divide and demonize," Romney said to the supporters who braved the chilly fall weather to attend. "President Obama promised to cut the deficit in half, but he doubled it. And his budget? It failed to win a single vote, Republican or Democrat, in either the House or the Senate. He said he would reform Medicare and Social Security and save them from pending insolvency, but he shrunk from proposing any solution at all."

Romney hit Obama hard on the theme of jobs: "Where are the nine million more jobs that President Obama promised his stimulus would have created by now? They are in China, Mexico, and Canada, and in countries that have made themselves more attractive for entrepreneurs and business and investment, even as President Obama's policies have made it less attractive for them here."

He threw Obama's campaign slogan, "Forward!" back at the president: "But to the 23 million Americans struggling to find a good job, these last four years feel a lot more like 'backward.' We cannot afford four more years like the last four years."

He charged that Obama had made the economic problems he inherited worse by the policies he adopted, ticking off the following list of failed initiatives:

- "In just four short years, the president borrowed nearly $6 trillion, adding almost as much debt held by the public as all prior American presidents in history.
- "He forced through Obamacare, frightening small business from hiring new employees and adding thousands of dollars to every family's health-care bill.

- "He launched an onslaught of new regulations, often to the delight of the biggest banks and corporations, but to the detriment of the small, growing businesses that create two-thirds of our jobs.
- "New business starts are at a thirty-year low because entrepreneurs and investors are sitting on the sidelines, weary from the president's staggering new regulations and proposed, massive tax increases.
- "Many families can't get mortgages and many entrepreneurs can't get loans because of Dodd-Frank regulations that make it harder for banks to lend."

Romney said energy prices were up in part because energy production on federal lands was down. He stressed that Obama rejected the Keystone Pipeline from Canada, while the Obama administration cut in half drilling permits and leases, even as gasoline prices soared to new highs.

"No, the problem with the Obama economy is not what he inherited; it is with the misguided policies that slowed the recovery and caused millions of Americans to endure lengthy unemployment and poverty," Romney concluded, indicting Obama for four years of failed economic policy while at the helm. "That is why 15 million more of our fellow citizens are on food stamps than when President Obama was sworn into office. That is why 3 million more women are now living in poverty. That is why nearly one in six Americans today is poor. That is why the economy is stagnant."

Romney explained to the Ames rally that his plan consists of the following five elements:

- "One, we will act to put America on track to a balanced budget by eliminating unnecessary programs, by sending programs back to states where they can be managed with less abuse and less cost and by shrinking the bureaucracy of Washington.
- "Two, we'll produce more of the energy we need to heat our homes, fill our cars, and make our economy grow. We will stop the Obama war on coal, the disdain for oil, and the effort to crimp natural gas by federal regulation of the very technology that produces it.

- "Three, we will make trade work for America. We'll open more markets to American agriculture, products, and services. And we will finally hold accountable any nation that doesn't play by the rules. I will stand up for the rights and interests of American workers and employers.
- "Four, we will grow jobs by making America the best possible place for job creators, for entrepreneurs, for small business, for innovators, for manufacturers. This we will do by updating and reshaping regulations to encourage growth, by lowering tax rates while lowering deductions and closing loopholes, and by making it clear from day one that unlike the current administration, we actually like business and the jobs business creates.
- "Finally, as we create more opportunity, we also will make sure that our citizens have the skills to succeed. Training programs will be shaped by the states where people live, and schools will put the interests of our kids, their parents, and their teachers above the interests of the teachers' unions."

Romney promised that taking these steps, the economy would come "roaring back" to create 12 million new jobs over the next four years. He pledged to "save and secure" Medicare and Social Security for present as well as future generations, and to restore the $716 billion Obama took from Medicare to fund Obamacare. He pledged to take a bipartisan approach as president, avoiding the politics of division and demonization he accused Obama of pursuing.

"I was elected as a Republican governor in a state with a legislature that was 85 percent Democrat. We were looking at a multibillion-dollar budget gap. But instead of fighting with one another, we came together to solve our problems," he stressed. "We actually cut spending—reduced it. We lowered taxes nineteen times. We defended school choice. And we worked to make our state business-friendly."

He concluded by urging voters "to rise to the occasion," noting he would resolve to make the century ahead "an American century."

MAINSTREAM MEDIA PANS ROMNEY ECONOMICS

Predictably, the response of the mainstream media was to pan Romney's plan.

"If you want to see how Romney's economic policies would work out, take a look at Europe. And weep," wrote *New York Times* columnist Nicholas Kristof.[8]

Kristof argued that Republicans have praised Germany and Britain, in particular, for implementing "precisely the policies that Romney favors," with the result that "those economies seem, to use a German technical term, kaput."

Kristof's point was to assert that any deviation from Obama's current policy of massive trillion-dollar deficit spending meant austerity, discounting Romney's contention that the economy can be stimulated by the type of supply-side economics that Ronald Reagan used to bring the US economy out of the doldrums of Jimmy Carter's presidency.

"Since Keynes, it's been understood that, in a downturn, governments should go into deficit to stimulate demand; that's how we got out of the Great Depression," he wrote. "And recent European data and IMF analyses underscore that austerity in the middle of a downturn not only doesn't help, but leads to even higher ratios of debt to economic output."

Kristof characterized as "empirically wrong" any attempt by Republicans to curb deficits and entitlement growth in the middle of an economic downturn. He suggested Obama print bumper stickers saying: "It Could Be Worse."

At the *Atlantic* magazine, staff writer Molly Ball, in an article entitled "Romney's Major Economic Speech That Wasn't," characterized Romney's speech as "substance-free promises to make things better, punctuated by Romney's new mantra of 'big change.'"[9]

She insisted that in the 2,700 words of the prepared text, the first 1,500 consisted of "a familiar critique of Obama and his campaign." Then, after eleven minutes in a twenty-minute speech, "Romney got around to reciting his five-point plan." She argued, without dissecting any of Romney's particular plans, that "the point of Romney's five-point plan and its *ad nauseam* repetition is to drill home the idea that he has a plan, not to produce a coherent economic blueprint." She noted that in focus groups, voters are clear that Romney has a five-point plan, but they cannot say what the plan is.

Just to be sure Romney did not gain advantage from the Ames speech, Ball added: "When voters, especially women voters, think primarily about the economy, Romney wins. When they think about other things—like whether pregnancies from rape are God-willed—Romney loses."

She concluded by noting that the Romney campaign "has spent the past several days avoiding comment on the furor over Indiana Senate candidate Richard Mourdock's rape remarks."

Rachel Streitfeld wrote a CNN article titled "Romney Pledges 'Big Change' but Offers Few Specifics," in which she dismissed the speech as a repeat of attacks Romney had given on the stump at rallies in Ohio a day earlier, charging the speech was long on promises and short on specifics. Streitfeld quoted Obama campaign spokeswoman Lis Smith, who tried to associate Romney with "the same failed policies that crashed our economy in the first place," suggesting Romney's economic plans would be a repeat of the economic policies of George W. Bush that the Obama campaign insisted were the cause of the nation's continued economic downturn.[10]

"True to form, Mitt Romney's most recent 'major policy speech' included dishonest attacks and empty promises of change, but no new policy," Smith told CNN. "That's because all Mitt Romney has is a one-point economic plan that he's been running on for two years: the very wealthy get to play by a very different set of rules than everyone else."[11]

OBAMA: "TAX THE RICH!"

At a campaign speech in Roanoke, Virginia, on July 13, 2012, in explaining why taxing the rich was fair, Obama articulated a fundamental socialist belief that those who are rich gain their wealth not as a result of their own skills, hard work, and individual initiative—core free-enterprise values—but through collective action. The rich, in Obama's worldview, take advantage for personal benefit of opportunities others have created through *their* skills, hard work, and individual initiative.

Here are the two key paragraphs from the Roanoke stump speech:

> There are a lot of wealthy, successful Americans who agree with me—because they want to give something back. They know they didn't—look, if you've been successful, you didn't get there on your own. You didn't get there on your own. I'm always struck by people who think, well, it must be because I was just so smart. There are a lot of smart people out there. It must be because I worked harder than everybody else. Let me tell you something—there are a whole bunch of hardworking people out there.
>
> If you were successful, somebody along the line gave you some help. There was a great teacher somewhere in your life. Somebody helped to create this unbelievable American system that we have that allowed you to thrive. Somebody invested in roads and bridges. If you've got a business—you didn't build that. Somebody else made that happen.

> The Internet didn't get invented on its own. Government research created the Internet so that all the companies could make money off the Internet.[12]

The line that created a firestorm of criticism was the comment, "If you've got a business—you didn't build that." Rush Limbaugh jumped on the line, claiming the fifty-second blurb from Roanoke was "perhaps the telling moment of Obama's presidency and his campaign." Limbaugh replayed Obama's comment, interpreting it as saying the people who have the wealth do not deserve it.

"They did it by stealing from you," Limbaugh paraphrased for his national radio audience. "They used work or labor from you that they didn't pay you for, not fairly. Or they ran businesses that cheated people or overcharged. Or they made too big a profit. They're no smarter than you are, and I'm here to get it back for you!"

Limbaugh argued that Obama was aiming to socialize profit so the government can claim it: "What [Obama] wants people to conclude is that profit was not possible, is not possible, without government first making it possible. And therefore, government owns it. It's government's profit."[13]

The socialist underpinnings of Obama's speech sounded similar notes to his exchange with Joe Wurzelbacher, who became known as "Joe the Plumber" during the 2008 campaign, when Obama said, "I think when you spread the wealth around, it's good for everybody."[14]

Income redistribution has been an Obama theme since 2008, much like his "tax the rich" rhetoric that emerged as a major campaign theme in 2012.

On February 2, 2012, a date yet early in the 2012 presidential election cycle, Obama used a National Prayer Breakfast speech as an opportunity to wrap his "tax the rich" mantra into a biblical theme, suggesting there was a moral justification for his claim the rich must pay their "fair share" of taxes:

> And when I talk about shared responsibility, it's because I genuinely believe that in a time when many folks are struggling, at a time when we have enormous deficits, it's hard for me to ask seniors on a fixed income, or young people with student loans, or middle-class families who can barely pay the bills to shoulder the burden alone. And I think to myself, if I'm willing to give something up as somebody who's been extraordinarily blessed, and give up some of the tax breaks that I enjoy, I actually think that's going to make economic sense.

But for me as a Christian, it also coincides with Jesus's teaching that "for unto whom much is given, much shall be required." It mirrors the Islamic belief that those who've been blessed have an obligation to use those blessings to help others, or the Jewish doctrine of moderation and consideration for others.[15]

THE OBAMA "FAIR SHARE" MANTRA

In his 2012 State of the Union speech given on January 25, 2012,[16] Obama repeated the "fair share" refrain four times (emphasis added):

- "We can either settle for a country where a shrinking number of people do really well while a growing number of Americans barely get by, or we can restore an economy where everyone gets a fair shot, and everyone does their *fair share*, and everyone plays by the same set of rules. . . ."
- "Second, no American company should be able to avoid paying its *fair share* of taxes by moving jobs and profits overseas. . . ."
- "But in return, we need to change our tax code so that people like me, and an awful lot of members of Congress, pay our *fair share* of taxes. . . ."
- "We don't begrudge financial success in this country. We admire it. When Americans talk about folks like me paying my *fair share* of taxes, it's not because they envy the rich. It's because they understand that when I get a tax break I don't need and the country can't afford, it either adds to the deficit, or somebody else has to make up the difference—like a senior on a fixed income, or a student trying to get through school, or a family trying to make ends meet."

Sitting with First Lady Michelle Obama in the gallery of the House of Representatives to be on view during the nationally televised broadcast of the 2012 State of the Union speech was billionaire investor Warren Buffett's secretary, Debbie Bosanek. The secretary had become an issue in Obama's "fair share" rhetoric after Buffett went public with the complaint that it was unfair that he paid a lower percent of his income in taxes than did his secretary.

On the day of Obama's 2012 State of the Union speech, however,

Paul Roderick Gregory pointed out in *Forbes* that Bosanek earns between $200,000 and $500,000 a year, dramatically reducing her value as a sob story. Moreover, Gregory noted that Buffett's taxes were primarily on investment earnings rather than income, thus making the comparison to his secretary's taxes an apples-to-oranges calculation.[17]

Still, with the television cameras watching, Obama proclaimed in the address, "Right now, Warren Buffett pays a lower tax rate than his secretary."[18]

Next, Obama proclaimed what he called the "Buffett Rule," namely that anyone earning more than $1 million a year should not pay less than 30 percent in taxes. Never has Obama referenced what the *New York Post* revealed: that Buffett's Berkshire Hathaway has owed the IRS as much as $1 billion in unpaid taxes going back a decade, as long ago as 2002.

"If Buffett really thinks he and his 'mega-rich friends' should pay higher taxes, why doesn't his firm fork over what it already owes under *current* rates?" the *New York Post* asked. "Likely answer: He cares more about shilling for President Obama—who's practically made socking 'millionaires and billionaires' his re-election theme song—than about kicking in more himself."[19]

WHY TAXES ARE NOT "FAIR"

Truthfully, the income tax schedule in the United States was never meant to be "fair." A "fair tax" is typically a flat tax applied to consumable goods or services, such that every consumer, regardless how rich or poor, pays the same identical tax when purchasing the same identical goods or services. The income tax code in the United States is and has always been a progressive tax, designed such that the wealthier a person or family is, the higher the income tax percentage that must be paid. When Obama charges that he wants the rich to pay their "fair share," what he is demanding is that the marginal rate taxed the rich be raised higher than it is today, without raising tax rates for those below a certain income threshold. In other words, Obama wants the income tax to be even more progressive than it is today, demanding the rich pay a larger proportion of their income in taxes than do those who earn lower incomes.

According to the Congressional Budget Office, the highest quintile of American taxpayers are the largest sources of federal revenues—including income taxes, Social Security payroll taxes, corporate income taxes, and excise taxes—paying an average rate of 25 percent of their household income for the four taxes combined. By comparison, the second quintile pays only about 10 percent of their household income for the four taxes combined, and the bottom quintile, less than 5 percent.[20] The conclusion should be clear: The rich are already paying more than their "fair" share of taxes.

Financial analyst Steve McCann, writing on American Thinker, posed the question, "What would the United States gain if in fact the government did confiscate the wealth of the so-called rich and taxed at 100% all the income above $200,000.00 per household per year?"

To answer the question, McCann turned to IRS statistics that indicated that in 2008, there were 6.9 million taxpayers that had adjusted gross income above $200,000. Taxing at 100 percent all income earned above and beyond the $200,000 threshold would have yielded the IRS a mere $221 billion—less than a quarter of annual deficit being piled up by the Obama administration.

McCann further pointed out that according to IRS figures there were 2.7 million adults with a net worth above $1.5 million. If the government were to seize all wealth above the $1.5 million threshold, Washington would earn a onetime windfall of $4 trillion—hardly enough when the national debt is approaching $17 trillion and the Obama administration is adding over $1 trillion every year since taking office.[21]

The numbers simply demonstrate that even "taxing the rich" at startling, draconian rates would have little effect on the massive spending and debt of the federal government.

Still, Obama was able to calculate that fanning the flames of class warfare, a "community organizing" tactic he learned from Saul Alinsky, would mobilize enough economic resentment to carry him to reelection.

In the first quarter of 2010, 48.5 percent of the US population lived in a household receiving some type of government benefit, ranging from food stamps to Medicare/Medicaid to unemployment insurance and Social Security payments, a number that has been increasing since the current prolonged economic downturn began in 2008.[22]

The dark underbelly of class envy is fear. By flaming the resentment of the growing number of American "have-nots," Obama was able to suggest the election of a Republican president in 2012 would mean reduction of entitlement programs and other forms of government benefits paid disproportionately to the poor and the unemployed in America today.

"Three years after the Hope and Change president took office, Hope turns out to mean high taxes and lots of regulations, and Change consists of celebrating the government's takeover of General Motors and belittling technological progress that destroys some jobs even as it creates others," wrote economics commentator and reporter Charles Gasparino in the *New York Post* the day after Obama's 2012 State of the Union speech. "The Great Uniter is all about class warfare. . . .

"But America is not (yet) Europe," Gasparino continued. "People here still aspire to be rich more than they hate success, no matter how many times the media extols the virtues of Occupy Wall Street and its attacks on the 1 percent."[23]

Gasparino also pointed out that Obama's class-warfare rhetoric alienates former supporters in the business community, including top Wall Street donors who helped Obama bankroll his 2008 presidential election victory.

"Would you rather keep . . . tax breaks for millionaires and billionaires or would you say let's get teachers back in the classroom?" Obama asked voters in Ohio during a speech given there in October 2011. "Now, the Republicans . . . they said, 'Well, this is class warfare.' You know what? If asking a billionaire to pay their fair share of taxes, to pay the same tax rate as a plumber or teacher is class warfare, then you know what? I'm a warrior for the middle class. I'm happy to fight for the middle class."[24]

Obama could pursue class-warfare themes successfully in the 2012 presidential campaign because shoring up his base was a required campaign strategy the moment David Axelrod, Jim Messina, and David Plouffe were reassured by their voter-intelligence demographic microanalysis that the key to victory was getting their reconstituted New Deal coalition to vote. The common element among the African Americans, Hispanics, union members, single women, and youth voters supporting Obama was that all felt economically disadvantaged. All feared they needed a government-supporting champion if only to hold their already precarious position on the US economic ladder.

"BLAME BUSH" MORPHS TO "BLAME ROMNEY"

Entering the campaign for reelection, the Obama campaign faced a major obstacle: in 2008, Obama had campaigned on his ability to turn around the economy, but in 2012, the nation was still struggling economically with a recovery that was weak at best. To win, Obama had to deflect criticism that continuing economic difficulties were a result of his policies.

One approach to claiming economic success was evidenced by the Obama administration's nebulous claim that the $787 billion economic stimulus plan succeeded in saving jobs as well as creating jobs. Arguably, economists could point to federal government stimulus spending to document jobs created, but how could the Obama administration prove jobs would have been cut except for the stimulus spending? In a little-noticed memo, Peter Orszag, then the director of the Office of Management and Budget, instructed that recipients of stimulus spending would no longer be required "to make a subjective judgment on whether jobs were created or retained as a result of the Recovery Act."[25] By only requiring reporting on jobs funded with Recovery and Reinvestment Act dollars, the memorandum eliminated the hypothetical "or saved" category.

At the time the memorandum was issued, December 18, 2009, the government website Recovery.gov listed 640,329 "Jobs Created/Saved as Reported by Recipients." Ed Pound, the spokesman for the Recovery Board, the agency in the federal government in charge of Recovery.gov, told ABC News that since the OMB had abandoned the category "jobs created or saved," Recovery.gov would drop the category also, reporting in the future something like "jobs reported by recipients where Recovery funds were expended."[26] Initially, Obama promised that his recovery plan would "save or create three to four million jobs over the next two years," despite consistent criticism that the "created or saved" number was pure fiction since there was no way to say with precision how many jobs were actually being "saved."[27]

What the Obama team learned with the "created and saved jobs" fabrication was that the mainstream media would faithfully report their claim. The end result was that regardless how high unemployment got, the Obama administration could claim it could have been worse, much like the Obama bumper sticker suggested by columnist Nicholas Kristof, namely: "It could be worse!"[28]

"You created a situation where you cannot be wrong," Montana Democratic Senator Max Baucus, chairman of the Senate Finance Committee, challenged Treasury Secretary Timothy Geithner on the "created or saved" formula. "If the economy loses two million jobs over the next few years, you can say yes, but it would've lost 5.5 million jobs. If we create a million jobs, you can say, well, it would have lost 2.5 million jobs. You've given yourself complete leverage where you cannot be wrong, because you can take any scenario and make yourself look correct."[29]

Interestingly, the Obama administration quit releasing reports on the stimulus program required by law after Obama economists in the last released report (at the end of the third quarter 2011) claimed to have created or saved only 2.5 million jobs, at a cost of $317,000 per job.[30]

The Obama administration also developed a facility for claiming cuts in the federal budget had been made that reduced the federal debt by trillions of dollars. The problem was the apparent budget savings were again accomplished by clever manipulation of the numbers. At various campaign rallies, Obama claimed his administration had a plan to reduce the federal debt by $4 trillion without requiring any congressional action. Typically, these so-called spending cuts are fabrications, predicated on reducing the increase in future spending, or in savings realized by wars the US does not intend to fight, such as are occasioned by pulling US troops out of Iraq and Afghanistan.

The truth is that federal spending has increased from $2.983 trillion in 2008, when Obama was running for president, to around $3.796 trillion in fiscal year 2011. So, too, the national debt increased $6 trillion, approximately 60 percent, in Obama's first term, with no sign the federal borrowing will decrease anytime soon in the Obama second term.[31]

Similar tricks have been played by the Bureau of Labor Statistics in reporting unemployment numbers under Obama. A convenient way to depress the unemployment rate is to declare chronically unemployed individuals are no longer in the labor force, hence no longer considered "unemployed." During Obama's first term, Americans "not in the labor force" increased by 8,332,000 to a record total of 88,839,000, according to BLS reports.[32]

The Obama administration also argued that the economic downturn that began in 2008 under President George W. Bush would have been worse without Obama's economic programs, including a willingness to allow the Federal Reserve to engage in repeated rounds of what was known as "quantitative easing," a program under which the Federal Reserve simply printed money to purchase US Treasury debt as well as various mortgage-backed securities. While the Federal Reserve argued the purpose of quantitative easing was to keep interest rates low, thereby stimulating a revival in the housing market, critics would argue that printing trillions of dollars to buy

Treasury debt created a liquidity-driven stock market surge unjustified by improvements in stock fundamentals and made the onset of hyperinflation more likely.

Still, the argument the economy would have been worse without Obama's Keynesian-justified federal budget deficits was almost identical to the contention that the $787 billion stimulus program "created or saved" jobs—neither contention was provable.

But in the final analysis, the Obama team fell back to arguing the economy inherited from George W. Bush was much worse than most economists realized at the time. Similarly, the Obama team argued the improvement of the jobless rate from a peak of 10.2 percent in October 2009 to less than 8 percent in the final months leading up to the 2012 election was due to Obama administration economic policies.

At a stump speech at Ohio University in Athens, Ohio, on October 17, 2012,[33] Obama bragged about a claimed economic recovery:

> "Four years ago, I said I would do everything I could, every single day, to dig us out of the hole we were left. And because of the incredible resilience of the American people, four years after the worst economic crisis of our lifetimes, we are moving forward again. We were losing 800,000 jobs a month. Now we've added more than 5 million new jobs, more manufacturing jobs than any time since the 1990s. The unemployment rate has fallen from 10 percent to 7.8 percent. Foreclosures are at their lowest in five years. Home values are on the rise. Stock market has doubled. Manufacturing is coming back. Assembly lines are putting folks back to work. That's what we've been fighting for. Those are the promises I've kept."

In the same speech, he also took a shot at Romney's economic plan:

> "Governor Romney continues to run around talking about his five-point plan for the economy. . . . But as we saw last night, the five-point plan really boils down to one point—folks at the very top get to play by a different set of rules than you do. So they can pay lower taxes. They can use offshore accounts. They can buy a company, load it up with debt, lay off the workers, strip away the pensions, send the jobs overseas—and still make a big profit doing it. It's the same philosophy that's been squeezing middle-class families for over a decade. It's the same philosophy that got us into this mess. And I have seen too much pain and struggle here in Ohio and all across the country to let us go down that path again."

Obama capitalized on the campaign's effort to portray Romney as a rich "vulture capitalist," charging that Romney made his money bankrupting companies and destroying jobs. This was the underpinning to Obama's argument that Romney's only real economic plan was to reduce taxes for the rich, like himself. Obama rejected this as "trickle-down economics," arguing that supply-side economics dating back to the Reagan era had done nothing to help the economically disadvantaged that constituted the core Obama voting constituency.

But the new wrinkle late in the campaign was to suggest that Romney's economic plan was the same economic plan that caused the economic downturn in the first place. The Democrats had argued that the Bush tax cuts had failed to stimulate the economy sufficiently to prevent economic downturn, so lowering taxes as Romney suggested was not seen as a solution. Blaming Bush had now morphed into blaming Romney, even though Romney had never spent a day implementing economic policy in the White House—something Obama had been doing for the last four years.

What all these approaches had in common was the Obama administration's determination to claim success for any and all positive economic news, while deflecting blame from adverse economic news—a feat accomplished by suggesting the economic news would have been even worse had Barack Obama not been on the watch. Truthfully, there was no way to know if improving unemployment numbers were a real trend or simply another bubble caused by the Federal Reserve continuing to pump fiat money into the economy.

Obama took pains to deny his vision of America was a socialist vision. Yet his message preying on class conflict and economic dissatisfaction reflected the classic socialist motif advanced in America since the 1930s. Saul Alinsky codified that message in his classic book titled *Rules for Radicals: A Pragmatic Primer for Realistic Radicals.*[34] Truthfully, Obama in 2012 was applying community organizing techniques to running for president, both in how he organized his grassroots GOTV effort to rely upon microtargeted data collected on individual voters and in the themes on which he chose to campaign.

The Romney campaign's message was a classical message of free enterprise. The Obama rejoinder was that unbridled capitalism, as exhibited by Romney's experience at Bain Capital, preyed on ordinary workers, eliminated jobs, and bankrupted companies, just so Romney and his capitalist associates could gain wealth. This was a message that would explain to the economically downtrodden in Obama's modern-day New Deal coalition that their economic disadvantage was no fault of their own, but instead was an inevitable product of capitalism allowed to run loose without protective government regulation.

The economically disadvantaged among Obama's core voters could look to him as a champion of social justice to redistribute income in their favor, taking from the rich to make sure an extensive safety net of social welfare programs protected the economically disadvantaged from poverty in difficult economic times. As the consequences of the severe global downturn that began at the end of George W. Bush's second term in office progressed, the economic misery extended into the middle class. Obama's message that he would not raise middle-class taxes in favor of taxing the rich fell on receptive ears.

Meanwhile, Romney struggled against an unreceptive mainstream media to gain attention for his supply-side message that lowering taxes across the board and reducing government regulations were the prescription to restore job creation in the US economy. Choosing class-warfare themes and strategies, the Obama camp decided the path to victory in 2012 rested in whipping up the base, not in reaching across the divide to attract undecided or GOP-leaning voters. Obama's campaign rhetoric could stay strident, attacking Romney as an unsympathetic rich guy who did not have an economic plan that would succeed to benefit the nation's disadvantaged and downtrodden. In a political environment where the certainty of continuing entitlement programs was more important to Obama's voters than the possibility of creating jobs, Romney's message that he was a capitalist who knew how small businesses could be made to thrive fell on deaf ears, except to supply-side Republicans already predisposed to embrace the message.

DETROIT: A CASE STUDY IN IDENTITY POLITICS

An illustration of how little Romney's vision could penetrate the thick cloud of Obama's identity-based politics is the city of Detroit, a once-bustling hub of industry that is today bankrupt. Detroit could desperately use Romney's vision to boost business, capital, and employment, but its residents clearly resonated more with the economy-crushing security blanket of Obama's welfare state.

Detroit, once the home of the US auto industry and Motown music, is suffering such a loss of population that a new urban renewal project calls for returning large sections of the city to farmland, as it was in the middle of the nineteenth century. City planners in Detroit are contemplating turning roughly one-quarter of the city's 139 square miles from urban to semirural land, with fruit trees and vegetable farms replacing the eerie landscape of empty buildings and vacant lots, according to a 2010 Associated Press report.

"People are afraid," Deborah L. Younger, executive director of Detroit Local Initiatives Support Corporation, told the AP. "When you read that neighborhoods may no longer exist, that sends fear."

On some Detroit city blocks, only one or two homes remain, surrounded by empty trash-filled lots and burned-out homes that scavengers have stripped of anything valuable. Detroit, according to one estimate cited by the AP, has as many as 33,500 empty houses and 91,000 vacant lots.[35]

Even the Romney family home, one of 292 homes in Palmer Woods, a high-end suburb in northwestern Detroit, was demolished because it was vacant. Mitt Romney's parents, George and Lenore Romney, owned the house from 1941 until 1953, when the family moved to the northern suburbs. As recently as 2002, the Romney house sold for $645,000, but after that it lapsed into foreclosure, bounced between several lenders, and fell into disrepair. In 2009, following complaints from neighbors, Wayne County declared the Romney family home "a public nuisance and blight" and ordered it demolished.

Mitt Romney told the *Wall Street Journal* that "it's sad" his childhood home was being razed, "but sadder still to consider what has happened to the city of Detroit, which has been left hollow by fleeing jobs and liberal social policies."[36]

French photographers Yves Marchand and Romain Meffre, in an expensively printed 2010 book titled *The Ruins of Detroit,* have documented graphically the decline of Detroit as a thriving urban environment, taking dozens of beautifully detailed color photographs of abandoned homes, office buildings, and factories in the decaying city.[37]

Detroit's population, at a peak in 1950 with a total of more than 1.8 million people, was the nation's fourth largest city. But by 2005, Detroit's population shrank to an estimated 850,000, with estimates in 2012 indicating the city has now dropped below the 700,000 mark.[38] Detroit in 2010 had one of the highest percentages of African-American residents of any city in the nation, with the US Census Bureau estimating 82.7 percent of Detroit's residents were black.[39] The Census Bureau further estimated that 36.2 percent of Detroit's population lived below the poverty level from 2007 to 2011.[40]

The situation in Detroit is especially severe for the city's children. A January 2013 report from Data Driven Detroit revealed that 57.3 percent of Detroit's children lived in poverty in 2011, approximately three out of every five children, a 64.7 percent increase in child poverty in Detroit since 1999. The study found children accounted for 194,347 of Detroit's residents, about 27 percent of the city's total population.[41]

The study also found 81.9 percent of Detroit's children were African-American. In 2011, the state of Michigan approved a plan to close seventy public schools in Detroit, cutting the numbers of public schools in half by 2014, leaving only seventy-two. The goal, according to the plan's author, Robert Bobb, appointed the emergency financial manager of the eighty-seven-thousand-student Detroit Public Schools in 2009, is to eliminate the school system's current $327 million budget deficit.[42] According to the US Department of Education, only 7 percent of Detroit's eighth graders scored high enough on the department's National Assessment of Educational Progress test in 2011 to be rated "proficient" or better in reading, and only 4 percent scored high enough to be rated "proficient" in math.[43] Add to this a disproportionately high rate of teenage pregnancy and single mothers raising families without fathers in the black community, and the result is a formula for generational entrapment in poverty. The city's crumbling infrastructure is estimated to be operating $300 million short of municipal sustainability, and the city has become the crime capital of America, with seven of ten crimes going unsolved.[44]

Detroit has not had a Republican mayor since 1962. In February 2011, Detroit Mayor Dave Bing, a former NBA basketball player, offered Detroit police officers the opportunity to own an abandoned home in the city for the price of $1,000, in hopes of enticing some police to live in Detroit's inner-city neighborhoods. The plan offered to make two hundred tax-foreclosed homes in the East English Village and Boston-Edison neighborhoods, two of Detroit's more stable and historic neighborhoods, available to officers who agree to live in the homes. As an inducement to join the program, each officer would receive $150,000 in federal grants for home renovations.

"Detroiters want to live in safe, stable neighborhoods, and they deserve no less," said Bing, when announcing the plan. "This is just step one of many things that we're going to have to involve ourselves in as we bring our city back." Bing stressed that officers "living in neighborhoods have the potential to deter crime, increase public safety and improve relations between the community and sworn officers."[45]

At least 53 percent of Detroit's three thousand police live in the suburbs, and the percentage is higher for firefighters, reported the *Detroit News* in featuring Bing's announcement. The newspaper also noted Bing was using $30 million in federal Neighborhood Stabilization funds to implement the program. The city partnered with a long list of bureaucratic agencies to get approval for the plan, including the Detroit Land Bank Authority, the Department of Housing and Urban Development, Michigan State Housing and Urban Development Authority, the Michigan Housing Trust, and other private interests. The program involved safeguards that would require officers to repay money for the houses if they sell their homes to someone other than a police officer.[46]

Unemployment in Detroit has been consistently twice that of the state average since 2001. Data Driven Detroit found that Detroit unemployment reached a high of 24.9 percent in 2009. In 2011, 49.1 percent, almost half of Detroit residents between sixteen and sixty-four years of age, reported not working during 2010 and 2011; only 27 percent of the working-age population reported working full-time during the same period. In Detroit, black unemployment reached a peak of 25.7 percent in 2010, more than four times the 6 percent for black unemployment seen in Detroit in 2000, at the height of the technology-driven boom that characterized the dot-com bubble years.[47] In a ranking of black male employment rates in selected metropolitan areas between 1970 and 2010, employment among black males in Detroit declined 28.6 percent, the second worst in the nation (behind only Milwaukee), from a 1970 total of 71.6 percent of black males in Detroit employed to a 2010 total of only 43 percent of black males in Detroit employed.[48]

Bruce Dixon, managing director of the Black Agenda Report, chided President Obama for failing to mention African-American unemployment in his 2012 State of the Union address: "But despite levels of black unemployment not seen since the Great Depression of the 1930s, [African-American unemployment] went unmentioned," Dixon wrote. "Black concerns . . . are largely irrelevant to the president, and black communities powerless. Since the first black president is pretty much guaranteed the black vote anyhow, record black unemployment wasn't even worth acknowledging, much less lying about."[49]

Still, in the 2012 presidential election, Detroit voted 98 percent for Obama. In a city of approximately seven hundred thousand people, Romney was able to get only 6,016 votes.

The vote in Detroit affirmed that Romney's message of job creation through lower taxes, fewer regulations, and private enterprise was rejected in favor of Obama's message that continued government involvement in an expanded social welfare state was the promise of the future. For Detroit voters determined to vote for Obama, it is doubtful Romney or the Republican Party could have crafted a message that would have appealed sufficiently to get Detroit voters to change their minds. Romney's program to create jobs did not appeal to Detroit voters who had given up on jobs. Nor did Detroit voters care about taxes because it was unlikely any but a few were paying any income tax.

The African Americans who were 82.7 percent of Detroit's population voted for Obama for two reasons: first, because he was of African descent, and second, because of the calculation that Obama and the Democratic Party were more likely to continue the extensive social welfare programs on which these Detroiters, in a continuing bad economy, were dependent, to live even a marginal lifestyle. The likelihood was that after years of chronic unemployment and deepening poverty, the free-enterprise system espoused by Romney meant nothing or near nothing to African Americans struggling to get by in what remained of Detroit's once-thriving inner city.

The tragedy is that Detroit is only one of many Northern cities headed down this same path. Other cities include Cleveland, Pittsburgh, and Newark, where the concentration of impoverished inner-city African Americans is enough of a voting bloc to tip the balance of the state in favor of the Democratic Party, not only in the presidential election of 2012, but possibly in every presidential election to come in the foreseeable future.

The other side of the coin is the corruption engaged in by numerous mayors, council members, freeholders, and other city officials who prey on the people for their own personal enrichment, whether within the law or not. It is hard to imagine how cities like Detroit can emerge from what is becoming the prospect of generational entrapment in an environment where poverty and crime are pervasive.

The further tragedy is that the massive social welfare programs Democratic candidates offer cities like Detroit keep the lid on what otherwise is an inherently unstable and unlivable reality.

Obama's class-conflict message of "tax the rich" got Detroit voters to the polls, if only because the message appealed to their economic discontent, as Saul Alinsky would have predicted. A legitimate question remains: Did Obama's victory in 2012 mean Detroit will see any improvement in the economic condition of the city, any more than his victory in 2008 meant? Yet almost every voter in Detroit could be counted on by the Democratic Party to vote for Obama a second time in 2012.

TOWARD A WELFARE SOCIETY

Detroit, however, as a microcosm of people voting for the very policies that create the problems from which they want relief, is not alone in its self-defeating pattern, and current economic trends suggest many more cities may soon be joining it. What may appear to be merely racial and socioeconomic issues on the surface truly reveal even deeper, more startling trends beneath.

Some have argued, for example, that the only voting bloc Romney could rely on in 2012 was aging white voters, who are about to become a minority. Exit polls showed Romney won 59 percent of the white vote, while Obama won 93 percent of the black vote, 71 percent of the Hispanic vote, and 73 percent of the Asian vote.[50]

"If only white people had voted on Tuesday, Mitt Romney would have carried every state except for Massachusetts, Iowa, Connecticut and New Hampshire, according to the news media's exit polls," wrote historian and journalist Jon Weiner in *The Nation*. "Even in the deepest blue states, white voters went for Romney: 53 percent in California, 52 percent in New York, 55 percent in Pennsylvania."[51]

Noting that Romney won 6 percent more of the white vote than McCain won in 2008, Weiner argued from a leftist perspective that the vote showed racism, with liberals left disappointed, hoping whites who had opposed

Obama in 2008 "would learn toleration and acceptance of racial difference after four years with a black president in the White House." Interestingly, Weiner did not interpret as racism that 93 percent of African Americans voted for Obama, or that Obama got the lion's share of the minority vote in 2012 across all minorities, including Hispanics and Asians.

Romney voters were 88 percent white, argued left-leaning author Tom Scocca, writing in *Slate* magazine the day after the election.[52]

"White men are supporting Mitt Romney to the exclusion of logic or common sense, in defiance of normal Americans," Scocca wrote five days before the election. "Without this narrow, tribal appeal, Romney's candidacy would simply not be viable. Most kinds of Americans see no reason to vote for him."[53]

Lumping together Romney supporters such as Donald Trump, Clint Eastwood, Buzz Bissinger, and Meat Loaf, Scocca characterized Romney supporters as "one aging white man after another," concluding Romney's support was "a study in identity politics."

Interestingly, again, Scocca did not similarly characterize the support of blacks, Hispanics, and Asians for Obama in the same terms. Scocca portrayed Romney's campaign as being "scripted for white people." He portrayed Romney's message as "first of all, Obama hasn't accomplished anything, and second of all, [I'm] going to repeal all the bad things that Obama has accomplished." Then, he demeaned Romney's business career, saying Romney promises were empty and negative, promising only to do "something" about small business, restore America, cut taxes, and grow jobs. He claimed that for more than four years, Republicans have been "campaigning and propagandizing against an imaginary Obama." He charged that at the "most grotesque end of the fantasies" these unnamed Republican operatives have seen Obama as "a foreign-born, anti-colonialist Muslim," who "is a power-mad socialist and a dumb, affirmative-action baby, promoted all the way to the presidency by a race-crazed, condescending liberal elite." In sum, Scocca captured the spirit of the far left when he concluded the "white-people's bubble" was "a strange inverted world . . . full of phantoms and rumors."

In writing their 2002 book, titled *The Emerging Democratic Majority*, journalist John Judis and sociologist Ruy Teixeira predicted a fundamental realignment of the voters to produce a new, then-emerging Democratic majority based on progressive values and a postindustrial view of America.

The Democratic majority would bring together the following demographic groups: white working-class and middle-class Democrats; minorities, including blacks, Hispanics, and Asian-American voters; women voters, especially single, working women who are highly educated; and professionals, including highly educated tech specialists.

"These are products of a new postindustrial capitalism, rooted in diversity and social equality, and emphasizing the production of ideas and services rather than goods," Judis and Teixeira wrote. "And while some of these voters are drawn to the Democratic Party by its New Deal past, many others resonate strongly to the new causes the Democrats adopted during the sixties."[54]

The new causes included lifestyle issues such as support for abortion, acceptance of same-sex marriage, and "a new postindustrial metropolitan order in which men and women play equal roles and in which white America is supplanted by multiracial, multiethnic America."[55]

On page 70 of their book, the authors produced an electoral map of the United States in which the configuration of the states looks remarkably like the battleground fought between Obama and McCain in 2008 and between Obama and Romney in 2012.

The hard left is ushering in the newly emerging Democratic majority with a vengeance, determined to identify those who oppose Obama as racists, Baby Boomers rapidly aging into their senior years, and old-age and middle-class whites. Those who oppose Obama are seen as lacking a birth rate sufficient to keep up with the growing numbers of Hispanic immigrants.

Yet deeper at stake are the ideological issues dividing whites and minorities.

Romney's appeal fell flat among those on the political left precisely because his political and economic thinking is rooted in a view of capitalism and private enterprise that would have been assumed to be commonplace among previous generations of Americans.

Today's far left embraces an expansive government that has a right to intrude into the lives of all, not only from cradle to grave, but also on every imaginable social, political, and economic issue. Obama campaigned on the theme that the nation required an expanding regulatory structure deemed necessary to redress the imbalances caused by "unbridled capitalism." But he also campaigned on the idea that the EPA was right to ban coal because of climate concerns, and that the military should be forced to accept the LGBT community as well as women, because not to do so would violate civil rights. Obama insisted that women's rights demanded not only equal pay, but also free access to government-sponsored contraceptives and abortions.

The far left refused to hear Romney's challenge that an ever-expanding social welfare state based on a European model is doomed to incur unsustainable budget deficits. Even with entitlement programs now taking up 60 percent of all federal government expenditures, with no end in sight, the far left refuses to believe the inevitable consequence is bankruptcy. The far left sees income redistribution and "tax the rich" policies as necessary to achieve "social justice," rejecting the proposition that eventually the welfare state runs out of tax revenue to spend and hits the point where lending nations, foreign central banks, and international monetary agencies demand austerity as a condition of continued lending.

Unfortunately, the mad dash to make America a nation of Detroits is on. Under Obama, the United States is about to shut down coal production, increasing the nation's dependency on foreign oil at a time when alternative renewable energy sources, such as air and wind, have failed to prove themselves sufficiently robust or economically viable substitutes. With mounting federal regulations, including Obamacare, now a likely reality for Obama's second term, many small businesses across the nation will reduce employee counts or simply close their doors. Under Obama, the nation could well settle into a long-term structural economic downturn that cannot be reversed by applying classical Keynesian economic theories preaching the wisdom of deficit spending.

Regardless of whether the political left likes it or not, available data demonstrate welfare spending under Obama is shattering previous records, creating new all-time highs. The nation is approaching the point where 50 million Americans participate in food stamp programs.

In July 2012, the Department of Health and Human Services granted itself the authority to "waive compliance" with all the work provisions in the Temporary Assistance to Needy Families, or TANF, program. The work requirements had been crafted between Republicans, then led by House Speaker Newt Gingrich, and Democrats in Congress, resulting in legislation replacing the old Aid to Families with Dependent Children or AFDC program with TANF, a reform President Clinton declared to be "the end of welfare as we know it."[56]

In 1995, nearly one in seven children was on AFDC; within a few years under TANF, the welfare caseload was cut in half, while earnings and employment among single mothers soared.

"Roughly 3 million fewer children lived in poverty in 2003 than in 1995, including 1.2 million fewer black children, marking the lowest level of black child poverty in the nation's history," noted analyst Robert Rector at the Heritage Foundation.[57]

Releasing TANF from the necessity for work requirements may have been a popular election-year move for a president wanting to win welfare recipients' votes, but Obama's decision has sent welfare spending in the United States soaring toward the $1 trillion mark annually.

Roughly one-third the US population now receives aid from at least one means-tested welfare program each month, with average benefits estimated at approximately $9,000 per recipient. Today, eighty federal means-tested programs provide cash, food, housing, medical care, and social services to low-income people, with spending in these programs having increased more than one-third during Obama's first term. By 2022, at the current rate of increase, it is estimated there will be $2.33 in federal and state welfare spending for every $1 spent on defense.[58]

Social welfare benefits are now calculated to make up 35 percent of wages and salaries in the United States, up from 21 percent in 2000, and from 10 percent in 1961.[59] If federal welfare payments were converted to hourly wage cash payments, federal welfare payments would provide $30.60 per hour, forty hours per week, untaxed, to each household living below poverty, compared to $25.03 per hour, the median income in the private economy after accounting for federal income taxes.[60]

According to estimates by the Ludwig von Mises Institute, an advocate of the private enterprise economy, the typical welfare "client" in the United States receives an estimated annual sum of $32,500, which includes approximately $3,000 in cash, $14,000 in Medicaid, $10,000 in housing assistance, and $5,000 in food assistance. Since these welfare payments are untaxed, the Institute estimated the $32,000 sum was equivalent to a $45,000 annual salary before taxes.[61]

An alarming report coming out of the American Community Survey conducted by the US Census Bureau in 2010 indicated that more than half the family households in parts of the District of Columbia and Prince George's

County are run by single parents. That these areas have a high minority population, largely African-American and Hispanic, is not a coincidence, Ron Haskins, a senior fellow at the Brookings Institute, told the *Washington Examiner*. "About 70 percent of black kids are born outside marriage, and then you have those born in a marriage, about half of them end in divorce," Haskins said. "And first-generation Hispanics have a relatively low divorce rate . . . but once you get into the second generation that disappears."[62]

Haskins's comment reflects that increasing dependence on government welfare programs has historically led to family disintegration in the minority communities, a phenomenon that is increasing in speed and intensity under the Obama administration. The far left's agenda to expand social welfare programs in the name of "social justice" will only result in even more minority poverty, and thus the cycle of Detroit threatens to repeat itself generationally, with children doomed to live in poverty, as are their children in turn.

Yet this is not a racial problem as much as it is a direct result of the socialist agenda that has been imposed on America over the past few decades, largely by Democrats, with the assistance of an increasing number of centrist Republicans in Congress. The shift can be traced to the 1960s, when President Lyndon Johnson declared a "War on Poverty" in his first State of the Union address, delivered to a joint session of Congress on January 8, 1964, less than two months after John F. Kennedy was assassinated in the streets of Dallas, Texas.

The debate over poverty in America has since swung between the political left—as represented by Barack Obama in the 2012 presidential election, arguing for the need to establish at public expense a national guaranteed minimum income for every American—and the political right, as represented recently by Mitt Romney, arguing the only solution to poverty rests in creating strong families among the poor, educating children, and providing jobs.

Yet the fact remains that we have now had more than fifty years to test the proposition that Lyndon Johnson's social welfare formula is an effective way to combat poverty. With more than five decades of experience since Johnson's Great Society, it has not succeeded.

On January 25, 1988, President Ronald Reagan delivered a State of the Union address in which he declared that the War on Poverty had failed: "My friends, some years ago, the federal government declared a war on poverty, and poverty won."

Yet many Americans—indeed most, if the 2012 election results are indicative—are oblivious to the battle's results. The nation is clearly divided between what Judis and Teixeira identify as the new Democratic majority, identified here as the modern-day reconstruction of the New Deal coalition, and the emerging Republican minority, identified as what is left of the Nixon-Reagan majority, composed of white voters and Southern Evangelical Christians.

These two groups are divided by race, by economic philosophy, and by their vision for the future of the American family. The family headed by one man and one woman, traditionally identified as "husband and wife," was a core value to Nixon-Reagan voters. Today, the traditional family is under attack by various factions within the newly emerging Democratic majority. Same-sex marriage advocates join the LGBT community in demanding a new definition of the family. Radical feminists among single women voters also question why the union of a man and a woman is required to bear and raise children. So, too, in the African-American and Hispanic communities, families with fathers are not necessarily the norm.

Reagan continually returned to a simple but critical theme: without strong families, the poor would never emerge from poverty. Even more revealing, Reagan directly stated that federal antipoverty programs actually function to destroy families, thereby perpetuating a culture of poverty that persists across generations.

In 1965, Daniel Patrick Moynihan, who was then serving under a presidential appointment as assistant secretary of labor heading the Office of Policy Research and Planning, wrote a report titled *The Negro Family: The Case for National Action.*[63] Moynihan created a national firestorm of angry backlash and criticism, simply because he argued the cause of African-American poverty was the deterioration of the African-American family, not white prejudice and discrimination.

Moynihan began his controversial report with a sentence that left little doubt: "At the heart of the deterioration of the fabric of Negro society is the deterioration of the Negro family."

According to the US National Center for Health Statistics today, nearly 70 percent of all African-American babies are born to unmarried mothers. While the percentages are going up in the non-Hispanic white community as well, the comparable figures showed that in 2005, some 37 percent of white births were to unmarried mothers, approximately half the rate for African Americans.[64] Yet the rates of births to white, unmarried mothers are today where the comparable African-American births were when Moynihan first wrote his report.

With the rates of births to unmarried mothers rising among the white population to levels experienced by minority populations some fifty years ago, the problem is clearly not a problem of race, but of family dysfunction. When babies are born to single women, the unmarried mothers are forced to struggle to give sufficient time and attention both to child care and to fulfilling the economic needs of earning a living and educating children.

Romney failed in his attempt to debate the economic viability of the welfare state. In Obama's second term, will America continue its downward, Detroit-like cycle into welfare dependency, family disintegration, and entrapment in generational poverty?

8

WHO VOTED, WHO DIDN'T

Election fraud, whether it's phony voter registrations, illegal absentee ballots, shady recounts or old-fashioned ballot-box stuffing, can be found in every part of the United States, although it is probably spreading because of the ever-so-tight divisions that have polarized the country and created so many close elections lately.

—John Fund[1]

IN EVERY ELECTION ANALYSIS, after the votes are made official, two major questions usually remain left unanswered: Where were all the people who *didn't* vote? And just how many voted that *shouldn't* have?

Let's address the second question first.

David Kupelian, managing editor at WND, has described Obama's 2012 election strategy as bribing interest groups needed to establish a winning coalition: wooing women voters by accusing Republicans of waging "a war on women," changing his position yet again on same-sex marriage to buy homosexual votes, playing for Hispanic votes by issuing executive decrees that enact by presidential fiat key provisions of the DREAM Act, and bribing students with promises of student-loan rate extensions and homeowners with mortgage-reduction programs.[2]

But to get its candidate over the top with the last few votes necessary to win an election, the Democratic Party has engaged in the systematic vote registration of "a shadow group" of illegal aliens, felons, dead people, multiple-state voters, and assorted others in a massive, nationwide campaign to enable voter fraud. In a close election, as few as 100,000 fraudulent votes in a hotly contested battleground state could be calculated to tip the balance.

Of course, measures could also be taken to prevent this kind of voter fraud.

But the far left currently in control of the Democratic Party has engaged for decades in systematic voter fraud as an ongoing policy, masterminded by ACORN grassroots-style activists. To cover their tracks, these far-left experts in voter fraud have run a public relations campaign arguing that any attempt by the Republican Party to enact and enforce voter-ID laws is, by definition, a far-right racist plan designed to suppress the votes of minorities, knowing that African Americans, Hispanics, and Asians are likely to vote Democratic.[3]

Journalist John Fund, a student of voter fraud, has looked to Mexico to see how simple it should be to run a national presidential election that would virtually eliminate voter fraud.

In his 2004 book titled *Stealing Elections: How Voter Fraud Threatens Our Democracy*, Fund wrote:

> Ironically, Mexico and many other countries have election systems that are far more secure than ours. To obtain voter credentials, the citizen must present a photo, write a signature and give a thumbprint. The voter card includes a picture with a hologram covering it, a magnetic strip and a serial number to guard against tampering. To cast a ballot, voters must present the card and be certified by a thumbprint scanner. This system was instrumental in allowing the 2000 election of Vicente Fox, the first opposition-party candidate to be elected president in seventy years.[4]

The TSA asks airline passengers to present a valid, government-issued ID, yet the far left screams "voter suppression" and brings lawyers to litigate every effort made to pass voter-ID laws. What else can be concluded but that the far left wants voter identification left loose in the United States precisely because it intends to win elections by doing whatever it takes, including committing massive and systematic voting fraud?

By contesting vigorously with multiple legal challenges every attempt any state makes to enact voter ID laws, the Democratic Party calculated in 2012 to steal the election using techniques that could be denied and disavowed, even if discovered. The strategy was simple: overload the voter rolls with fraudulent voter registrations in battleground states, making sure anyone who showed up would be allowed to vote, whether or not the person could prove his or her identity, place of residence, or eligibility.

The techniques Democrats used to get Obama elected involved coaching students in how to vote for Obama in the state where they were attending college and again by absentee ballot in the state where their parents resided; encouraging Obama supporters to vote by absentee ballot in states where they formerly resided, as well as the state in which they currently reside; and finding voters to present themselves to vote by assuming the identity of someone Democratic campaign officials knew would not show up in person to vote, including deceased individuals still listed on voter registration rolls.

WND reporter Aaron Klein reported that Obama did not win a single state that requires a photo ID to vote, although he was victorious in four states that accept nonphoto identification—Ohio, Virginia, Colorado, and Washington. These four states accept as legitimate identification current utility bills, bank statements, and paychecks.[5]

THE ACORN MACHINE

While working as a community organizer in Chicago, a young Barack Obama worked for Project Vote, a voter-registration project conducted by ACORN, a radical activist group that "has become synonymous with corruption, complicity in the subprime mortgage crisis and especially voter fraud."[6]

Matthew Vadum, senior editor at the Capital Research Center, documents in his 2011 book *Subversion Inc.: How Obama's ACORN Red Shirts Are Still Terrorizing and Ripping Off American Taxpayers*, a policy of ACORN founder Wade Rathke to engage in "Maximum Eligible Participation," a plan to swamp voter rolls with low-income people.[7] The idea was to implement the Cloward-Piven strategy, named after sociology professors Richard Cloward and Frances Fox Piven, a New York–based husband-and-wife team that in the 1960s developed a radical plan to collapse capitalism and usher in a socialist state by placing on government at all levels a demand to pay out welfare benefits to the point where governments went bankrupt. Rathke's idea was that welfare recipients, who are "naturally inclined to support political candidates promising to steal the wealth of productive members of society and redistribute it to the poor," ought to be allowed to register to vote in the same welfare offices where they apply for benefits.[8]

ACORN voter-registration drives have been distinguished by duplicate registrations, errors, and omissions, and a large number of overtly fraudulent names registered, including names of actors and actresses, as well as nationally known sports figures.

ACORN is also distinguished by a history of criminal indictments and convictions for voter fraud. Judicial Watch found that Amy Busefink, a former deputy regional director of ACORN, while under indictment for voter fraud in Nevada, still managed an online voter-registration program for the 2010 election campaign in Colorado, the goal of which was to allow people without a driver's license or state ID to register to vote online.[9]

Over the last forty years, before independent journalists exposed the rampant fraud, ACORN had received an estimated $79 million in federal grants.[10] At its peak, ACORN could call on some four hundred thousand members across the country to implement its programs.

"ACORN was arguably most successful at registering hundreds of thousands of low-income voters, though that mission was dogged by fraud allegations, including that some workers submitted forms signed by 'Mickey Mouse' or other cartoon characters," wrote the *Washington Times* in a 2010 investigative report.[11]

Perhaps the most famous case of ACORN voter fraud involved nineteen-year-old Freddie Johnson, bribed by ACORN with cash and cigarettes to register to vote seventy-two times. "Sometimes, they come up and bribe me with a cigarette, or they will give me a dollar to sign up," Johnson confessed.[12]

Although widely reported that ACORN has disbanded, the organization has merely adapted to increased media scrutiny by having local offices adopt new corporate names that mask the continuing affiliation with the parent ACORN organization.

But, seriously, how rampant is voter fraud? Is it merely a drop in the bucket, as many news outlets and Democratic pundits proclaim, or is it a significant problem?

A Pew Center on the States study in February 2011 discovered 24 million registrations on the nation's voter rolls, about one of every eight, have serious errors. The errors included 1.8 million dead still registered to vote, with an additional 2.75 million registered as active voters in more than one state.[13] In August 2012, the Pew Center on the States reported[14] on a database created by News21, a national investigative reporting project that details state by state 2,068 cases where voter fraud has been litigated, with 23.7 percent of the cases involving absentee-ballot fraud, 19.3 percent voter-registration fraud, and the remaining 57 percent of the cases comprising a variety of issues, including noncitizens casting ineligible ballots and voter-impersonation fraud.[15]

The voter-registration system maintained by the states is plagued with underfunding and understaffing issues that prevent validating one-by-one voter eligibility, let alone checking whether voter registration information, including name and address, is correct. In 2008, the Ohio GOP challenged that approximately 200,000 of 666,000 voters who had registered since the beginning of the year had records, including driver's licenses and Social Security numbers, written on voter registrations that did not match records in other government databases.[16] The reality is that unless a voter moving to another precinct or another state *requests* to be removed from voter-registration rolls, most state voter-registration systems have no way to know if the voter still resides at the address originally registered.

NONCITIZENS VOTING

Beginning in May 2012, Florida's Republican governor, Rick Scott, publicly alleged that as many as 180,000 registered voters in his state may be illegal immigrants who are not US citizens. The state of Florida sued the US Department of Homeland Security to gain access to its federal citizenship database, the Systematic Alien Verification for Entitlements Program, or SAVE, so the list of suspect voters could be authenticated.[17] The Florida Department of State and the Florida Department of Highway Safety compiled the list by comparing voter registration information with driver's license information.

In retaliation, MoveOn.org, the leftist organization funded in part by billionaire progressive activist George Soros, ran a series of television ads in Florida opposing the effort to validate the citizenship of the registered voters in question.

"Republican Governor Rick Scott tried to kick 180,000 people off the voter rolls in his state and is now suing the Department of Justice after they stepped in to stop him," said a fundraising e-mail authored by MoveOn.org on June 27, 2012. "Rick Scott's racist voter purge—which directly targets Latino voters—is so egregious that every one of the 67 supervisors of elections in the state—Democrats, Republicans, and independents—has so far refused to carry it out."[18]

In 2012, Romney lost Florida by fewer than 75,000 votes, making significant the possibility that 180,000 Hispanic voters were on the voting rolls despite questions about their citizenship and eligibility to vote. Looked at from this perspective, the political left was determined to fight the state of Florida over 180,000 challenged voters, a tiny percentage of the nearly 11.5 million voters registered to vote in Florida's 2012 presidential election.[19]

In May 30, 2012, the US Department of Justice ordered Florida's election division to halt the systematic effort to purge the state's voter rolls of noncitizens. In a two-page letter to Florida election officials, T. Christian Herren, the DOJ's lead civil rights voting lawyer, explained that Florida's effort appeared to violate the 1965 Voting Rights Act protection of minorities and the regulations of the 1993 National Voter Registration Act provisions governing voter purges.[20]

Two weeks later, on June 11, 2012, the Florida secretary of state nonetheless filed a lawsuit against DHS to gain access to the SAVE database.

"For nearly a year, the US Department of Homeland Security has failed to meet its legal obligation to provide us the information necessary to identify and remove ineligible voters from Florida's voter rolls," said Florida secretary of state Ken Detzner in a press release explaining the lawsuit. "We can't let the federal government delay our efforts to uphold the integrity of Florida elections any longer. We filed a lawsuit to ensure the law is carried out and we are able to meet our obligation to keep the voter rolls accurate and current."[21]

On June 27, 2012, a US District judge rejected the federal government's attempt to obtain a restraining order to block Florida, ruling that though federal laws prohibit the systematic removal of voters close to an election, the laws do not refer to noncitizens.[22]

The controversy continued into September 2012, as voter-advocacy groups sought to pursue a lawsuit to limit the number of voters challenged over citizenship from 180,000 to a few hundred.

In the end, the Florida controversy left open many questions about Hispanic voter registration. With the Obama administration's decision to implement key provisions of the DREAM Act by executive action, the questions remain open: for instance, whether new privileges extended to the children of illegal immigrants would include voter registration, even if the child in question had not yet obtained US citizenship.

In a speech at the LBJ Library at the University of Texas–Austin, Attorney General Eric Holder attacked voter-ID reforms as a return to the unjust racism of Jim Crow laws, calling up images of the hoses, bullets, bombs, and billy clubs that African-American voters had to confront before President Johnson pushed the Voting Act of 1965 through Congress.[23] This followed Holder's refusal to allow a Department of Justice investigation into accusations of civil rights violations made against members of the New Black Panther Party who allegedly menaced white voters in Philadelphia in 2008, making it clear the DOJ under Holder was unwilling to pursue a policy of race-neutral enforcement of voting-rights laws.

In a six-to-three decision on April 28, 2008, in the case *Crawford v. Marion County Election Board*, the Supreme Court upheld voter-ID cases, provided the same requirements were imposed on all voters. The case was widely interpreted as a major defeat for the Democratic Party and the efforts of the far left to preserve voting-registration methodologies that put ineligible voters on the rolls.[24]

Yet in 2012, the landscape for voter-ID laws being passed by various states was still confusing, with leftist voter-advocacy groups continuing to file legal challenges. On October 2, 2012, a Pennsylvania judge blocked a key component of a state law requiring strict photographic identification to vote from being implemented in the presidential election to be held the following month.

"Voter-ID laws have been taken off the table in Texas and Wisconsin," wrote Ethan Bronner in the *New York Times* on October 2, 2012, a month before the national election. "The Justice Department has blocked such a law in South Carolina, which has appealed in federal court. In Florida and Ohio, early voting and voter-registration drives have been largely restored. New Hampshire is going ahead with its law, but voters who do not have the required document will be permitted to vote and have a month to verify their identity."[25]

Strict voter-ID laws remained in Kansas, Indiana, Georgia, and Tennessee. Pennsylvania settled on a compromise for the election on November 6, 2012. Poll workers in Pennsylvania were permitted to ask to see a voter's ID, but voters were not required to comply, with the state anticipating legal clarification following the election.

At the conclusion of the 2012 presidential election, the cochair of Romney's Wisconsin campaign, state Senator Alberta Darling, claimed Romney would have won Wisconsin had a voter-ID law been in place.

"We're looking at all sorts of different precincts and all sorts of same-day registrations," Darling said. "I know people will go, 'We don't have fraud and abuse in our elections.' Buy why, why can't we have voter ID when the majority of people in Wisconsin wanted it, we passed it, the governor signed it? Why should one judge in Dane County be able to hold it up?"[26]

After a Wisconsin judge blocked enforcement of Wisconsin's voter-ID law, the Wisconsin Supreme Court declined to take the case.[27] Obama won Wisconsin with 52.8 percent of the vote, a margin of victory over Romney of approximately 213,000 of over 3 million votes cast. In the last days of the campaign, as noted earlier, Romney traveled to Wisconsin for a rally, convinced by the campaign's internal polls that the election had narrowed such that he had a chance of winning.

Aaron Gardner of Media Trackers, in a review of voter data for Colorado, a state without voter-ID requirements, found voter-registration rolls in ten counties had numbers larger than the total voting age population residing in the county.[28]

When Media Trackers requested comment on the "vote bloat" in Gilpin County, Chief Deputy Gail Maxwell explained, "This is just a reminder Gilpin is a gaming community. These voters come and go!"

Unconvinced, Gardner noted that all ten of the suspect counties reported vote turnout greater than the national average, while nine out of ten also showed voter turnout well above the Colorado average.

A separate analysis conducted by the Franklin Center showed that in 2012, seventeen of Colorado's sixty-four counties had registration greater than 100 percent of the US Census voting-age population; an additional nine counties had voter-registration rates of 95 percent or higher.

"There is a higher voter-fraud potential in areas of unmanaged voter lists and areas of high voter-list bloat measured by inactive voters," commented Franklin Center's Earl F. Glynn, on reporting the data.[29]

In 2012, as noted earlier, Colorado was a swing state the Romney campaign visited frequently in the final weeks before Election Day. Obama won Colorado by 51.2 percent, with a margin of approximately 138,000 votes out of just over 2.5 million votes cast.

Four days prior to the election, Colorado was also one of six states to which the Republican National Committee sent a letter warning of detected voting irregularities in which voting machines were registering votes for Obama when the voter desired to cast a vote for Romney.[30] The report in Colorado stemmed from a voter in Grand Junction who complained that a vote he cast for Romney on a touch-screen voting device was registering as a vote for Obama. After investigating the complaint, an elections clerk in Grand Junction pulled the voting machine out of service.[31]

THE UNION ADVANTAGE

To actually implement a nationwide voter-fraud system, however, a political party would need an army of boots on the ground willing to do whatever it takes to get its candidate elected. In 2012, the Democrat Party had such an army.

The Service Employees International Union, better known as the SEIU, announced in a press release dated June 19, 2012,[32] that the nation's fastest-growing union, with 2.1 million members, was launching "the largest and most-targeted political field campaign in the union's 91-year history to re-elect President Obama and to win other key elections in eight battleground states." The SEIU announcement specified the union would target both union and nonunion members, "with an emphasis on African American and Latino communities, younger voters, union households and other working people—on an unprecedented scale." The SEIU committed to knocking on more than 3 million doors and holding 1 million conversations across the nation, with the majority of the work focused in Colorado, Florida, New Hampshire, Nevada, Ohio, Pennsylvania, Virginia, and Wisconsin.

"Our boots-on-the-ground effort will be bold and targeted," said Eliseo Medina, SEIU International secretary treasurer, repeating what sounded like Democratic Party talking points. "Far too much is at stake this election cycle. We are using our human and capital resources to stand by candidates who will stand up for working people and not return the country to failed policies of the past. We know our communities can make a difference when they go to the polls."

The SEIU announced the field campaign for Obama would include the following: aggressive paid and volunteer GOTV efforts; large-scale civic engagements with community partners in the African-American and Latino communities; major paid media campaigns; and coordinated voter-education and voter-protection programs. The launch of the program included a joint, SEIU/Priorities USA Action, $4 million, Spanish-language television and radio ad campaign in Colorado, Florida, and Nevada. Rank-and-file SEIU members were authorized to take time off their jobs to become member political organizers, or MPs, assigned to reach out to fellow union members to focus on African Americans, Latinos, union households, and other working people. By Election Day, the SEIU program included a volunteer recruitment program aimed at getting more than a hundred thousand union and nonunion members volunteering to help reelect Obama.

"We are going full force on this get out the vote effort because we cannot allow the voices of working people to be drowned out by the corporations and elected officials beholden to the interests of the elite," said Gerry Hudson, SEIU international executive vice president. "Mitt Romney and other extremist candidates have made clear that their vision is an America where the rich get more of the nation's wealth and the rest of us face cuts in critical services such as education and health care. Working people literally can't afford Romney's agenda."

Brandon Davis, SEIU national political director, elaborated on what was characterized as an "extreme, far-right agenda to suppress votes, scapegoat public workers, deny women access to health care, refuse to consider a fair pathway to citizenship, and otherwise drown out the voices of working people."

Unions like the SEIU gave the Democratic Party free boots-on-the-ground workers key to any successful voter-registration drive—rife with fraud or not—or GOTV effort. A video taken by an amateur at a Romney rally in Bedford, Ohio, showed protestors, most of whom were African-American, chanting slogans like "Romney, go home!" and "We don't need no bad economy," acknowledging on camera that they were paid eleven dollars per hour by SEIU organizers and that they had been bused into the suburb.[33]

At the end of October 2012, SEIU president Mary Kay Henry told reporters, "We are fired up and ready to go."[34]

Henry confirmed she had made campaign-related stops in nineteen cities in October, including Columbus and Toledo in Ohio, and Las Vegas, Milwaukee, and Detroit. She confirmed the rest of the SEIU's leadership team had been following similarly brutal travel schedules, with the goal to put twenty-five thousand volunteers in the field for the final days of the race. Henry further explained SEIU union members from safely blue states were being transferred into battleground states like Colorado and Nevada, and that targeted outreach teams were under way to Latino and African-American communities, including special teams aimed at combating efforts Henry claimed Republicans were making to intimidate minority voters and suppress turnout.

While the Bureau of Labor Statistics reported unionization rates have fallen over the last twenty years and even during Obama's presidency,[35] at the same time, the SEIU, a union that focuses on government employees, has expanded under Obama. From the start of taking office, Obama has made a concerted effort to place at the center of his administration Andy Stern, the former president of the SEIU whom reporter and commentator Michelle Malkin has described as the "militant left-wing social worker-turned-union heavy."[36]

Furthermore, Diana Furchtgott-Roth, a former chief economist at the US Department of Labor and a current senior fellow at the Manhattan Institute for Public Policy, has argued Obama did everything he could in his first term to help unions.

"His stimulus package was directed at public-sector unionized workers," she wrote. "His executive order on project labor agreements required large construction projects to hire unionized workers. Obama supported the misnamed Employee Free Choice Act, which would have taken away workers' right to a secret ballot in elections for union representation and would have imposed mandatory binding arbitration on employers and workers who could not agree on a contract."[37]

In the GM and Chrysler bankruptcies, Obama ignored well-established corporate law, awarding to UAW union workers stock in exchange for their debt position, bullying senior secured creditors to stand aside—a move calculated to appeal to auto workers in Michigan and Ohio that experts estimate cost taxpayers about $23 billion.[38]

Again, Romney was probably right that the smart solution would have been to allow GM and Chrysler to go directly into bankruptcy, so the courts could administer an orderly reorganization. But Obama, thinking ahead to 2012, and seeing an opportunity to play politics with the unions, was not about to let a good crisis get away. After all, Obama knew, even in the midst of the 2008–2009 bailout of GM and Chrysler, just how important union workers would be to his reelection ground game.

The voter-intelligence, computer-driven GOTV system created in 2008 under the direction of campaign manager Jim Messina was expected to be robust and effective operating on its own in 2012. But the voter-intelligence system buoyed by the union boots-on-the-ground GOTV effort was even more certain to give Obama the advantage he needed to ensure reelection, even if voter enthusiasm and turnout in 2012 were, as anticipated, less than in 2008.

"VOTE EARLY, VOTE OFTEN"

The union advantage was especially valuable in states where the Democrats were able to pass laws expanding voting beyond Election Day itself. Innovations including early voting, absentee voting on demand, and same-day registration gave fraudsters ready to be loose with the rules the opportunity to utilize nonvoters' names in various schemes, including sending someone to the polls who claimed to be the voter involved. In states where no voter ID is required, precinct workers generally have no way to tell if a voter is the person he or she claims to be when that person shows up to vote or ask for an absentee ballot. Also nearly impossible to detect are voters registered in more than one state who use early voting laws to facilitate their travel from one state to another so they can vote twice.

In the field, union workers supplemented Obama paid campaign workers and volunteers. With information provided by the Obama GOTV computer system, this army of fieldworkers used the extra days of early voting to increase the odds that a time could be found to bring every possible Obama supporter to the polls.

By the end of October, Michael P. McDonald, associate professor at George Mason University in Fairfax, Virginia, and spokesman for the United States Election Project, reported that about 10 million voters had cast ballots nationwide, with early voting on a pace likely to exceed the 41 million early votes cast in 2008. McDonald concluded that with the election less than two weeks away, Obama had an advantage in Iowa and Nevada, with Romney holding a slight lead in North Carolina.[39] In the end, the United States Election Project reported 32,311,399 early votes were cast in 2012, approximately one-third of the total votes cast. Obama's advantage held in Iowa, where Democrats were responsible for 41.9 percent of the early voting, compared to 32 percent for Republicans; and in Nevada, where Democrats were responsible for 43.9 percent of early votes cast, compared to 36 percent for Republicans.[40]

Nevada clearly demonstrates the growing importance of early voting. In Nevada, early voting represented 68.97 percent of all votes cast, with absentee mail-in votes constituting 9.17 percent and in-person voting on Election Day responsible for only 21.86 percent of all votes cast.[41]

In assessing the impact of early voting, admittedly, it is difficult to know if one party or the other is simply banking in advance voters who would have shown up on Election Day or if the party is actually bringing in to vote early voters who otherwise would not have voted at all.

In Ohio, however, a study of early voting in 2008 conducted by Northeast Ohio Voter Advocates found that in five counties analyzed, African Americans voted early in person heavily and far out of proportion to their percentages of voters or percentages of adults in those counties. "The disproportionate 'excess' use of EIP [early in-person voting] (rather than vote-by-mail or election day voting) by African Americans ranged from an over-representation of about 50% to 260% in different counties," the report concluded.[42]

Other clues suggest Republican and Democrat GOTV efforts do not utilize early voting in the same way. In 2012, extremely long lines at polling places were observed in Ohio after early voting was reduced from five weekends before the election to only the weekend right before Election Day.[43] In October 2012, a federal appeals court ruled against Ohio's Republican Secretary of State Jon Husted in favor of the Obama campaign, allowing hours to be extended in the final days before the election. Husted took the case to the Supreme Court, only to have the Supreme Court refuse to hear it.[44]

On Election Day, long lines were evident in African-American precincts around Cleveland in Cuyahoga, as well as in the counties and precincts in inner-city Columbus and Cincinnati, with reports of people lining up to vote as early as at 4:00 a.m. The same was not true in Ohio's rural white counties and precincts.

During the afternoon of Election Day, Ohio's Republican Governor John Kasich made a series of concerned calls to state and national GOP leaders, including to advisors in the Romney campaign, concerned that turnout in Ohio's white precincts might not be enough to overcome the surge being observed in African-American voting.

This would suggest the Romney campaign's effort to increase early voting totals in 2012 may have resulted only in banking Republican votes Romney would have gotten anyway on Election Day, while the Democrats had employed techniques that were successful in using early voting to bring in voters who otherwise might not have voted on Election Day.

Particularly damaging to Democrats' claims of innocence in 2012 was a series of undercover videos taken by James O'Keefe and his Project Veritas, showing Democratic Party campaign workers and volunteers being willing to advise voters how to commit voter fraud, including how to register and vote in more than one state.[45] The videos also demonstrate how difficult it is to get your name removed from the voter registration rolls after you have moved and how easy it is to get an absentee ballot to vote in a second state, even if in the second state the voter's registered name is different from the voter's current legal name.[46]

One video demonstrated how easy it was for illegal immigrants and non-citizens to vote in states like North Carolina that do not require voter ID, or for persons to vote after stealing the identities of registered voters who are dead.[47]

Also exposed by O'Keefe's undercover video cameras were students voting for Obama in the state where they were attending college, as well as voting by absentee ballot in their home state.

A clear point of O'Keefe's videos is that early voting statutes provide ample time to explore and implement voter-fraud schemes.

O'Keefe further exposed judges and state voting officials who imposed lax voter-registration processes because they supported the "open election" procedures favored by Democrats who charge voter-ID laws are racist by nature.

O'Keefe's videos also caught salaried employees of the DNC who worked for the Obama campaign in Organizing for America offices advising undercover Project Veritas reporters on how to vote twice, including in more than one state—clearly demonstrating the Democratic Party was engaging in voter fraud in 2012.[48]

MISSING WHITE VOTERS

And now to the other unanswered question—where were all the people who *didn't* vote?—for the presidential election of 2012 was not only a story about the demographic explosion among nonwhite voters and the Democratic campaign workers engaging in systematic practices of voter fraud; it was also about a large number of white voters not showing up.

Sean Trende, the senior election analyst at Real Clear Politics, pointed out in the aftermath of Romney's defeat the "missing white voters" were a mystery in the 2012 election that Republicans need to solve to understand more completely the reasons Romney lost. Based at the time on projections from yet incomplete ballot reports, Trende was nonetheless able to estimate that in 2012, minority voting increased by about 2 million voters from 2008, but white voters disappeared from the polls to the tune of nearly 7 million "missing" voters.[49]

Clearly, key to Obama's victory was, as David Kupelian argued, engaging in voter fraud and boosting the number of voters Obama gained by bribing with government benefits the various components of the New Deal coalition he had assembled. Also key was the work Messina had done creating "the Cave" in Obama's Chicago headquarters, assembling a world-class group of computer geeks dedicated to identifying and communicating with likely Obama voters one by one. Had Obama not engaged in voting fraud or had he lacked what amounts to about an order-of-magnitude edge over the Republicans in voter-intelligence computer technology, he may well have lost another 1 or 2 million votes on the road to being retired as a one-term president.

Still, Romney has to be taken to task for failing to meet a major goal of his campaign strategy: namely, to significantly better the voter total achieved by McCain in 2008.

Going into the election, Romney's top advisors believed Romney would lose unless he got more votes than McCain. Romney campaign managers in state after state during the last three weeks of the campaign rattled off statistics attempting to prove they had done more door knocks and made more phone calls than McCain four years earlier. Yet, when the totals were counted, the Romney GOTV computer system crashed on Election Day, and Romney's vote total was less than a million more than the GOP's 2008 candidate.

The following table, constructed by Trende, makes clear the white vote in America still commands by far the largest total vote of any demographic subgroup in the nation. While Romney had a 20-point advantage with white voters, Obama still got an estimated 39 percent of the white vote, compared to 59 percent for Romney.[50] The table shows nearly 6.7 million fewer white voters voted in 2012 than voted in 2008. Assuming a 39/59 percent split among the 2008 white voters who did not vote in 2012, this would have given Romney 3,953,000 additional votes and Obama an additional 2,613,000 votes. Adding some 1.3 million votes to Romney's total may have tipped several key battleground states into Romney's column, including possibly both Ohio and Florida.

Number of Votes
Cast by race/ethnicity
2012 and 2008

	2012 (est)	2008	Difference
White votes (according to exits)	91,916,995.80	98,597,791.50	(6,680,795.70)
African American votes	16,596,124.24	16,301,501.53	294,622.71
Hispanic votes	12,766,249.42	11,042,952.65	1,723,296.77
"Other" votes	6,383,124.71	5,915,867.49	467,257.22

When Trende further factored into the analysis a normal growth of the various voting-age populations over the past four years and assumed a 55 percent turnout, he concluded there were actually about 8 million fewer white voters than could have been expected in 2012. If the correct figure of missing white voters in the 2012 election was 8 million, and we assume the same 39/59 percent split, Romney would have received an additional 4,720,000 votes, compared to Obama's 3,120,000 additional votes, giving Romney a 1.6-million additional vote advantage. White voters who stayed home may have very well cost Romney the election.

"So who were these whites and why did they stay home?" Trende asked. "My first instinct was that they might be conservative evangelicals turned off by Romney's Mormonism or moderate past. But the decline didn't seem to be concentrated in Southern states with high evangelical populations."

To answer this question, Trende conducted a detailed analysis of white voters in his home state of Ohio. He noted turnout remained high in the counties clustered around Columbus in the center of the state and in the suburban counties around Cincinnati in the Southwest of the state. He observed these are heavily Republican counties filled with white-collar workers. Where Trende found the turnout was disappointing was in the rural portions of Ohio, especially in the southeastern portion of the state. These counties have been hit hard by the recession, unemployment is high and economic growth has been negligible in recent years.

"My sense is these voters were unhappy with Obama. But his negative ad campaign relentlessly emphasizing Romney's wealth and tenure at Bain Capital may have turned them off to the Republican nominee as well," Trende concluded. "The Romney campaign exacerbated this through the challenger's failure to articulate a clear, positive agenda to address these voters' fears and self-inflicted wounds like the '47 percent' gaffe. Given a choice between two unpalatable options, these voters simply stayed home."

Interestingly, the southeastern portion of Ohio was one region in the country where the Romney campaign believed their message about Obama's "war on coal" was having a major impact. Trende stressed that elections are won and lost only on who shows up, not on who *might* have shown up. Still, figuring out who did not show up to vote and why is key to any postmortem analysis seeking instructive lessons for the future.

Byron York, chief political correspondent of the *Washington Examiner*, also wondered "why a large group of voters [in Ohio], carefully cultivated through personal contacts and putative supporters of Mitt Romney, just didn't show up at the polls."[51]

York noted that in 2008, when Obama first won Ohio, blacks were about 11 percent of the electorate. In 2012, blacks—who are now 12 percent of Ohio's population—were 15 percent of the electorate. "There has been no population explosion of African Americans in those four years," York noted. "Obama simply succeeded in getting more black voters to the polls than he did four years ago."

York further observed that given the high level of enthusiasm for Obama four years ago, as reflected in Ohio by a large black turnout, with 97 percent of blacks voting for Obama, a higher black turnout seemed impossible to most Republican strategists.

"That four-percentage-point increase in black turnout produced about

200,000 votes, more than Obama's winning margin in the state," York wrote.

The white vote in Ohio was just the opposite. Four years ago, white voters were 83 percent of the electorate, York observed, but in 2012, white voters were 79 percent.

"There has been no implosion of the white population in Ohio in those years," York wrote. "There was simply lower turnout among whites—somewhere in the 200,000 range, which is, again, more than Obama's winning margin."

York's explanation is similar to Trende's explanation: Obama attacked Romney hard early in the campaign, while Romney fought a lackluster campaign, refusing to fight back.

York wrote: "There are several theories about those missing white voters, but the most plausible is that the ones who were undecideds or weak Republicans were deeply influenced by Obama's relentless attacks on Romney in May, June, July and August. A steady stream of negative ads portrayed Romney as a heartless, out-of-touch rich guy, and Romney didn't really fight back. The missing white voters didn't like Obama but were also turned off by the Republican, so they stayed home. That's the theory, at least; Republicans will know more when they actually interview lots of those nonvoters."

York quoted Mark Weaver, a veteran Ohio Republican strategist, who said: "Obama won Ohio because he did what Bush did in 2004—surprised pundits by increasing turnout in his base. Also, by demonizing the undefined Romney, he tamped down Romney's ability to motivate weak Republicans to turn out."

Also, in 2004, Ohio was a primary target of the attack by the Swift Boat Veterans for the Truth, questioning in a series of television ads the truthfulness of John Kerry's war record as a supposed Vietnam War hero who had received three Purple Hearts the SBVFT considered suspect, and castigating Kerry for his role as the leading national spokesman for the Vietnam Veterans against the War after Kerry returned home. While Karl Rove, a chief strategist for George W. Bush's reelection campaign in 2004, disavowed the SBVFT message, the attack raised questions about a central image Kerry intended to portray to the American people from the moment he appeared at the Democratic National Convention in Boston to accept the presidential nomination. Kerry began his acceptance speech by saluting and saying, "Reporting for duty."

Professional establishment politicians like Karl Rove can be counted on to eschew negative campaigning in their public comments, despite repeated scientific evidence validating the impact negative campaigning has on voters. Clearly, when outside PACs aligned with the Democratic Party characterized Romney as a rich "vulture capitalist" who gained his wealth by bankrupting companies and firing middle-class workers, Obama campaign strategists knew what they were doing. The independent PAC attack portraying Romney as an unsympathetic rich guy set up Romney for a knockout punch with moderate voters not deeply committed to either candidate. Obama delivered that knockout punch by repeating the Saul Alinsky–style class-warfare campaign theme of "tax the rich" in every stump speech he gave in the closing weeks of the 2012 presidential campaign. In states like Ohio, the economic downturn made voters suspect of any politicians they perceived had not personally felt economic pain at one point or another in their lives. Romney's emphasis on supply-side economics was an intellectually compelling argument to conservative Republicans. The argument did not have the same motivating effect on moderate voters, including many centrist Republicans in Ohio's rural counties.

THE MORMON QUESTION

Mormon Craig L. Foster, a historian and scholar of the religion, posed precisely the Mormon question Romney faced in running for president: "Because Mormons believe in what most Americans see as alien, even non-Christian, doctrines and strange practices, can a Mormon be trusted to preserve, protect, and promote the common good of the United States as president?"[52]

The Mormon religion has been castigated for a number of practices and beliefs most Christians consider peculiar if not bizarre, including at one time the acceptance of polygamy, the preaching that Jesus Christ visited the Americas after his crucifixion, and the belief that Satan was appointed by God to rule the earth. Such doctrines lead many Christians to define the Mormon faith not as a variant Christian religion, but as a cult.

Foster cited a poll taken in November 2006 showing 43 percent of all voters and 53 percent of evangelical Christians would not vote for a Mormon, a percentage Foster took to be an underestimation given that people generally do not want to admit their bias.[53]

In analyzing the 2008 campaign, Foster noted obvious press bias when the Associated Press published an article in February 2007 titled "Romney family tree has polygamy branch." In contrast, the mainstream media neglected to mention the polygamy at the heart of Barack Obama's life story, in that Obama's father, the Kenyan Barack Obama, had multiple wives and was married to a woman in Africa at the same time he married Ann Dunham and conceived the future president.[54]

On October 7, 2011, Robert Jeffress, pastor of First Baptist Church in Dallas, Texas, caused a commotion at the Values Voter Summit when he warned against voting for Romney because "Mormonism is not Christianity," claiming the decision for evangelical Christians is whether "we prefer someone who is truly a believer in Jesus Christ or someone . . . who is part of a cult."[55]

Keying off the outburst by Jeffress, the next salvo came from Christopher Hitchens, internationally known for his atheist views.

"The Mormons apparently believe that Jesus will return in Missouri rather than Armageddon: I wouldn't care to bet on the likelihood of either," Hitchens wrote in an October 17, 2011, article in *Slate* magazine that examined what he characterized as Romney's Mormon problem. "In the meanwhile, though, we are fully entitled to ask Mitt Romney about the forces that influenced his political formation and—since he comes from a dynasty of his church, and spent much of his boyhood and manhood first as a missionary and then as a senior lay official—it is safe to assume that the influence is not small."[56]

Hitchens, however, wrote nothing in 2008 or 2011 asking Obama to explain his past association with communist poet and journalist Frank Marshall Davis in Hawaii or the praise Obama lavished on Malcolm X in writing his autobiography.

On November 23, 2011, the Pew Form on Religion and Public Life published an important survey on Romney's Mormon faith. The conclusion was that Romney's Mormon faith would be a factor in the GOP primaries, but not in the general election.

The Pew Research Center found that about half of all voters and 60 percent of evangelical Republicans knew that Mitt Romney was a Mormon. The study further found that evangelical Protestants, a key element of the GOP electoral base, are more inclined than the public as a whole to view

Mormonism as a non-Christian faith.

Republicans who replied Mormonism was not a Christian religion were found to be less likely to support Romney for the GOP nomination, but these same Republicans were prepared to back Romney overwhelmingly in a run against Barack Obama in the general election.

When asked if the 2012 election were a choice between Mitt Romney and Barack Obama, 87 percent the GOP respondents said they would support Romney, compared to only 9 percent who would support Obama.

"There is no evidence that Romney's Mormon faith would prevent rank-and-file Republicans, including white evangelicals, from coalescing around him if he wins the GOP nomination," the executive summary of the Pew report read. "Rather, the same Republicans who may have doubts about Romney's faith are among the most vehement opponents of Barack Obama. Fully 91% of white evangelical Republican voters say they would back Romney over Obama in a general election matchup, and 79% would support Romney strongly. Overall, white evangelicals would be among the strongest Romney supporters if he is the GOP nominee challenging Obama next fall."[57]

Romney's approach to the issue in 2011 was to maintain silence over his faith, treating the issue of Mormonism as a nonissue.

Immediately after Pastor Jeffress forced the topic of Romney's faith onto the headlines in October 2011, reporters trailing Romney in New Hampshire began peppering him with questions. CNN reported that Romney kept silent, shaking hands with crowds in the granite state, while aides shouted, "No questions," in an effort to quiet the press.

CNN further reported that late in the day, the persistence of the press on this issue irritated Romney.

"I do press avails and then I answer questions that are important questions in the length that I want to do but what I don't do is in a group like this is [*sic*] stop and rattle off questions to people just as we walk along," Romney shot back to the press.[58]

Exit polls further showed Romney's Mormon faith did not hurt him in the 2012 election.

The *Washington Post* reported the day after the election that 78 percent of white evangelical Christians went for Romney, up from 74 percent for John McCain in 2008. Moreover, evangelical Christians turned out to vote equally for Romney and McCain, with the *Washington Post* reporting that white evangelical Christians were 26 percent of the electorate in both 2008 and 2012.[59]

In the final analysis, the Pew study was correct: During the 2012 presidential campaign, prominent evangelical leaders came out in support of Romney.

On October 11, 2012, roughly a year after the outburst by Pastor Jeffress at the Value Voters Summit, Billy Graham, ninety-three, held a much-publicized personal meeting with Mitt Romney in his North Carolina home.

"It was an honor to meet and host Gov. Romney in my home today, especially since I knew his late father, former Michigan Gov. George Romney, whom I considered a friend," Graham said. "I have followed Mitt Romney's career in business, the Olympic Games, as governor of Massachusetts and, of course, as a candidate for president of the United States."

Graham praised Romney's character: "What impresses me even more than Gov. Romney's successful career are his values and strong moral convictions. I appreciate his faithful commitment to his impressive family, particularly his wife Ann of 43 years and his five married sons."

He made it clear he prayed with Romney: "It was a privilege to pray with Gov. Romney—for his family and our country. I will turn 94 the day after the upcoming election, and I believe America is at a crossroads. I hope millions of Americans will join me in praying for our nation and to vote for candidates who will support the biblical definition of marriage, protect the sanctity of life and defend our religious freedoms."

So as to leave no doubt, these quotations were published in full on the Billy Graham Evangelistic Association website, along with photographs of Billy Graham and Mitt Romney sitting together in discussion in the study of the evangelist's North Carolina home.[60]

The press coverage of Romney's meeting with Billy Graham was favorable. The *Washington Post* reported Romney asked Graham for his prayers, and "the ailing evangelist came through by praying with the Republican presidential candidate and offering his support."

"I'll do all I can to help you," the newspaper reported the evangelist said.[61]

Yet, there is more to the story about Romney's faith. Did Romney's Mormonism have any impact on the millions of white voters who stayed away from the polls in 2012?

JFK'S APPROACH

In 1960, John Kennedy's presidential campaign struggled with how best to handle the issue that JFK, if elected, would be the nation's first Roman Catholic president.

The issue was controversial, given the prejudice many Protestants held toward the pope, who ruled the Catholic Church as the Bishop of Rome—a controversy that dated back to the sixteenth-century division known as the Protestant Reformation, in which prominent European religious leaders, including John Wycliffe, Martin Luther, and John Calvin, led a theological revolt against Rome and the authority of the Catholic Church.

The concern among top JFK advisors, including Bobby Kennedy, was that the issue of their candidate's Catholicism if not addressed directly could lead to a whisper campaign that just might cost the Democrats the election to Richard Nixon, who was born and raised a Quaker.

To resolve the issue, Kennedy's advisors turned to empirical research, a bold move in an era in which seasoned professionals in smoke-filled back rooms still made most political decisions, relying only on their personal experience and intuition to argue out differences.

The Kennedy camp consulted Simulmatics, a pioneering data corporation that had developed 480 social descriptions of voter profiles that could be used in computer simulations to test electoral outcomes. At that time, the Kennedy camp considered the results of the computer analysis so "top secret" that each copy of the final report "was seen only by those who had to see it," with copies distributed within the campaign numbered so as to ensure privacy and facilitate accountability should there be a leak.[62]

The results were surprising.

Simulmatics reported to the JFK campaign that surfacing the issue of religion would cause eleven states, totaling 122 electoral votes, to move away, but would pull six states, including three out of the four largest, worth 132 electoral votes, into the Democratic Party camp.

"The simulation shows that there has already been a serious defection from Kennedy by Protestant voters," the Simulmatics report read. "Under these circumstances, it makes no sense to brush the religious issue under the rug. Kennedy has already suffered the disadvantages of the issue even though it is not embittered now—and without receiving compensating advantages inherent to it."[63]

Remarkably, the advice of these early computer-expert, voter-intelligence researchers was that JFK would actually gain votes by being confrontational on the issue of religion—exactly the opposite strategy of the silent treatment the Romney campaign preferred when deciding how to deal with his Mormon issue.

Within three weeks of receiving the Simulmatics report, JFK traveled on September 12, 1960, to Houston, where he gave his now famous speech on religion to the Greater Houston Ministerial Association—a speech widely covered by broadcast national television news at the time.[64]

Kennedy's risk was arguably greater than Romney's. Kennedy knew he had the Catholic vote in 1960 the same way Romney should have known he would have the evangelical Christian vote in 2012.

A Democratic Party opponent who was a Protestant or an evangelical Christian would have split the religious vote in 2012. But many evangelical Christians still felt uncertain concerning the depth of Obama's commitment to Christianity.

By daring to confront openly the issue of his Catholic religion, JFK forced the topic on the agenda. In so doing, he solidified the resistance to his candidacy on the part of many Protestants who were already inclined to vote against him. What JFK accomplished in his favor was to win over Christians who were inclined to be sympathetic to his candidacy but were afraid to address the issue openly. Once the issue was in the open, JFK and his supporters could make clear his Catholic faith would not open the door for the pope in Rome to dictate to him in matters of politics.

Kathryn Lofton, a professor of religious studies at Yale University, has argued persuasively that Romney lost not because he was a Mormon, but because he was not Mormon enough. She says that successful presidential candidates explain to the electorate how the strangest parts of themselves make sense. She praised Obama for transforming his "itinerant childhood and complicated genealogy" into a story average Americans could understand and relate to. Romney's mistake, she contends, was his failure to unveil the relationship between his particular religious experience and his vision of America.

Eloquently, Lofton explained:

> He should have announced at every pit stop that he had met the world through his missionary work; that he came from a good Christian home that emphasized the principles of hard work and self-sacrifice; that he keeps a weekly calendar guided by the principles of Stephen R. Covey; and keeps a marriage because he believes those commercials are right—diamonds are forever, and so is this bond. He should have proclaimed his financial success was the result of all this earnestness, and explained private equity as just another way to organize free enterprise. Not because it's a crafty re-framing of his biography, but because it is also true: it's true to the very thing his supporters find so solid, and his detractors find so discomfiting, about Romney."

Lofton wanted Romney to tell his story. She longed for him to provide an account of himself as a pioneer, missionary Mormon, presenting himself to the American public as a "naively stalwart, and almost always inadvertently gallant, hero."[65]

As Election Day approached, the Romney campaign made more use of Ann Romney, who was particularly effective in communicating an emotional message of how Mitt had stood beside her through her trial with cancer.

The Romney that emerged from Ann's description was a loving father, dedicated to his children, who worked hard and earned money, but knew the line was drawn so that family and God came first.

Had the message been proclaimed openly early in the campaign, Obama's public relations and media henchmen may never have succeeded in portraying Romney as a money-hungry "vulture capitalist" who only cared about sucking the blood out of blue-collar companies to enrich himself.

That image was not the true Romney.

The true Romney was a deeply religious man who believed the core values of the American dream, regardless how corny those values might seem to far-leftist Democratic operatives.

The true Romney could have explained how he was tired of compromising with the radical ideals of the politically correct left and regretted ever having done so, even though he was still determined to work with Democrats in Congress, believing he could bring to the nation the same type of impressive economic turnaround he could argue he had helped accomplish in Massachusetts.

WHAT DONALD TRUMP PROVED

In the first months of 2011, Donald Trump made impressive gains in the polls, pressing forward with his improbable presidential candidacy.

In a remarkable poll reported in April 2011, Trump led the field with 14.3 percent of Republican and Republican-leaning respondents saying they would vote for the billionaire real estate mogul if their state party primary were held that day, compared to 14.1 percent for second-place Mike Huckabee and 13.5 percent for Mitt Romney.[66]

How did Trump do it?

Trump dared to venture headfirst into politically incorrect territory, questioning fundamental gaps in Obama's nativity story and his birth narrative. Why were Barack Obama's college transcripts still sealed? Was he enrolled at Occidental College as a foreign exchange student? When he was with his mother and Muslim stepfather in Indonesia, did Obama actually become an Indonesian citizen, as his grade school enrollment cards in Jakarta suggested? Why was the Hawaii Department of Health three years into the Obama presidency still refusing to show the American public the original, 1960 pen-and-paper records documenting Obama's birth? Was Obama hiding that he was born abroad? Was he hiding that his Indonesian stepfather had legally adopted him as a child? Under article 2, section 1 of the Constitution, either might have compromised his eligibility to run for president by rendering him not a "natural-born citizen."

These were questions the Democrats had asked in 2008 regarding McCain's birth in the Panama Canal Zone. Why were these questions somehow illegitimate to ask about Obama?

Trump withstood the Democratic ridicule, launched with an intensity that could only be explained by surmising senior Democratic operatives knew honest answers could be lethal to Obama's reelection hopes.

Trump's presidential aspirations looked in early 2011 as if they might be successful precisely because Trump dared to confront Obama directly, completely disregarding the threat of the mainstream media to ridicule Trump and destroy his reputation as a serious player if he persisted in demanding to see records as mundane as Obama's original 1960 birth certificate and his grade school records.

The mainstream media dismissed as absurd polls showing one-third or more of Americans and an even higher percentage of Republicans believed Obama was lying about his past,[67] possibly to cover up a foreign birth. The mainstream media continued to support Obama, even after proof emerged that Obama had allowed his book publicist to promote Obama's literary efforts by proclaiming in print for years that Obama was Kenyan-born.[68]

The air came out of Trump's campaign only after April 27, 2011, when Obama released from the White House what he claimed was a computer copy of his original birth certificate.

Trump's downfall was that he did not advance immediately the suspicion the document was forged by demanding to have the original document, supposedly held in the Hawaii Department of Health vault, subjected to independent verification by a team of court-qualified forensic experts.

Trump's lame claim responding to Obama at his own press conference held the same day was that he was "proud" of himself for forcing the president to release his birth certificate. This reaction fell flat with a large and growing segment of the American people that wanted to see Obama subjected to rigorous questioning that was tough and unafraid.[69]

"THE BEST DEFENSE IS A GOOD OFFENSE"

What Trump proved in 2011 was what Jack Kennedy's advisors knew in 1960: the American voting public becomes energized when a presidential challenger is willing to confront a sitting president, demanding accountability.

In 1960, JFK confronted Eisenhower as much as he confronted Nixon, inventing a "missile gap" with Russia in a willingness to attack as weak on defense the sitting president who as a US Army general had won World War II serving as the Supreme Allied Commander. Kennedy won in 1960 because his campaign always thought as if he were behind. JFK never worried that he might blow a lead in the polls because he stirred up the press with a controversy.

Romney's advisors in direct contrast became cautious the minute they perceived Romney had a lead in the polls after the first debate. When it came to controversy, Romney's campaign advisors virtually put the candidate in hiding, especially after observing how vehemently the mainstream media attacked him for "jumping the gun" with his press conference remarks in the immediate aftermath of the Benghazi attack.

To be successful, a presidential candidate must be willing to attack the press as much as the opposing candidate. Romney campaign advisors, thinking properly, should have welcomed the opportunity to charge the press with bias in the process of attacking the Obama White House for its willingness to lie in its determination to manipulate the news.

The voters who stayed home were not white evangelical Christians. The voters who stayed home were Republicans who decided Romney was truly no different from Obama.

Establishment "me-too" Republicans, since the era of Tom Dewey, have been so anxious to get press approval that they are unwilling to engage in the type of knock-down, drag-out politics required to convince American voters a Republican deserves to occupy the White House.

In 2012, the true enthusiasm gap was a Republican problem.

Yes, Democrats who voted enthusiastically for Obama in 2008 were disappointed at how little Obama had delivered on his campaign promises in his first term in office. But Obama's constituency was composed of interest groups defined by identity politics: African Americans, Hispanics, single women, union workers, and youth bribed by Obama with future benefits if he were reelected. Even if disappointed with results in Obama's first term, his coalition was still willing to vote for Obama one more time, on the conviction they would gain more if Obama won than if Romney won.

Republicans could not win by bribing its base, since Republicans promising interest group concessions would not be nearly as credible as Democrats making the exact same promise.

The only way Romney could have won was by going on the offensive—pounding home how and why Obama's economic policies were bound to produce resumed deepening economic woes, while charging Obama's foreign policy was doomed to produce more Benghazi attacks as the Middle East under Obama was heading once again into chaos.

Remarkably, Romney allowed Obama to cakewalk to victory.

Obama got away preaching Saul Alinsky class warfare, when Romney should have been accusing Obama daily of being nothing more than another "tax-and-spend Democrat" running budget deficits that gave him no hope of delivering on his campaign promises.

Instead, Romney stayed on positive themes that were so lofty in their principles that ideological opponents in the mainstream media could dismiss

Romney altogether as a Republican idealist lacking in practical plans voters could rely on to make a difference if put into practice.

THE RON PAUL EFFECT

Tragically for Romney, another bloc of white voters that likely stayed at home was one of the GOP's most fervent subgroups, the Ron Paul supporters.

Ron Paul managed to get 177 delegates to the Republican National Convention in Tampa, Florida, in August 2012, even though he never won a single primary. The Republican National Committee was hostile to the Paul delegates from the beginning. Paul had no chance to be an insider in the GOP establishment. His attacks on the Federal Reserve and deficit spending rang true for the Tea Party, but truthfully the GOP under President George W. Bush had been a big-spending party, especially after promoting and getting through Congress programs such as government-funded prescription drugs.

At the beginning of the Republican National Convention, Ron Paul supporters had plans to make a statement at what was shaping up to be a Mitt Romney coronation. According to GOP rules, a candidate for president needed only five states' support recognized on the floor so that votes could be cast for that candidate in first-round balloting. Ron Paul delegates calculated they had a chance with five states—Louisiana, Oregon, Massachusetts, Oklahoma, and Maine.[70] But the GOP establishment was not pleased. Paul delegates pushed ahead with their various schemes to make a statement at the convention, even if it meant embarrassing Romney and the Republican establishment.

The Republican National Committee was determined to prevent the first-round ballot from being a contest.

In a move that appeared calculated to embarrass Paul delegates, the RNC seating chart placed the delegations from Nevada, Louisiana, Maine, Minnesota, and Oklahoma at the outer fringe of the convention floor.

What the Republican establishment wanted was a ceremonial roll call that could quickly be declared nomination by acclamation.

Instead of following conventional procedures in which candidates with no chance of winning the nomination generously cede their delegate votes to the presumptive nominee, Paul quietly encouraged his supporters to use procedural mechanisms available to them to take a majority of delegates from

Nevada, Iowa, and Minnesota. At the commencement of the convention, suffice it to say Paul supporters saw the chance to make a political statement, while RNC establishment officials saw the Paul activists as meddling in the scripted program media consultants to the party had crafted to get maximum exposure for Romney's message.

To the rescue of RNC establishment insiders came the Romney campaign's top lawyer, Washington attorney Ben Ginsberg, who pushed through rule changes that were designed to prevent the Paul delegates from making a statement at the convention. One rule change enabled the Republican National Convention to make decisions without the full approval of the full convention; another, clearly aimed at Paul supporters, eliminated unbound delegates in a statewide presidential caucus or primary, requiring all delegates to be allocated to the winner or distributed proportionately according to the results.[71] The rule changes crafted by Ginsberg appeared to have been designed as tools the GOP establishment could use to block any meaningful grassroots challenge that might arise from within the party in the future.[72]

Zeke Miller at BuzzFeed.com reported from Tampa that Ginsberg pushed through the RNC rules committee changes that would make it impossible for supporters of one presidential candidate to override the will of voters at a state convention, as Paul supporters did in Iowa and Nevada.[73] Miller stressed that the rule changes gave "the Republican establishment a new tool to keep at [bay] Tea Party initiatives that threaten to embarrass or contradict party leadership and stray from a planned message."[74]

Virginia delegate Morton Blackwell, a highly respected conservative GOP leader for decades, objected to the rule changes. "There are very large numbers of people who supported other candidates, in particular Ron Paul, who will see this as an attack on their behavior," he protested, warning that Paul voters might be so disaffected they could vote for the Libertarian Party candidate.[75]

An equally serious risk was that Paul voters would just stay home, insulted that their candidate had been shut out of the Republican National Convention by a lawyer-engineered maneuver designed to block out their message.

To add fuel to the fire, RNC officials denied Paul a chance to address the convention floor from the podium.

Shut out from addressing the convention, some ten thousand raucous Ron Paul supporters crowded into the Sun Dome arena in Tampa on the Sunday before the Republican convention convened, anxious to cheer their candidate.

When it came time to speak, Paul joked that he had just received a call from Republican Party leaders offering him an hour to speak at the convention on Monday, the opening day, about whatever he wanted.[76] Even though Paul's comment was in jest, angry Paul voters claimed injustice when the RNC decided to cancel the first day of the convention because of Hurricane Isaac.

There is no question Ron Paul voters stretched the policy scope of the GOP, with their libertarian views on social issues, including legalizing marijuana, and their foreign policy views, which most resemble the advice George Washington gave in his farewell address to the troops to avoid foreign entanglements.

Still, by antagonizing the Paul delegates at the convention, the GOP threw away a group of highly motivated Republicans that might have been induced to support the Romney-Ryan ticket if only they had been given a chance to make their statement at the GOP convention in Tampa.

In two key battleground states—Ohio and Florida—the margin of votes by which Romney lost to Obama was less than the number of votes received by Ron Paul in that state's primary, and in three states—Virginia, Connecticut, and New Hampshire—the margin was close.

Political website Policymic.com identified this as the "Ron Paul effect," arguing that Mitt Romney could have won the election if only the GOP establishment had seated Paul delegates appropriately and treated them with respect.[77]

Instead, the GOP establishment decided to advance the Romney-Ryan ticket, not realizing that by disrespecting the Paul delegates in Tampa, the GOP risked losing the support and enthusiasm not only of the Paul supporters throughout the nation, but also of the tens of thousands of Tea Party conservatives who had been impressed during the primaries with Paul's message.

HURRICANE SANDY

Nature did Romney no favors, either.

Hurricane Sandy made landfall on New York and New Jersey on Monday, October 29, 2012, just one week before the election.

On Sunday, October 28, senior campaign advisor Kevin Madden told reporters at the conclusion of a Romney-Ryan rally in Celina, Ohio—itself a last-minute reschedule after the campaign cancelled rallies Romney had originally planned to attend in storm-affected Virginia that day—that the campaign was adjusting campaign activities so as not to complicate Hurricane Sandy emergency and relief operations.

"The schedule we have locked down for now involves the states not directly impacted by the storm," Madden said. "Our top concern is for the safety of the people in harm's way."

Late that Sunday, the Romney camp cancelled plans for Governor Romney to travel to New Hampshire for campaign rallies on Tuesday.

Reporters asked Madden if the hurricane would disrupt the news cycle such that the Romney campaign might not be able to make the planned closing argument in pivotal East Coast states, including Virginia and New Hampshire.

"It's been a long campaign and a lot of folks have gotten a lot of information about both campaigns," he responded. "Right now the safety of the people in the states affected by the storm is the top concern of the campaign, not additional campaigning."

Madden reinforced this point by telling reporters the Romney campaign has halted fundraising in states likely to be affected by the storm, including DC, Virginia, Pennsylvania, North Carolina, New York, and New Jersey.

On Tuesday, October 30, before flying to Tampa, Florida, to wait out the storm, Romney held a campaign event in Kettering, Ohio, billed as a "storm relief" event, in which attendees were asked to bring nonperishable foods and other items for storm victims. Romney appeared at the event in a button-down blue dress shirt, with his sleeves rolled up to his elbows and no tie.

The attempt to look informal and ready to engage in storm-relief work was belied by the gray, nicely pressed slacks and dress shoes that rounded out the Romney look that day. Romney began by picking up a microphone and addressing the crowd packed into the James S. Trent Arena. To Romney's side were white tables piled high with food products and items useful in an emergency, including flashlights and batteries, as well as toothbrushes, blankets, and toilet paper. The idea was that after giving a short speech on the storm, Romney would help pack the goods to be shipped to storm victims.

But the *Washington Post* did not hesitate to point out "there remained many trappings of a campaign rally, including the soundtrack and a biographical Romney video."

Romney explained the message to the crowd: "We're going to box these things up in just a minute and put them on some trucks, then we're going to send them into, I think it's New Jersey. There's a site we've identified where we can take these goods and distribute them to people who need them."

The *Washington Post* further noted that as he wrapped up his remarks, Romney added that entertainer Randy Owen, of Alabama, was asked to be present, with the idea that his music would make this "an enjoyable music setting." Owen was a featured guest at the rally originally scheduled for Kettering that day. The *Washington Post* also observed that the canned goods and other donations were "a cover charge" for supporters to hear the band's performance. While Romney and Ohio's Republican Senator Rod Portman packed items in bags, Romney ignored a pool reporter who asked nearly a dozen times if Romney planned to eliminate FEMA if he were elected president.[78]

The next day, President Obama traveled to New Jersey to tour the storm damage with New Jersey's Republican governor, Chris Christie.

Obama showed up wearing a casual blue sports shirt and blue zip-up jacket, khaki pants, and low-cut outdoor shoes. Arriving in *Air Force One*, Obama and Christie traveled in a White House helicopter to tour the devastation on the Jersey Shore. What resulted was an invaluable campaign photo op in which the Republican governor gushed over the president's visit.

"Governor Christie has put his heart and soul into making sure the state of New Jersey bounces back stronger than ever before," Obama told the press during the tour.

Christie thanked the president, saying the two men had a "great working relationship" and that the president had "sprung into action immediately." A New Jersey congressional delegation, including New Jersey Democratic Senator Bob Menendez, was present for the president's press conference with Governor Christie at the conclusion of the tour.[79]

For Romney campaign top advisors, the hurricane was politically devastating. Obama got nationally televised coverage of his trip to New Jersey, featuring him at his presidential best, appearing concerned and determined to bring relief.

Even though the subsequent response of the White House and FEMA was predictably disappointing, the television images showed Obama and Christie cooperating in what appeared to be a genuine friendship, as well as a bipartisan political effort, that allowed both to seem as if they were overlooking politics in their concern for the victims of the disaster.

Exit polls showed Obama's hurricane response was an important factor in the decision made by two out of every five voters.[80]

Clearly, Obama gained political advantage by using the power of his office as president to play the disaster for the emotion of the moment. Romney, even had he rushed into the disaster area to make a personal appearance, would have been criticized by a hostile mainstream media for making matters worse by requiring valuable law-enforcement resources to be diverted from disaster relief to protect the presidential candidate.

Where the press presented Obama as a savior, the mainstream media would have ravaged Romney for showboating.

Before the storm hit, Romney's top advisors had hopes their candidate was surging to somewhere between a three- and five-point advantage over Obama in the polls. While the storm was dominating national news, Gallup suspended daily polling. When Gallup did resume polling after the hurricane, the final poll before the election, on November 5, 2012, the day before the voting, showed Romney up by one point, with 49 percent for Romney and 48 percent for Obama.[81]

Any lead Romney had before Hurricane Sandy struck was erased by the storm, which millions of Americans told exit pollsters was the final deciding factor in making up their minds.

The storm, intervening as it did on the final days of the election, leaves room in an admittedly close election for the Romney camp to conclude the election was lost by an act of God.

Those more jaded observers of politics, looking for a mundane explanation, observed that Hurricane Sandy just topped off a long list of events in which a skilled team of Obama political operatives bettered the Romney team.

Viewing Hurricane Sandy as an opportunity, team Obama maneuvered the mainstream media once again to frame Romney as a Massachusetts rich guy who did not get his hands dirty in disaster relief.

At the same time, a loving mainstream media packaged Obama as a president who cared about the poor and downtrodden and was willing to show up to see the storm's destruction in person because he cared about people, not politics.

9

A NATION DIVIDED AGAINST ITSELF

A house divided against itself cannot stand.
—Abraham Lincoln, June 17, 1858, address accepting Illinois Republican Party nomination for US Senate[1]

Elections have consequences. I won.
—President Barack Obama, comment to House Majority Leader Republican Representative Eric Cantor, Republican—Virginia, January 2009[2]

ELECTIONS DO HAVE CONSEQUENCES, not only depending upon who was the ultimate victor, but also depending upon how the candidates conducted themselves in the course of the electoral campaign.

Obama may have won reelection in 2012, but the way he conducted his reelection campaign divided the United States more severely than the nation has been divided since the days of the Civil War. Systematically, Obama pitted various demographic groups that constituted his reassembled modern-day New Deal coalition against the economic advantages realized disproportionately by white America.

The division of the nation was clear just by looking at a county-level red/ blue map of 2012 election results. Remove the Obama-controlled urban areas where minorities typically reside and even solidly blue states, like California and New York, have the potential to turn red. Or, gather together a sample of photographs from Romney rallies and Obama rallies and eyeball the predominantly white audience attending Romney rallies compared to the racially mixed audience characterizing Obama rallies.

On Monday, January 21, 2013, in the public ceremony where he took the oath of office a second time, Obama swore on the Lincoln Bible, reminding the world of his personal identification with Abraham Lincoln.

But there is a major difference between the two presidents. The emancipation set in place by the Civil War ended in a series of Supreme Court decisions perhaps best symbolized by *Brown v. Board of Education*, 347 US 483 (1954), in which *de jure* freedom and equality of rights were fully conferred upon African Americans, ending a disgraceful legal history that traced back to the failure of the Founding Fathers to ban slavery when writing and signing the US Constitution. Yet *de jure* freedom conferred only equality of opportunity, with a series of laws and Supreme Court decisions in the 1960s making it clear that in the United States racial discrimination risked civil and possibly even criminal penalties.

In 2012, Obama promised more than *de jure* freedom; he also promised what sounded like *de facto* equality. This was a different standard, declaring no group in America should be economically disadvantaged in reality, even if it required income redistribution effected by taxing the rich to achieve "social justice."

By arguing the rich should "pay their fair share," Obama articulated a fundamental principle of socialism that philosopher John Rawls, a prominent professor at Harvard in the years Obama attended Harvard Law School, formulated in the argument that the concept of "justice" included the concept of "fairness."

In campaigning on Saul Alinsky class-conflict themes, Obama suggested the government could enact taxes that take from the rich to give to the poor.

While the Robin Hood theme might sound good in principle, Obama failed to address the much harder question, namely, do we as a nation really want to apply concepts of justice viewed as fairness to social distinctions commonly identified by sociologists, political scientists, and demographers?

Affirmative action programs applied to schools that demanded busing white children from South Boston to African-American public schools in Roxbury ended up in such social discord that the Supreme Court in the 1990s began pulling back. Ultimately, even the Supreme Court pulled back from strict adherence to the policy articulated in *Swann v. Charlotte-Mecklenburg Board of Education*, 402 US 1 (1971), which held busing constitutional as a method of forcing public school racial integration.[3]

Yet, by stirring this pot once again, was Obama really ready to suggest that social justice in America would not be achieved until income and property were redistributed such that his voter coalition of African Americans, Hispanics, single women, union workers, and youths were economically as well off as middle-class, or possibly even upper-class whites?

For politicians willing to demagogue the issue of demographics in America, the current era offers new and almost limitless possibilities.

Open borders have produced a wave of Hispanic immigration unprecedented in America; the growing secularization of the nation along with a Supreme Court–authorized banishing of the Judeo-Christian God from the nation's public schools and squares has encouraged the rise of alternative lifestyles and increasing demands for "social justice" from the LGBT community; single-parent families are growing in numbers; and youth are marrying later, divorcing more often and bearing fewer children. These are major demographic changes that will demand years if not decades to be absorbed into an America that is vastly different from the United States Baby Boomers knew in their growing-up years.

Then there is the question of the economic standard Obama would say all Americans are entitled to enjoy. He has made clear his concern that the Constitution is generally "a charter of negative liberties" – what the federal government cannot do – rather than positive rights. But would Obama insist every adult in America should be entitled to own a home? Does every adult have a right to a job paying more than minimum wage? Does every student in America have a right to go to college?

The Democratic Party under Obama has placed a bet on the proposition that FDR-like bribing of interest groups targeted through identity politics may form a generational hold on a newly emerging Democratic majority.

The decision to demagogue demographics is a tricky game. Consider the following:

- Can the Democrats count on always being able to divide demographic groups to their electoral advantage?
- What happens to a Democratic majority if a mounting federal deficit and continuing trillion-dollar federal budget deficits limit the ability of a Democratic president or a Democratic Congress to deliver to their constituent groups the economic goodies promised?
- What happens if conflicting economic needs competing for available jobs, housing, and schools divide minorities against one another?
- What happens if the inability of the Obama administration to deliver everything promised results in a crisis of rising expectations that fuels political violence, much as happened in US cities across the nation in the 1960s, after the Watts riot in Los Angeles in 1965?
- How long will whites, still a majority in the United States today, continue to pay for escalating and possibly endless demands of the Obama coalition for current and expanding entitlement programs?

By applying a concept of social justice to the mixed demographics of the United States, Obama has opened a Pandora's box that runs the risk of reigniting in America battles like the nation witnessed in the streets of Boston between black and white parents in the 1970s.

The problem is acute when we consider Obama made these promises as the United States continued to head toward financial insolvency. The national debt now exceeds the nation's gross domestic product. If the United States is forced into financial austerity on the model of what has happened in recent years to the European Union, which entitlement programs will be cut first? Dire choices of this nature almost necessarily invite protests, demonstrations, and possibly even civil violence.

The GOP has responded to Romney's loss by imposing a "me-too" orthodoxy on Republican Party politics, threatening to shut out Ron Paul supporters and Tea Party patriots from full participation in the Republican

Party's inner workings and decision making. In so doing, the Republican establishment may have badly underestimated the degree to which conservatives in America are on the verge of a tax revolt.

The Republican establishment is clearly desperate to reach out now to Hispanics. But how willing are true conservatives to see passed in Congress a comprehensive immigration bill before the US border with Mexico is secured? A "me-too" GOP that tries to out-Democrat the Democrats when it comes to handing out social welfare benefits to interest groups defined by identity politics is almost certain to fail, if only because the strategy is likely to alienate the GOP's conservative base.

Out of the bankruptcy of capitalism forced by an ever-expanding social welfare state, extreme leftists in the Democratic Party may believe they will have the long-awaited opportunity to re-create the USA as a true socialist state. This may be what Obama meant when he suggested his reelection offered the opportunity to destroy the Republican Party, once and for all, burying the idea of free enterprise and individual freedoms.

The way Obama conducted his election campaign raises a modern-day version of the question Abraham Lincoln proposed on the eve of the Civil War: How long can a nation divided against itself endure?

KEY DEMOGRAPHIC TRENDS

Subtle distinctions among demographic groups in the United States determine their electoral significance. Major demographic trends will continue to evolve and perhaps become even more distinct as the 2014 midterm election and the 2016 presidential election approach. Consider, for instance, the following trends in demographics likely to be of major import in the upcoming elections:

- *Historically, whites have been much more likely to register and to vote than other minorities—but that may be changing.* Estimates for the presidential election in 2008 were that for every 100 Hispanics residing in the United States, only 19 would vote, and for every 100 Asians, only 22 would vote. Comparable numbers for whites were 52 voters for every 100, and for blacks 40. If the United States passes amnesty legislation, however, the voter participation figures for Hispanics and Asians are likely to increase closer to comparable rates for African Americans.[4] With the Obama candidacy in 2004 and 2008, voting participation rates among African Americans increased dramatically, approaching rates for whites. It is unclear if the participation rates for blacks would remain equally high for a white Democratic Party candidate in 2016.

- *The white population of America will become a minority within the next thirty years.* The non-Hispanic white percentage of the population is expected to peak in 2024, at 199.6 million, then taper off and fall by nearly 20.6 million from 2024 to 2060. Meanwhile, the Hispanic population is expected to more than double from 53.3 million in 2012 to 128.8 million in 2060. The black population is expected to increase from 41.2 million in 2012 to 61.8 million by 2060. The Asian population is expected to double from 15.9 million in 2012 to 34.4 million in 2060. All minorities, now comprising approximately 37 percent of the population today, are projected to increase to 57 percent of the population by 2060. White Americans are projected to become a minority for the first time in 2042.[5] In California, the Hispanic population is projected to outnumber the white population within the next year, while in New Mexico, non-Hispanic whites are already a minority, at 40.2 percent.[6] Departure of high-income individuals and families from California into adjoining states and increased Hispanic immigration into the Southwest are likely to make the Western states of Idaho, Utah, Colorado, Arizona, and New Mexico increasingly Democratic-voting states.[7]

- *The Democratic Party is losing its hold on the fewer and fewer working-class white voters.* In 1940, 58 percent of workers were whites holding manual, service, or farm jobs, whereas by 2006, that figure had fallen to 25 percent. The prototypical member of the original New Deal coalition was an ethnic white voter in a unionized factory, with the coalition including most blacks and nonunion workers, as well as Jews and Southerners. By the 1960s, working-class whites—a demographic subgroup that declined in numbers along with the economic prosperity and increasing educational levels associated with the post–World War II era—became disaffected with new demands being taken on by the Democratic Party, including environmental concerns, the civil rights movement, pressure from the LGBT community for equal rights, and demands of radical feminists for equal access to the workforce, for free access to government-sponsored contraceptives, and for government-funded abortion on demand. In the 2004 election, Democrats ran a 13-point deficit among working-class whites in large cities and an 18-point deficit in the suburbs, with the results worst in rural areas, where Democrats lost two to one, with 66 percent voting Republican.[8]

- *Marriage in the US is declining, while single-parent families are increasing.* Demographic statistics show the US population is delaying marriage, with the median age at which a first marriage occurs going from 22.8 to 27.1 years for men between 1960 and 2003, and from 20.3 to 25.3 for women. At the same time the rate of divorce for women more than doubled between 1960 and 1980, from 9.2 divorces each year per 1,000 women married in 1960, to 22.6 a year per 1,000 women married in 1980. Furthermore, the percentage of children under eighteen living in households with only one adult present has increased from under 5 percent in 1972 to over 22 percent by 2002. The rate of unmarried teen pregnancy has increased, especially among minority populations. Demographers are beginning to conclude that marriage has declined as the central institution under which households are organized and children raised.[9]

- *America is becoming a more secular society, with fewer Americans with strong religious affiliation, except among evangelical Christians.* Democrats have been adding support from the less observant and nonobservant members of their constituencies, while Republicans have gained from evangelical Christians. Americans unaffiliated with any religious denomination have grown from 4.6 percent of the population in 1944, during World War II, to 14.4 percent of the population in 2004. In 2004, 71.9 percent of the religiously unaffiliated voted for Kerry, while 83 percent of observant, white, evangelical Protestants voted for Bush. Demographers have found that while the unaffiliated and nonobservant have been growing among Protestants and Catholics, church attendance by observant, mainline evangelical Christians has grown slightly in recent years. Hispanics tend to be overwhelmingly Catholic and disproportionately observant, while increased immigration has brought a mix of additional religions to the United States, including Islam, with the nontraditional religious among the recent immigrants voting largely Democratic.[10] Demographers project that by 2024, 20 to 25 percent of US adults will be unaffiliated. That trend, combined with the growth among non-Christian faiths from a diverse mix of immigration, will mean that by the 2016 election, or possibly by 2020 at the outside, the United States will have ceased to be a white, Christian nation. Looking farther ahead, by 2040, Christians will be only around 35 percent of the population, and conservative, white Christians, a key component of the Republican base, will be only one-third of that, a minority within a minority.[11]

- *Millennials, who vote overwhelmingly Democratic, are coming of voting age in large numbers.* Millennials, those born between 1978 and 2000, numbering approximately 103 million Americans, are adding 4 million new voters each year. Millennials in 2008 voted for Obama by a 66 to 32 percent margin. By 2020, the first year all Millennials will have reached voting age, some 90 million will be eligible voters, representing just fewer than 40 percent of America's total voters.[12]

Demographers with progressive political views have observed these demographic changes enthusiastically, believing "the potential for true progressive government is greater than at any point in decades," with the electorate making a commitment to a progressive vision of government, international values, and economic and political policies "that could transform the country in a way that has not been seen since FDR and the New Deal."[13]

Writing of Obama's reelection in 2012, political scientist and sociologist Ruy Teixeira, one of the first to identify a new emerging Democratic majority, and his colleague John Halpin, both currently senior fellows at the Center for American Progress, wrote on November 8, 2012, two days after the election: "Obama's strong progressive majority—built on a multi-racial, multi-ethnic, cross-class coalition in support of an activist government that promotes freedom, opportunity and security for all—is real and growing, and it reflects the face and beliefs of the United States in the early part of the 21st Century."

In glowing terms, Teixeira and Halpin credited Obama's win to a message that "everyone gets a fair shot, everyone does their fair share and everyone plays by the same rules."

Teixeira and Halpin praised Obama for the stimulus bill, for the bailout of the auto and financial sectors, for passing Obamacare, and for expanded rights for women, Latinos, and LGBT families.

To make their message painfully clear, Teixeira and Halpin added a warning for the Republican Party: "The GOP must face the stark reality that its voter base is declining and its ideology is too rigid to represent the changing face of today's country."[14]

Yet even at the peak of success, politics can take dramatic and unexpected turns.

In November 1972, when Richard Nixon crushed Democratic presidential hopeful George McGovern, who could have imagined that only a few months later, in August 1973, Nixon would be forced to resign over a burglary in the Watergate complex? On February 1, 1979, when Ayatollah Khomeini returned to Tehran for the first time after fifteen years in exile and Jimmy Carter welcomed the Iranian revolution as a "breath of fresh air in the Middle East," who would have imagined that Carter would be defeated in the November 1980 election after failing for 444 days to end the ordeal of Iranian terrorists holding hostage US embassy personnel in Tehran?

In their enthusiasm over Obama's 2012 reelection, progressives quickly forgot how a surge in Tea Party conservatism had allowed the GOP to capture a majority in the House of Representatives in the 2010 midterm elections.

Leftist postmortem evaluations that today credit Democratic Party policies and favorable demographic trends for the 2012 victory rarely factor in an important consideration: In November 2010, Obama was not on the ballot.

Will the Democratic Party do as well in 2014 and 2016 when Obama is likewise not on the ballot?

How much of the Democratic victory in 2008 and 2012 was due to Obama's charisma, his ability as a celebrity to command attention in the pop culture relevant to Millennials?

Democratic Party strategists opening champagne at Obama's 2012 reelection may soon have to answer these questions. If it turns out the election victory was due more to Obama's personal popularity and celebrity, the enthusiasm with which American voters have embraced a radical progressive agenda may soon diminish.

When riding a trend, either upward or downward, it is hard for all but the most discerning to imagine the trend will not continue forever.

The pattern of political history is that a currently emerging Democratic electoral majority is likely to be followed by yet another newly emerging

Republican electoral majority, albeit with different demographic characteristics from those that identified the last Republican electoral majority arising in the Nixon years and reaching a peak in the Reagan years.

DEMOCRATIC TROUBLES IN DEMOGRAPHIC PARADISE

Furthermore, will the economic interests of Hispanics and Asians remain sufficiently identified with the economic interests of African Americans such that all three groups retain loyalty over time to the Democratic Party?

Today the interests of the two minorities are similar because both see the Democratic Party as a means to seek continued government benefits while their struggle to achieve economic advancement continues.

Yet there is evidence Hispanics are achieving economic gains more rapidly than African Americans. A report by the University of Georgia's Selig Center for Economic Growth at the Terry College of Business predicts a surge in the economic buying power of Hispanics and Asians in the United States, at a rate significantly higher than is predicted for African Americans.[15] Hispanic buying power is expected to grow 50 percent in the next five years, from $1 trillion in 2010 to $1.5 trillion in 2015. The relatively young Hispanic population means that disproportionately more Hispanics are starting their careers and moving up the ladder economically. Increased entrepreneurial activity and an expected rising level of educational activity also predict the upward mobility of Hispanics.

Asians, as a group, are much better educated than average Americans and therefore hold many top-level jobs in management, professional, and scientific specialties. Over the next few years, Asian buying power is expected to grow 42 percent, from $544 billion in 2010 to $775 billion in 2015.

The same study found economic hardship likely to persist in the African-American community.

From a prerecession peak in January 2008 through July 2010, the number of employed African Americans dropped by more than 1.3 million, and unemployment among African Americans soared from 8 percent to 15.6 percent. In the past decade, the number of jobs held by African Americans decreased by 270,000, suggesting the recession has erased more than a decade's worth of job growth in the African-American population.

The report noted that the relatively low median age of African Americans made the group especially vulnerable to economic downturns, since young adults are more exposed to recessions than those more established in their careers.

The report concluded the youthful demographic profile of African Americans, combined with rising levels of education attainment and a high rate of business formation, will result in an increase in buying power from $957 billion to $1.2 trillion, an increase of 25 percent—noticeably less than the projected rate of increase for Hispanics and for Asians.

Numbers and projections aside, however, demonstrated tensions between Hispanics and African Americans are already evident in Southern California. Latino gangs have waged a campaign to force black families out of Compton, according to Los Angeles County Sheriff's Office officials. As reported by the *Los Angeles Times*, on January 25, 2013, four Hispanic youths riding in a black SUV accosted an African-American resident of Compton, telling him that they were gang members and his family was not allowed to live in their area because they were black. The gang members shouted racial insults and violent threats until the man ran for home. They then climbed from the SUV and began beating him with metal pipes.

"The gang members drove off, but returned to the family's home accompanied by 15 to 20 more gang members who swore at the family, used racial insults and told them that blacks were not allowed in the neighborhood."[16]

The *Los Angeles Times* reported that Compton, with a population of 97,000, was predominantly black for many years, but it has gone through enormous demographic change and is now 65 percent Latino.

In 2008, the *Los Angeles Times* reported that hate crimes rose to their highest level in five years in 2007. This is documented by the annual report of the Los Angeles County Human Relations Commission, which showed hate crimes rose by 28 percent, to 763 incidents, led by attacks between Latinos and blacks, with vandalism and assault leading the way. The *Times* further stated that many incidents were not included in the report, such as a series of crimes involving attacks against Latinos in which low-wage workers were robbed and beaten, allegedly by African Americans.[17]

In September 2012, the New York Police Department released a report that showed 96 percent of all shooting victims and 97 percent of all shooting suspects in the city were black or Latino; the report further showed that 90 percent of the New Yorkers stopped and frisked by police were black and Latino.[18] Social science data have demonstrated that an influx of Hispanic workers into a city increases unemployment and violence in the African-American community, typically caused by a large number of Hispanic immigrants who move into an urban area and displace blacks from low-skilled jobs.[19]

WND reporter Colin Flaherty has done more reporting than any other journalist on what appears to be skyrocketing black-on-white crime, violence, and abuse. The incidents are not widely known, largely because of a virtual blackout in the mainstream media. The news blackout results from concerns that reporting on escalating black violence would be considered inflammatory or even racist. Still, Flaherty has quietly and systematically documented hundreds of examples of black mob violence in more than seventy cities, big and small, throughout the nation.[20]

In New York City, for example, an epidemic of flash mobs of thirty to fifty African-American youths has terrorized newsstands and convenience stores, leaving New York City police at a loss regarding how to respond to stop the violence.[21] Security video cameras throughout the nation have captured hundreds of black mobs terrorizing the elderly, the LGBT community, young people, Asians, and white people in general. For reasons of political correctness, news sources rarely identify the perpetrators in these violent incidents by race, choosing instead to characterize them only as "groups of teens" or "mobs of youth," seldom specifying "African-American teens," or "mobs of African-American youth."

With tightening state and local budgets, the ability of municipalities to maintain adequate law enforcement protection is now in question.

In February 2013, the Chicago police department announced that officers would no longer respond immediately to 911 calls for incidents of criminal damage to property, vehicle thefts, garage burglaries, or other crimes where the suspect is no longer on the scene and the victim is not in immediate danger. The policy change was made to free up the equivalent of 44 police officers a day for patrol duty.[22] In 2011, in order to close a Chicago budget gap of $636 billion, Chicago Mayor Rahm Emanuel ordered police superintendent Garry McCarthy to cut $190 million from his budget, despite campaigning on a promise of putting 1,000 more police on Chicago's streets.[23]

In California, the Sacramento Police Department has lost more than 300 sworn officers and civilian staff in a cut of more than 30 percent of its budget since 2008; in Los Angeles, the police department implemented plans at the end of 2012 to lay off 160 civilian employees in an effort to keep sworn officers active.[24] Sacramento's cuts were so deep the police department laid off sworn officers; eliminated the vice, narcotics, financial crimes, and undercover gang squads; thinned the auto theft, forensic, and canine units; and sent many detectives back to patrol. The Sacramento Police Department was reduced to conducting follow-up investigations for only the most serious crimes, like homicide and sexual assault. The Los Angeles County district attorney estimated in 2012 that 1,400 street gangs exist in the county,[25] with the majority of the gangs known to involve either Hispanic or African-American youths that without massive police presence tend to war against one another, destroy neighborhoods with graffiti, and engage in a variety of crimes, including drug dealing, murder, and extortion.

A key factor in ending a Democratic majority that had developed in the 1950s and 1960s was having the American public witness the gains that had been registered by the civil rights movement deteriorate into the urban race riots of the late 1960s. Similarly, increasing violence in the Hispanic and African-American communities today runs the risk of a backlash against the Democratic Party. The adverse reaction will accelerate as a growing number of Americans realize that government welfare programs do not generate private-economy jobs and that government handouts are not a path to generating self-esteem or producing long-lasting economic advancement.

John McWhorter, associate professor of linguistics at the University of California–Berkeley and a contributing editor to the Manhattan Institute's *City Journal*, in a study published by the Cato Institute, noted the high percentage of African-American youth in black communities drawn into selling drugs, an especially lucrative activity given the high prices created because drugs remain illegal. "The result is usually spells in jail, as well as a failure to build the job skills for legal employment that serve as a foundation for a productive existence in middle and later life," McWhorter wrote.[26]

With reductions in police protection forced by state and local government budget crises, how many US cities will be abandoned to nearly unstoppable minority gang crime and youth drug-dealing?

Ironically, if Hispanics and Asians advance economically at a faster rate than African Americans, a Hispanic and Asian emerging minority middle class is likely to reject Democratic efforts to benefit African Americans at their expense. Will Hispanics and Asians remain enthusiastic about high taxes if the economic redistribution goes to other minorities, including African Americans, left behind because they have accomplished less within the private economy?

None less than Ruy Teixeira acknowledged how similar economic forces affected white working-class voters, a core constituent in the 1930s FDR coalition, breaking them away from the Democratic Party ranks in the 1970s. Working-class white voters abandoned Democrats when high rates paid to fund welfare went to minorities and aggressive affirmative action policies raised doubt about the Democrats' ability to manage the economy.

The Reagan revolution, Teixeira concedes, resulted in Republican electoral success after white working-class voters saw that Republican arguments about government regulations, high taxes, and high spending were reasonable explanations for the stagnant economic growth amid high inflation the nation was experiencing in the Carter years. Teixeira observed that in the 1980 and 1984 elections, Reagan averaged 61 percent support among the white working class, compared to an average of 35 percent support for his Democratic opponents, Jimmy Carter and Walter Mondale.[27]

ARE MILLENNIALS A LOST GENERATION?

A series of studies published by the Pew Research Center have demonstrated the prolonged global downturn that began at the end of George W. Bush's presidency has had the hardest impact on Millennials, those born between 1978 and 2000.

In February 2012, Pew reported the share of young adults eighteen to twenty-four currently employed, 54 percent, is the lowest such percentage since the government began collecting data in 1948. The 15 percent gap in employment between the young and all working-age adults is the widest in recorded history. Further, young adults employed full-time have experienced a greater drop in weekly earnings, down 6 percent, than any other age group.

The study reported that 82 percent of the public surveyed claimed it is harder for young adults today than it was for their parents' generation. At least seven in ten claimed it's harder now to save for the future (75 percent), pay for college (71 percent), or buy a home (69 percent).[28] These results suggest Millennials may be one of the first generations in America to conclude their lives will not be better off economically than the lives of their parents or possibly even their grandparents.

The Pew study released in February 2012 also demonstrated that tough economic times have changed Millennials' lifestyles. Pew recorded that 31 percent of young respondents have postponed either getting married or having a baby, and approximately one in four have moved back with their parents after living on their own. Among all eighteen- to thirty-four-year-olds, about half (48 percent) say they have taken a job they didn't want, just to pay the bills, with more than one-third (35 percent) saying that, as a result of the poor economy, they have decided to go back to school. The Pew study noted that in a 1993 *Newsweek* poll, 80 percent of parents with young children said children should be financially independent from their parents by the age of twenty-two, a view held by only 67 percent of parents today.[29]

Commenting on the February 2012 Pew study, Chris Miles, the editor at PolicyMic.com, asked whether Millennials are "a lost generation," a term typically applied to the young men and women who fought World War I in England.

"Millennials are more and more so decrying their place in society," Miles wrote. "Many of us graduated right as or right after the bottom fell out of the economy. With few job options and holding suffocating college debt, Millennials have been funneled into unappealing and soul-sucking job positions that are anything but the starts to the career tracks they had hoped for."[30]

The economic plight of Millennials caused author Audrey Farber to question whether her Ivy League college degree was worth the effort and the expense.

"Did I really peak at 18?" Farber asked. "Much to the shock and chagrin of our parents' generation, rather than building an investment portfolio or 401k while sitting behind a desk for 40 or more hours a week, we are working in bakeries, coffee shops, and restaurants until the rest of our lives fall into place, convinced they never will."[31]

A Pew survey published in December 2012 showed that Millennials as a result of their difficult job experiences display a generation gap when their attitudes toward important public policy questions are compared with older Americans'. Older adults by a lopsided margin of 66 percent to 21 percent say protecting Social Security and Medicare is more important than reducing the public debt, a position held by only 48 percent of those aged eighteen to twenty-nine, with 41 percent of this younger group saying it is more important to reduce the debt.

"In effect, each age group endorses priorities that reflect its generational self-interest," concluded Kim Parker, in reporting on the research for Pew.[32]

More than half of respondents ages eighteen to twenty-nine (52 percent) said maintaining Social Security and Medicare benefits at their current levels will put too much of a burden on younger adults, a position only 35 percent of those sixty-five and older thought was correct.

"If it persists much longer, this era of high joblessness will likely change the life course and character of a generation of young adults—and quite possibly those of the children behind them as well," wrote Don Peck, feature editor for the *Atlantic*. "It will leave an indelible imprint on many blue-collar white men—and on white culture. It could change the nature of modern marriage and also cripple marriage as an institution in many communities. It may already be plunging many inner cities into a kind of despair and dysfunction not seen for decades."

Ultimately, Peck worried, the jobless era for Millennials "is likely to warp our politics, our culture, and the character of our society for years."[33]

The economic plight of Millennials raises important questions regarding whether or not Millennials in their pursuit of self-interest could turn as they age against the self-interest of various other subgroups in the Obama coalition:

- Will Millennials continue paying the high levels of taxation required to fund generous government-funded welfare for minorities, especially when escalating federal budget deficits place huge interest repayment burdens on them?
- Will the current support Millennials show for Democrats continue if the Obama administration's trillion-dollar deficits in its second term fail once again to stimulate enough growth in the private economy to reduce unemployment to the 5 or 6 percent level associated with prosperous economies in the post–World War II era?
- Are Millennials as they mature willing to support the Democratic Party's progressive agenda if limited employment opportunities in the private economy risk their generation's becoming a permanent "lost generation" in an economy that never recovers entirely, in which their prospects to marry and

have children keep getting pushed back later in life, risking that they might simply become too old?

- Are Millennials now living with parents for economic reasons willing to also pay for parents' senior years in an era when Millennials suspect Social Security and Medicare will be dried up by the time they retire?

Already, the economic reality of living in a welfare-laden state—like New York—is having an impact on those who would otherwise champion such welfare programs.

Bloomberg reported that Obama won New York City in the 2012 election with 81 percent of the vote, the highest recorded for a candidate in more than a hundred years. How did Obama achieve this impressive result?

"The results underscore New York's decades-long status as a Democratic bastion where most voters are racial and ethnic minorities," Bloomberg's Greg Giroux concluded.

Of New York City's 8.2 million people, 29 percent are Hispanic, 23 percent are non-Hispanic black, and 13 percent are non-Hispanic Asian, Bloomberg reported, citing 2011 estimates from the Census Bureau.[34]

But on January 28, 2013, Josh Margolin of the *New York Post* reported, "An increasing number of financial firms, especially private and hedge funds, are fed up with New York's sky-high city and state taxes and are relocating to the business-friendly climate in Florida's Palm Beach County. And they're being welcomed with open arms—officials in Palm Beach recently opened an entire office dedicated to luring finance hot shots down South."[35]

There's no income tax in Florida, compared to New York, where state and local governments took $14.71 of every $100 earned in 2010, Margolin noted. How willing will Millennials be to pay the exorbitant taxes required to fund minority poverty in cities like New York, simply for the privilege of living or working in the Big Apple?

Neither can simply moving out of Manhattan solve the problem of paying for New York City. As Empire State taxpayers, all residents of New York state share the privilege of paying for welfare programs aimed at New York City's minority poverty.

A WAR ON RELIGION

The Obama coalition's long-term stability is further threatened by religion, a historical hotbed for turning minor differences into full-scale battles.

In January 2012, Pope Benedict XVI warned Roman Catholics in America a growing antireligious sentiment was threatening their religious liberty. "It is imperative that the entire Catholic community in the United States come to realize the grave threats to the Church's public moral witness presented by a radical secularism, which finds expression in the political and cultural services," the pope explained to a group of bishops from the Mid-Atlantic states who were in Rome to meet with Vatican officials.[36]

Ten days later, on Sunday, January 29, 2012, letters penned by Catholic authorities across the country were read to parishioners, conveying the pope's message and strongly opposing the requirement in Obamacare that employers, including the Catholic Church, provide health-insurance plans that include contraceptive and abortion coverage.

The letter from the Archdiocese of Washington, DC warned organizations "will be placed in the untenable position of having to choose between violating the law and violating their conscience."

In the Diocese of Phoenix, Arizona, the letter called for resistance: "We cannot—we will not—comply with this unjust law. People of faith cannot be made second-class citizens."[37]

In Pittsburgh, Bishop David Zubik wrote that President Obama had told Catholics, "To hell with your religious beliefs."[38]

The Obamacare health-care rule was popular among the feminists and single women that Obama was counting on for victory in 2012, but why was he willing to take the risk of offending Catholics?

The Obama campaign calculated that the Catholic population in the United States is becoming increasingly secular, with a diminishing percentage remaining observant churchgoers. With the secularization of the Catholic laity has come a reduced adherence to the Church's teachings on reproductive issues. Exit polls showed Catholics, who were 25 percent of the electorate, voted 50 percent for Obama and 48 percent for Romney. This was despite the pope's strong condemnation of the Obamacare features requiring a wide range of Catholic employers, including Catholic hospitals and adoption services, to provide health care for their employees that is in direct contravention to Church teachings on sexual behavior. The difference between observant and nonobservant Catholics was clear in that Catholics who attend weekly mass voted for Romney by 57 to 42 percent.[39]

Furthermore, analysis by Pew Research found that while Catholics voted for Obama 50 to 48 percent, Hispanic Catholics voted for Obama 75 percent to 21 percent.[40] This is a clear indication identity politics overrode religious politics when it came to Hispanic Catholics choosing to vote for Obama.

In waging a "war on religion" by forcing the Catholic Church to provide employee insurance offering contraception and abortion services, the Obama campaign took a big risk. Based on popular vote, the majority of Catholics have voted for the winner in every presidential election since 1972.

The Obama administration position also raised serious First Amendment questions about freedom of religion. But once again, given the superior voter intelligence of the Obama campaign, the risk was properly ascertained so that Obama's campaign advisors understood they were not risking Obama's reelection by holding to their position on Obamacare. In other words, the Obama campaign calculated the president could play contraceptive and abortion issues to win over feminists and single women voters—a decision Obama strategists knew would energize the Obama base—without having to risk losing the Catholic vote.

What is also clear is that the Catholic Church hierarchy failed to get the message out to the faithful in a convincing manner.

"Judging from the faith-based issues that dominated headlines, though, it's likely that religious peoples, especially Catholics, will be thinking through more viable ways to reach adherents (particularly those who do not attend church weekly) in order to get them better synced up with the issues," concluded journalist Billy Hallowell.[41]

Still, the slight against Catholics has the potential to explode in Obama's face.

If Democrats persist and the Catholic Church decides to close Catholic institutions in the United States—including more than 200 universities with 750,000 students enrolled; 6,980 Catholic elementary or secondary schools; the nation's 600 Catholic hospitals; as well as 1,400 Catholic long-term care centers—the shockwave would resonate across the country.

Furthermore, Catholic offices, charities, and service organizations spend billions of dollars annually helping the needy in America. What if they were forced to close doors? There is a precedent for this. Jonathan V. Last, a senior writer for the *Weekly Standard*, noted in reporting the above statistics that in 2006, Boston's Catholic Charities closed its adoption services, considered one of the most successful in the nation, after Massachusetts law required the organization to place children in same-sex households.[42]

Should the Catholic Church all but decide to pull out of the United States, the backlash among religious voters, including evangelical Christians who side with Catholics on the issue, may be an order of magnitude more severe than Obama strategists have so far calculated.

A separate religious rift deliberately underreported by the Obama-loving mainstream media is the growing number of Muslims within Democratic Party ranks.

At the Democratic National Convention in Charlotte, North Carolina, on Wednesday afternoon, September 5, 2012, a strange issue came to the floor. Rebroadcast repeatedly on national television that evening was a raucous controversy that erupted over a move to restore to the party's platform a reference to "God" and the recognition of Jerusalem as Israel's capital. Fox News reported correctly that a loud group of delegates shouted, "No!" from their seats in the convention hall. Convention chairman, Los Angeles Mayor Antonio Villaraigosa, had to call three times from the convention rostrum for a vote that the "Ayes" had it before he could restore the disputed language. In an embarrassing television moment, Villaraigosa struggled on the third try over whether or not to ignore the crowd booing before he finally gaveled the vote to an end. Watching the vote being taken a third time, it was by no means certain the chairman got the two-thirds vote needed to restore the provisions.[43] What was underreported was that Muslim delegates were responsible for the controversy.

Fox News reporter John Roberts from the convention floor called the incident "an unforced error," saying it was "inexplicable" why the provisions were taken out from the 2008 Democratic Party platform.[44]

Apparently, the explanation was that Muslim delegates to the DNC demanded the platform changes in the first place.

"Democrats need to feel included, it doesn't matter what religion you are," Noor Ul-Hasan, a Muslim delegate from Salt Lake City, told TPM.com, explaining that including God in the Democratic Party platform might make people feel uncomfortable. "To have God in there, people who don't believe in God, you've got to have those people included."

She was equally determined that the reference to Jerusalem had to be removed: "We have two Muslims in our delegation, and we have two Jews as well. We work together. But I think if they told me they were going to make a Muslim city be the capital, I think we'd be dividing our Democrats. That's why I'm in the Democratic Party—because I don't want to be divided."[45]

Evidently it never occurred to Noor Ul-Hasan that by removing God and Jerusalem from the platform, Democrats were dividing themselves from a very large bloc of voters the Obama campaign did not want to offend, namely, Christians and Jews.

The number of Muslim delegates at the Democratic National Convention has quadrupled since 2004, the *Washington Post* reported. The Washington-based Council on American-Islamic Relations, or CAIR, estimated there were more than one hundred Muslim delegates representing twenty states.[46] This put Muslims at approximately 5 percent of the DNC delegates, when Muslims constitute less than 1 percent of the US population.[47]

As demonstrated in Charlotte, Muslim activists within the Democratic Party can exert a policy impact disproportionate to the number of Muslims in the US population. But the critical question remains: Are Democrats now willing to challenge traditional Judeo-Christian beliefs by including Muslims within the base of the party?

Nor should radical feminists, single mothers, and the LGBT community welcome Muslims into the Democratic Party coalition without appreciating yet another risk: Are Muslims in the Democratic Party ready to embrace their lifestyles?

What will the Democratic Party do in the future when faith-based Muslims turn not only on the God of the Christians and the Jews, but also on contraceptives, abortion, and same-sex marriage?

HOW BIG THE DEMOCRATS' TENT?

Immediately after the second inauguration, President Obama undertook a campaign-style speaking tour to promote congressional gun-control legislation in the wake of yet another tragic elementary school shooting.

Obama also decided to engage in the continuing controversy over whether the Boy Scouts of America should admit openly gay scouts and leaders.

"My attitude is that gays and lesbians should have access and opportunity the same way everybody else does, in every institution and walk of life," Obama told Scott Pelley of CBS News in an interview broadcast immediately preceding the Super Bowl. "The Scouts are a great institution that are promoting young people and exposing them to opportunities and leadership that will serve people for the rest of their lives. And I think nobody should be barred from that."[48]

The issue did come up during the 2012 campaign, and not surprisingly a 1994 video of Mitt Romney taking the same position resurfaced, a moment in the campaign that did not gain Romney favor with his conservative base.

But during the 2012 presidential campaign, Obama eschewed campaigning for gun-control legislation—a position that would have cost him votes from gun-association members—and he did not press the Boy Scouts to open their ranks to gays—a position that would have cost him votes from Boy Scout and Girl Scout families around the nation, even though he quickly pounced on the issues after his election.

The Democratic Party is constantly pushed by left-wing interest groups to champion a wide range of causes—from environmental issues, such as "Save the Whales" and global-warming fears, to demands to fight with Christian organizations over Obamacare demands and LGBT lifestyles. But can Democrats effectively juggle all the concerns of their coalition without offending others within their tent?

In the first weeks of Obama's second term, for example, EPA officials began imposing coal-use restrictions, resulting in closing several coal-burning power plants. While global warming alarmists could be expected to welcome this move, inner-city African-American families struggling with poverty were faced with higher energy costs.

Once again, political scientist and sociologist Ruy Teixeira has warned that it was a similar proliferation of causes that cost the Democrats the majority crafted together by the original FDR New Deal coalition.

"If race was the chief vehicle by which the New Deal coalition was torn apart, it was by no means the only one," Teixeira wrote. "White working-class voters also reacted poorly to the extremes with which the rest of these new social movements became identified. Feminism became identified with bra burners, lesbians, and hostility to the nuclear family; the antiwar movement with appeasement of third world radicals and the Soviet Union; the environmental movement with a Luddite opposition to economic growth; and the move toward more personal freedom with a complete abdication of personal responsibility."[49]

Building a winning electoral coalition is difficult enough, but holding the coalition together so as not to antagonize elements within the coalition is a feat the Democratic Party has failed to accomplish with any permanency. Obama's modern-day version of the New Deal coalition promises to be difficult to manage as Obama's second term in office progresses. No government could ever satisfy all the conflicting interest-group promises Obama made to secure his reelection.

AUSTERITY IS NO FUN

Spending cuts meaningful enough to reduce federal budget deficits significantly risk imposing austerity measures on voting constituencies key to Obama's coalition. Reducing Social Security or Medicare benefits, for example, has become "the third rail" of American politics, lethal to the future career of any professional politician that would dare propose benefit reductions for current recipients or for those nearing eligibility. Cuts in welfare payments, including the US Department of Agriculture's food stamp program, risk a serious backlash by key constituencies in the Obama modern-day New Deal coalition as well.

Politicians on both sides of the aisle find it easy to vote for the increased spending required by expanding the social welfare state. Voting for meaningful cuts is a much more difficult business.

In Greece, austerity measures demanded by the European Union and international monetary authorities as a condition of continued lending have brought tens of thousands of people to demonstrate in the streets, occasioned by near riots where protestors in violent outbursts have thrown stones and bottles at police.[50]

Nothing would cause cracks in the Obama interest-group coalition faster than to reduce current levels of social welfare payments. Even if we attempt to exempt senior citizens from cuts, who should get hit first? How about welfare mothers? Or should we reduce instead the public assistance for Hispanic families seeking to educate children in public schools or reduce the ability of illegal immigrants to seek medical treatment in public-hospital emergency rooms? Shall we abandon students currently receiving federal tuition loans for college? Maybe we should cut unemployment benefits in an economy where long-term unemployment has become the "new normal"?

Austerity cuts to social welfare programs are impossible to make in a way the affected interest groups within the Democratic Party coalition will consider fair, if and when the cuts affect them directly. Austerity cuts to social welfare programs are impossible to make without the Democratic Party's losing key factions within the party's base.

CRACKS ALREADY APPEARING?

Despite their celebrations of victory, Democrats face the reality that not all is rosy in their national majority. The Obama claim to have won a "mandate" to implement a broad, progressive policy agenda is arguable only when considering national election results. While Romney lost the presidential election, the GOP won a series of impressive victories in state elections. The electorate's decision to elect Republican governors and state legislators, while Obama won reelection and the US Senate majority remained Democratic, is one more indication that the nation is divided.

Currently, thirty states have Republican governors, and in all but five of those (Iowa, Maine, New Jersey, New Mexico, and Nevada), the GOP also controls the state legislature. Additionally, seventeen states—including two with Democratic governors (Arkansas and Missouri)—have Republican legislative majorities strong enough to override gubernatorial vetoes.[51]

"While the party's Washington contingent is struggling mightily, the GOP retains full control of nearly half the state governments across the nation," wrote national politics reporter Aaron Blake in the *Washington Post*. "And that control, combined with the just-completed round of redistricting, has set up Republicans to hold onto many of those state governments—and by extension, the US House of Representatives—for potentially the next decade."[52]

Grover Norquist, president and founder of Americans for Tax Reform, has stressed that GOP gains in state elections undermine "the collective wisdom among the talking heads on TV, editorial boards across the country and the consultant class on both the right and the left . . . that the Republican Party is on the ropes and basically needs to become more like the Democratic Party if it wants to survive."[53]

candidate Rove supported.

To make matters worse, the much-touted Romney ground game collapsed when the GOTV computer system operated out of Romney campaign headquarters crashed on Election Day, leaving thousands of paid campaign workers and volunteers in precincts around the nation not knowing which voters to get to the polls.

Democrats increased their majority in the Senate by 2 seats, to a total of 53 seats, and Republicans who controlled the House of Representatives by 242–191 seats in the 112th Congress ended up with a slimmer margin of 232–200 seats in the 113th Congress that began January 22, 2013.

THE BOEHNER "PURGE"

The knee-jerk reaction of the GOP establishment was that conservatives and Tea Party extremists were responsible for the loss.

On December 3, 2012, just shy of a month after Election Day, in a spirit of retaliation, Boehner removed, for being uncooperative with the GOP leadership, four conservative congressmen from leadership positions: Reps. Justin Amash, R-MI, and Tim Huelskamp, R-KS, from the House Budget Committee; and Reps. David Schweikert, R-AZ, and Walter Jones, R-NC, from the Financial Services Committee.

"It's little wonder why Congress has a 16-percent approval rating," Huelskamp told US *News* the day after the House Steering Committee informed him he had been ousted. "Americans send principled representatives to change Washington and get punished in return. The GOP leadership might think they have silenced conservatives, but removing me and others from key committees only confirms our conservative convictions. This is clearly a vindictive move and a sure sign that the GOP establishment cannot handle disagreement."[2]

At a Heritage Foundation event on December 4, Amash, who considers himself part of the Libertarian wing of the GOP, was equally angry. "For a party that's trying to expand its base and reach out to young people, I think it's pretty outrageous," he said. "It's a slap in the face to all young people who are thinking about being Republicans, want to be a part of this party, and are being told, 'Well, if you disagree with leadership just a couple times we're going to send you home . . . you don't get to participate.'"[3]

Party–candidate controversies from the 2010 midterm elections over which they were still simmering:

- The first involved Christine O'Donnell, the Tea Party member who lost as Republican nominee for the US Senate in Delaware when controversies developed over various comments Democratic Party opposition researchers found in her background, including a claim that masturbation was a sin equivalent to adultery and that she had dabbled in witchcraft though she had never joined a coven.[7]
- The second involved Sharron Angle, the Republican nominee for the US Senate in Nevada. Senate Majority Leader Harry Reid won his fifth term beating Angle, after she made a series of bizarre comments, including saying, "I hope that's not where we're going, but you know if this Congress keeps going the way it is, people are really looking toward those Second Amendment remedies." In another instance, she reportedly said, "My goodness[,] what can we do to turn this country around? I'll tell you the first thing we need to do is take Harry Reid out."[8] To many listeners, both comments sounded like threats.

The GOP 2008 presidential nominee, John McCain, a prominent member of the establishment GOP, continues to bristle over being rebuffed by conservatives in Congress when he attempted to introduce comprehensive immigration reform legislation during the administration of George W. Bush. Establishment GOP leaders believe conservative members of Congress at that time supporting the Minutemen—a precursor to the Tea Party movement—cost McCain the election in 2008 by throwing the Hispanic vote into the open arms of the Democratic Party.

After Romney's defeat, what was brewing in telephone calls and private meetings among prominent big-money contributors and establishment GOP leaders was the idea the GOP would be a lot better off if only conservatives could be disciplined and Tea Party activists dismissed from the GOP as fringe political extremists.

ps and state legislatures positions the party
te spending, even if Democrats in the US
dlocked over meaningful spending cuts.[54]
reasingly looking toward states like Kansas,
Brownback has eliminated taxes on nearly
ns operating in the state and turned over
o private health insurers to reduce costs.
r Rick Snyder pushed through the state
t keeps unions from requiring workers to
es, even in companies covered by union
Governor Bobby Jindal is exploring plans
replace the state's income tax.
publican Party's strength comes from
ernors Association's ability to expand
r the future," said RGA chairman Bob
usiasm for the victories won in 2012 at

Republican governor, Scott Walker,
ng effort to recall and replace him with
emocratic Party challenger. The recall
S history—came after union workers
state's capital after Walker pushed
re prohibiting state and local govern-
except cost-of-living adjustments to
ion after an executive order Indiana's
sued in 2005, effectively eliminating
ees. "It has helped us in a thousand
naround here," Daniels told the *New*
n was to impose a pay freeze for state
erations where possible, and require
ore to receive health insurance.
a new law that restricted teachers'
g between school corporations and
d benefits.[58] Additional accomplish-
ol-voucher law, privatizing welfare,
hicles.[59]

"THE ARCHITECT" EXACTS PARTY DISCIPLINE

As Boehner began his "purge" of the undesirables, Karl Rove—a GOP centrist masquerading as a conservative—moved forward to assume the leadership role of "enforcer" for the GOP establishment and their big-money friends.

Once again, the establishment GOP in the aftermath of Romney's defeat repeated the mistakes made by the Rockefeller wing that controlled the GOP from the 1940s through the 1960s. Somehow, establishment Republicans seem to assume if only the GOP could be a lot more like the Democratic Party, the GOP would win more elections. Once more, the GOP was risking falling into exactly the same trap Phyllis Schlafly identified in her self-published 1964 book, *A Choice, Not an Echo*. As seductive as the thinking may be to the political centrists that form the core of the establishment GOP, "me-too" Republican candidates have been easy prey for professional Democratic Party operatives since FDR knocked off Willkie in 1940 and Dewey lost twice, first to FDR in 1944, then to Truman in 1948.

On Saturday, February 2, 2013, Jeff Zeleny of the *New York Times* reported that Rove's Super PAC, the American Crossroads Project, planned to finance a new organization aimed at recruiting "seasoned candidates" and protecting Senate incumbents from "challenge by far-right conservatives and Tea Party enthusiasts who Republican leaders worry could complicate the party's efforts to win control of the Senate."[9] The new organization, to be called the Conservative Victory Project, is intended to counter other organizations "that have helped defeat establishment Republican candidates" over the past two decades. Zeleny also reported the Conservative Victory Project "is the most robust attempt yet by Republicans to impose a new sense of discipline on the party, particularly in primary races."

"There is a broad concern about having blown a significant number of races because the wrong candidates were selected," Steven J. Law, the president of American Crossroads, told the newspaper. "We don't view ourselves as being in the incumbent protection business, but we want to pick the most conservative candidate."

Law specifically mentioned the Conservative Victory Project would engage in "hard-edge campaign tactics," including television ads, against candidates GOP establishment leaders see as unelectable and a drag on efforts to win seats in Congress.

The Rove announcement created an immediate firestorm of criticism from within the ranks of the GOP. David Bossie, head of Citizens United—the organization responsible for the Supreme Court decision paving the way for Super PACs to be created in the first place—penned an attack on Rove, titled "The Civil War Has Begun."[10] He argued that Rove's new organization was "nothing more than an attempt by establishment Republicans to cull the conservative movement," calling "laughable" claims by Rove's Conservative Victory Project that it could cure the ills of a disappointing 2012 election cycle.

Bossie pulled no punches. "At least Karl Rove and company are finally out front with their disdain for the conservative movement, and I am thankful for it," he wrote, concluding that Zeleny's article in the *New York Times* was "our Lexington and Concord" in a battle Bossie predicted would be "a long, hard slog against the establishment."

Bossie was outspoken denouncing Rove and his associates as Republican establishment henchmen: "Karl Rove and his cabal would sell out on any issue if it means more power in the short-term, for they don't stand for anything."

Bossie attacked Rove for having supported a long list of "Big Government causes," including "the fiscally crippling expansion of Medicare, the anti–free speech McCain-Feingold campaign finance act, and the plan to reward illegal behavior when it comes to immigration reform." He also charged that "under Rove's watch" federal spending in the Bush administration was out of control.

"Rove is no conservative," Bossie attacked. "His decisions are made free of principle, with the deciding factor always being how he and his failing establishment try to cling to power."

Bossie rejected the proposition that sending to Washington more free-spending, big-government Republicans would accomplish anything other than increasing the national debt and hastening a financial decline.

"Conservative donors must think twice about giving Rove money in support of this road to nowhere," Bossie admonished, characterizing Rove not as the architect of Bush's reelection, but as deputy chief of staff, an architect of disaster.

"President Bush was mired in the 30% approval range through most of his second term," he noted. "Those low approval numbers spurned by the genius of Karl Rove brought us President Barack Obama and Obamacare.

The opposite of a permanent Republican majority, you might say."

The controversy intensified when Brent Bozell, chairman of ForAmerica, a conservative PAC, and president of the Media Research Center, went on the WMAL-FM radio show *Mornings on the Mall* in Washington, saying he was particularly annoyed at Rove and his partner Steven Law for invoking William F. Buckley's famous admonition to support the most conservative candidate who is electable.[11]

Bozell has an unimpeachable connection to Buckley, for the conservative icon was his uncle and his father's debate partner at Yale.

"I'm listening to them echo the mantra of William F. Buckley, which was to support the most electable conservative," Bozell said on the morning radio show. "It's offensive to me that they even had the word *conservative* in their title. This is an effort that has spent years supporting one moderate after another over conservatives. The only conservatives who won last year were tea party conservatives, the very same candidates they want out of business."[12]

Bozell argued that Rove's organization was nothing more than an attack on the Republican base, and he pointed out that Rove supported Charlie Crist, the Florida Republican governor who became a Democrat after losing a reelection bid, as well as the late Senator Arlen Specter, who also became a Democrat after losing to a Republican challenger. Bozell explained Rove was only trying to cover up the hundreds of millions of dollars he wasted after fraudulently accepting money from Republican donors on the proposition that only he, Karl Rove, knew how to win elections.

"Karl Rove and company were so disastrous (New York Mayor Mike) Bloomberg called them the number one disaster of 2012," Bozell continued. "Donald Trump called them a waste of money. They had such terrible results in 2012 that they're frantically looking to blame somebody for what they did."

Jonathan Collegio, a colleague of Rove at American Crossroads, followed Bozell on the WMAL-FM *Mornings on the Mall* radio show the next day, but only added fuel to the fire.

"Bozell is a hater, and he has a long sordid history hating Karl Rove," Collegio said on air. "He has weird personal axes to grind."[13]

Collegio argued that the GOP has lost several elections over the last two cycles not because the GOP message was defective but the GOP recruited candidates he described as "undisciplined, who are unable to stay on message, who made clumsy mistakes and had difficulty fundraising."

Collegio argued the point was to avoid losing elections unnecessarily, and that the goal was only "to elect the most conservative folks possible in the primaries who are also capable of winning general elections; this way we are not forfeiting the seats to the Democrats and the liberals."

But the comments attacking Bozell at the end of the interview overwhelmed any attempt Collegio was making to portray the Rove effort as balanced, or to represent that Rove was not at war with GOP conservatives or the Tea Party. Collegio subsequently apologized to Bozell,[14] an apology Bozell did not accept.

Bozell's response came in a letter addressed to Steven Law, president of American Crossroads, written by Washington-based author and publicist Craig Shirley, on the stationery of Citizens for the Republic, a conservative advocacy group headed by Shirley.[15]

"Mr. Bozell is what we call in our movement a 'legacy.' He has devoted his life to the cause of American conservatism as did his father, Brent Bozell II, who wrote 'Conscience of a Conservative' for Barry Goldwater," Shirley's letter began. "Maybe you've heard of Brent's uncle, Bill Buckley, whose words you misquote and twist as the basis for your organization enough to falsely suggest you know something about him. You may have heard of his other uncle, Jim Buckley, a former US senator, or Brent's mother, Patricia Buckley Bozell—both important figures and writers in our conservative movement. Ronald Reagan often saluted the contributions of the Bozell and Buckley families to the cause of American conservatism."

Shirley's letter then demanded Collegio resign.

"Mr. Collegio calling Mr. Bozell a 'hater' publicly on WMAL radio this morning reflects the language of the establishment Republicans. It is the divisive language of the left," he wrote. "Rather than engaging in an intellectual debate, you, Mr. Collegio, Mr. Rove, and others in the consultant class attack good conservatives and Tea Party leaders and members. On behalf of the conservative movement, we are demanding you terminate Mr. Collegio. An apology is not acceptable."

Shirley concluded the letter by arguing that American Crossroads and "the so-called Conservative Victory Project" had marginalized themselves by the attacks on Bozell: "The sheer audacity of political consultants maligning a beloved and critically important player in American history is simply a bridge too far. You obviously mean to have a war with conservatives and the Tea Party. Let it start here."[16]

Conservative radio host Mark Levin joined the attack, saying on the air that Rove and his colleagues needed "a hard, swift kick" off the public stage.[17]

"No one lost as much on election night," concluded Amanda Terkel, senior political reporter and politics managing editor at Huffington Post.[18]

Terkel reported that through various American Crossroads organizational structures, Rove spent a total of approximately $390 million on Republican candidates in the 2012 election, making his groups the largest single outside force of the 2012 election.

"The results were bleak," Terkel continued. "According to the Sunlight Foundation, American Crossroads, Rove's super PAC, saw just a 1 percent return on its investments. Crossroads GPS, the political nonprofit arm, saw a 14 percent return."

Terkel further reported GOP billionaire donors were livid over Rove's lack of performance. "There is some holy hell to pay," she wrote. "Karl Rove has a lot of explaining to do . . . I don't know how you tell your donors that we spent $390 million and got nothing."

She further noted Donald Trump went after Rove the day after the election, writing on Twitter: "Congrats to @KarlRove on blowing $400 million this cycle."

Writing in the *Wall Street Journal* the day after Election Day, Rove attempted to dodge blame, claiming Obama was "lucky" to win the election.

"This time, the October surprise was not a dirty trick but an act of God," Rove argued. "Hurricane Sandy interrupted Mr. Romney's momentum and allowed Mr. Obama to look presidential and bipartisan."[19]

The conclusion Rove did not want to face was this: blaming true conservatives and Tea Party activists for Romney's defeat in an election the GOP could have won is not convincing, especially when Rove spent tens of millions of dollars with the result that the Democrats defeated every candidate Rove supported.

If Rove was such a genius at picking good candidates, why did candidates sponsored by American Crossroads lose?

SCHLAFLY: "NOW IT'S TIME FOR ROVE TO GO!"

On the final morning of the Republican National Convention, Karl Rove gave an exclusive breakfast briefing of seventy of the GOP's biggest campaign contributors. Rove bragged about how his Super PAC, American Crossroads, would persuade undecided voters in crucial swing states to vote against President Obama.

Then, when detailing plans for various Senate and House races, Rove joked, "We should sink Todd Akin. If he's found mysteriously murdered, don't look for my whereabouts!"[20]

Not everyone was amused. Eagle Forum founder Phyllis Schlafly took offense at Rove's obvious hostility to Akin.

"Karl Rove has made himself toxic to Republicans by his incredibly offensive and dangerous statement suggesting the murder of Congressman Todd Akin of Missouri," Schlafly said in a statement calling for Rove's resignation. "Any candidate or network who hires Rove will now be tarnished with this most malicious remark ever made in Republican politics."[21]

Nor was it good enough for Schlafly when Rove picked up the telephone and apologized to Akin for the remark.

"A private phone call by Rove to Akin to sort of apologize does not erase the public offense," she said. "At the very least Rove should make a public apology. But even that can't wipe out his gross political mistake."

Schlafly was angry. "Rove has been calling on Todd Akin to resign," she continued, "but the one who should resign because he made an embarrassing, malicious and downright stupid remark is Karl Rove."

Schlafly herself had not been pleased with Akin's comments over rape. But she was offended that Rove had ridiculed publicly a sitting US congressman who had a good record as a conservative, even if his remarks on abortion had been ill considered.

Rather than speaking with Akin privately, in an attempt to persuade him to withdraw from the race voluntarily, Rove made a laughingstock of Akin before prominent GOP donors who otherwise might have been inclined to contribute directly to Akin's campaign. With additional funding in August 2012, Akin might yet have won the election, despite his comments being under attack by the political left. After all, Schlafly had won major victories against radical feminists in her long and distinguished career, despite being attacked and ridiculed. A prominent example was Schlafly's famous campaign to defeat the Equal Rights Amendment.

But Schlafly's animosity toward Rove went deeper than the controversy over Akin. Schlafly had repeatedly fought Rove in the years of George W. Bush's presidency over numerous legislative initiatives she had considered ill-advised from a conservative public policy point of view. An example was the Security and Prosperity Partnership that Bush declared in a joint summit meeting with Mexico and Canada in 2005—without seeking congressional approval. Another example was Bush's nomination that same year of his legal counsel from Texas, Harriet Miers, to be an associate justice of the Supreme Court. Repeatedly, in the years Rove advised Bush, Schlafly felt neither was acting like a true conservative.

In writing *A Choice, Not an Echo,* Schlafly made an impact on the GOP by arguing the party needed to pick truly conservative GOP candidates if it wanted to win presidential elections, not establishment GOP candidates that were nothing more than an echo of their Democratic Party counterparts. Her point was that the GOP establishment, in attempting to control candidates and elections, tends to approve only "safe," establishment-approved candidates that espouse only centrist policy positions virtually indistinguishable from the policy positions of their Democratic Party opponents. The "me-too" Republican candidates that get the seal of approval from the GOP establishment tend to be an "echo" of their Democratic counterparts. GOP establishment candidates today like McCain and Romney tend to lose presidential elections just as Willkie and Dewey did in the 1940s.

What Schlafly wanted was a true "choice," the type of truly conservative candidate she knew from experience the Republican Party establishment disdained. In advocating for "a choice, not an echo" in 1964, Schlafly was largely responsible for Arizona's Sen. Barry Goldwater getting the GOP presidential nomination that year. Nor was she discouraged by LBJ's landslide victory over Goldwater in 1964. Schlafly attributed LBJ's win to the nation's continued mourning over JFK's assassination. Undaunted after Goldwater's loss, Schlafly began championing Ronald Reagan as a GOP presidential candidate.

"The kingmakers recognized Goldwater as a Republican they could not control," Schlafly explained in her 1964 book. "They started from the premise that the Republican Convention must nominate anybody but Goldwater."[22]

That analysis, as far as Schlafly was concerned, applied equally in 2012, when Rove and the GOP establishment continued to express animosity toward conservatives and Tea Party activists within the GOP ranks for precisely the same reason. Today, as in 1964, the GOP establishment rejects those in the Republican Party that the GOP establishment does not control.

"The kingmakers are playing for high stakes—control of federal spending—and they do not intend to lose," Schlafly warned.

Then as now, Schlafly saw through the motivation of GOP leaders to realize that for people like Rove, politics is about money. The difference for Schlafly and the true conservatives within GOP ranks is that for them, politics is about principle. Goldwater lost in 1964, but Schlafly did not give up. Reagan won the presidency in 1980, a feat he may never have accomplished had Schlafly not written *A Choice, Not an Echo* some sixteen years earlier.

How ironic was it that the highlight of the Conservative Political Action Conference 2013 was Pat Caddell, the Democratic Party pollster who came to prominence engineering Jimmy Carter's 1976 presidential win over Gerald Ford, after Ford pardoned Richard Nixon for any and all Watergate crimes that caused him to be the first president in US history to be forced to resign?

"When you have the Chief of Staff of the Republican National Committee and the political director of the Romney campaigns, and their two companies get $150 million at the end of the campaign for the 'fantastic' get-out-the-vote program . . . some of this borders on RICO [the 1970 Racketeering Influenced and Corrupt Organizations Act] violations," Caddell said. "It's all self dealing going on. I think it works on the RICO thing. They're in the business of lining their pockets."

Caddell charged the GOP is in the grips of what he called the "CLEC"—an acronym for the "consultant, lobbyist, and establishment complex"—a concept he modeled on President Eisenhower's famous warning concerning the "military-industrial complex" that Eisenhower issued in his farewell address to the nation from the White House.

"Just follow the money," Caddell told the audience. "It's all there in the newspaper. The way it works is this—ever since we centralized politics in Washington, the House campaign committee and the Senate campaign committee, they decide who they think should run. You hire these people on the accredited list [they say to candidates] otherwise we won't give you money. You hire my friend or else."[23]

WHY SCHLAFLY IS RIGHT

In the aftermath of Romney's stunning defeat, Schlafly continued to advise the GOP not to move to the center. Her basic argument is that in their lust for power and money, the GOP establishment is tone-deaf to the public policy arguments that excite not only the conservative base of the Republican Party but also millions of centrist voters that pollsters typically categorize as "independents." Reagan was famous for drawing "Reagan Democrats" into the GOP.

A quick comparison between Reagan and Romney makes the point. A brief review of Reagan's history in politics reveals a wealth of thoughtful and insightful expressions he gave to conservative ideals that captured the imagination of a generation of American voters. Reagan had a gift for explaining complex ideas in simple terms that average Americans could understand easily.

In a radio broadcast on November 16, 1976, Reagan was discussing the cost of government: "The point I'm making," he explained, "is that somewhere there must be a figure beyond which we can't go in the growth of the government without wiping out those in the private sector who pick up the entire tab."[24]

That should have been an effective answer to explain why Obama's plan to solve the government's fiscal problem by taxing the rich would not work. Instead, in the first presidential debate, Romney—in explaining what government programs he would cease to fund—mentioned he would stop the subsidy to PBS.

Romney said to moderator Jim Lehrer, a PBS employee, "I'm sorry, Jim. I'm going to stop the subsidy to PBS. I'm going to stop other things. I like PBS. I love Big Bird. I actually like you, too. But I'm not going to keep on spending money on things to borrow money from China to pay for it."[25]

In the second debate, Obama attacked Romney for failing to say which specific government programs he would cut. "We haven't heard from the governor any specifics beyond Big Bird and eliminating funding for Planned Parenthood in terms of how he pays for that," Obama quipped.

The point is that Reagan, willing to speak plainly and directly, could explain in one sentence why unlimited growth in government spending would not work. At some point we would hit negative results, where increased taxes would undermine the growth in the private sector required to pay those taxes. It is hard to think of a simpler or more eloquent expression of what came to be known as "supply-side economics."

Romney, faced with a similar question, ended up attacking Big Bird, a fanciful TV character loved by millions of children for several generations now, opening himself up not only to Democratic Party derision but to an image it would be hard to shake out of voters' minds. Somehow, that Romney would consider terminating Big Bird fit with the image Democrats had painted of him as a heartless "vulture capitalist."

The problem with GOP-establishment candidates like Romney is that he feared a straight answer would offend centrist voters dependent on the programs or benefits Romney targeted. The end result was that Romney sounded vague, without the specific details voters associate with a real plan.

In contrast, Reagan was known for straight talk, for saying what he meant and speaking in a clear way that left little doubt in the listener's mind about what was his point.

OBAMA SETS STAGE FOR A GOP CONSERVATIVE

In 1964, Schlafly properly judged the nation would embrace a true conservative when and if the GOP actually ran one for office. She warned that the GOP establishment would undermine Goldwater, even after he was nominated.

But by 1980, when the Republicans nominated Reagan, the welfare state had expanded dramatically, with LBJ enacting many New Deal social reforms, including the 1965 voting rights bill and the 1965 housing bill. When Jimmy Carter could not devise policies to get the United States out of stagflation and long gasoline lines, Reagan had an opening.

Obama's reelection may well mark a turning point where the majority of American voters realize runaway spending—with entitlement programs now consuming 60 percent of the federal budget and growing—is leading America into fiscal crisis.

The Tea Party prefigures the development of a tax revolt and the demand for a return to smaller, constitutional government.

States suing the federal government over programs with open-ended unfunded liabilities for the states could lead to a day when states exercise the Tenth Amendment to the Constitution and pull out of federal programs that DC has no constitutional power to enact.

Romney lost in large part because as a centrist candidate advanced by the GOP establishment, he backed away from directly confronting and challenging Obama. Had Romney kept pressing Obama on his record in office, as he did in the first debate, moderate Republicans may have come out to vote in sufficient numbers to defeat Obama.

Truthfully, Romney blew a great opportunity. In 2012, President Obama's reelection was anything but certain. Obama was vulnerable because in his first term he had failed to deliver real, sustainable economic gains for the key constituents in his voting coalition. What had he materially done to make sure African Americans, Hispanics, single women, union workers, and young voters were better off economically in 2012 than they were in 2008?

Yet when moderate Republicans discovered Romney was just another "me-too" candidate who by the third debate went out of his way to agree with Obama repeatedly, they legitimately asked, "Why vote for him?"

As Schlafly pointed out in writing *A Choice, Not an Echo*, voters want to see a presidential election conducted like a heavyweight prizefight. But when Romney was unwilling to stand toe-to-toe with Obama, centrist voters lost interest.

Obama won because he appealed to his core base with a class-conflict message his supporters consumed with enthusiasm.

The true advantage was the Obama campaign voter-intelligence computer system permitted top campaign advisors to run simulations demonstrating to Obama that he would gain more voters by making his message more radical, refusing to moderate the message to appeal to voters in the middle. If moderate Democrats stayed home, so what? Obama's top campaign strategists calculated Obama would win anyway, simply by energizing African-American voters, Hispanics, single women, union workers, and youth to vote for him a second time.

Romney never managed to free himself from the "callous rich guy" image the Obama campaign spent millions to create in a policy designed to frame Romney the moment he became the likely GOP nominee. The Romney camp, not appreciating the risk, did not immediately retaliate by portraying Romney as a faithful husband who had stood with his family through difficulties and a breadwinner who earned his living building companies, not destroying jobs.

To top it off, radicals in the Democratic Party engaged in massive, systematic voter fraud by registering ineligible voters nationwide. They taught Obama supporters how to vote in more than one state, gaming absentee voting and early voting, and resisting with legal challenges every voter-ID law passed. If Obama needed an extra push to win the election, Democrat insiders quietly calculated that liberalizing voter registration and eliminating voter-ID requirements would give Democrats the unfair advantage needed to tip the balance in their favor.

To beat the Democrats in future elections, Republicans need to press for voter-ID laws, while challenging state election officials on a continuous basis to scrub registration lists for voters who have moved or died.

But even this will not be enough.

The GOP will not emerge successful if it continues to believe it must pander to the interests of Democratic Party subgroups.

The GOP cannot out-Democrat the Democrats.

Rather than pushing for more "rights" or immigration reform that does not first secure the borders, GOP leaders must explain to African Americans, Hispanics, and single women that their most secure route to a prosperous economic future is through a private enterprise system in which jobs are revived through lower taxes and reduced government spending and regulation.

The same holds true for unions and youthful voters. Unions pressing for unfair or unsustainable benefits do not advance the best interests of union members, not if unions cause workers to lose jobs. Young voters want satisfying and well-paying jobs commensurate with the level of their education. The best way to fulfill these aspirations is not through Democratic Party promises of government jobs, but through Republican Party strategies proven to create private-sector jobs.

Rather than marginalize Tea Party activists, the GOP should capitalize on their political enthusiasm to build a new Republican majority.

With Obama now a lame-duck president unable to run for reelection under the Twenty-Second Amendment to the Constitution, the GOP is in position to regroup while the Democrats must search for another presidential candidate to replace Obama.

Given Obama's star qualities, the Democratic Party will have to search hard to find an equally charismatic replacement.

Schlafly is right. Republicans will win elections only by ignoring establishment GOP pundits whose main interest is to get rich by siphoning off millions of dollars from billionaire GOP donors.

Republicans must nominate strong, conservative candidates who are skilled in deflecting the efforts of Democratic Party operatives to discredit them.

The Republican Party has ample conservative talent rising through the ranks in state governments, as well as in the US House and Senate.

The goal must be for Republicans to increase their majority in the House and gain a majority in the Senate during the 2014 midterm election, positioning the GOP to recapture the White House in 2016.

The future of the Republican Party is bright, provided leaders of the party have the courage to articulate conservative principles with conviction.

After two terms of Barack Obama's presidency, the nation will be ready to return to a smaller government bound by the Constitution and to revitalize private enterprise with lower taxes and fewer regulations in order to stimulate a US economy to new heights of prosperity.

The message of our Founding Fathers, understood correctly, is a unifying message of "one nation under God, indivisible, with liberty and justice for all." Ronald Reagan had the charisma to deliver this message to a receptive nation. Other Republicans, following Reagan's example, must aspire to do so once again.

The 2016 presidential election could become a turning point.

The message of this book is that conservatives and Tea Party activists working within the Republican Party must have the courage and conviction of belief to make their message heard, beyond party leaders, to the American public.

The voters even in 2012 were anxious for a candidate willing and able to proclaim a truly conservative, Republican message in the heat of a fully engaged and well-contested presidential contest.

Republican voters were let down in 2008 and 2012. They need not be in 2016. But to make sure this doesn't happen, conservatives and Tea Party patriots working within the ranks of the GOP must make sure a charismatic conservative with the ability to win surfaces.

NOTES

PREFACE: NO SURPRISE

1. Theodore H. White, *The Making of the President 1960: A Narrative History of American Politics in Action,* reissue ed. (New York: Atheneum, 1961; New York: Harper Perennial, 2009), xvii. Citations refer to the Harper Perennial edition.

CHAPTER 1: A CRUSHING DEFEAT

1. Clinton Rossiter, *The American Presidency* (Baltimore and London: The Johns Hopkins University Press, 1987), 168.
2. Dan Hodges, "The Mathematical Beauty of the Electoral College, the Billion-Dollar Political Rubik's Cube," *Telegraph* (UK), October 18, 2012, http://blogs.telegraph.co.uk/news/danhodges/100185573/the-mathematical-beauty-of-the-electoral-college-the-billion-dollar-political-rubiks-cube/.
3. Helene Cooper, "Obama Kicks Off Eight-State Campaign Tour," *New York Times,* October 24, 2012, http://thecaucus.blogs.nytimes.com/2012/10/24/obama-kicks-off-nine-state-campaign-tour/.
4. Ibid.
5. "Battle for White House," Real Clear Politics, http://www1.realclearpolitics.com/epolls/2012/president/2012_elections_electoral_college_map.html.
6. Karl Rove, "Election 2012: State of the Race," Rove.com, http://www.rove.com/election.
7. "Dick Morris Stands by Prediction: Romney Will Win 325 Electoral Votes," Real Clear Politics, November 5, 2012, http://www.realclearpolitics.com/video/2012/11/05/dick_morris_stands_by_prediction_romney_will_win_325_electoral_votes.html.
8. "Dick Morris: 90% Chance Romney Wins, 60% Chance It's a Landslide," Real Clear Politics, November 6, 2012, http://www.realclearpolitics.com/video/2012/11/06/dick_morris_90_chance_romney_wins_60_chance_its_a_landslide.html.
9. *Wikipedia,* s.v. "Karl Rove," http://en.wikipedia.org/wiki/Karl_Rove.

10. Kevin P. Phillips, *The Emerging Republican Majority* (New York: Arlington House, 1969), 26.
11. Ibid. See especially pages 26–27 and 198–99.

CHAPTER 2: NO ORDINARY ELECTION

1. Quoted in Garry Wills, *Nixon Agonistes: The Crisis of the Self-Made Man*, First Mariner Books ed. (New York: Houghton Mifflin, 2002), 67.
2. The Ripon Society, "'*We are Americans and we will figure this out.*' Speaker Boehner Discusses Challenges Facing the Nation and the Republican Party in Address to the Ripon Society," News from the Ripon Society, January 23, 2013, http://www.riponsociety.org/news_1-22-13.htm.
3. Ibid.
4. Phillips, *Emerging Republican Majority*.
5. Wills, *Nixon Agonistes*, 68.
6. Ibid., 69.
7. Answers Corporation, WikiAnswers, http://wiki.answers.com/Q/Who_said_socialism_works_until_you_run_out_of_other_people's_money.
8. Wills, *Nixon Agonistes*, 76.

CHAPTER 3: WHAT YOU DON'T KNOW *WILL* HURT YOU

1. David Plouffe, *The Audacity to Win: The Inside Story and Lessons of Barack Obama's Historic Victory* (New York: Viking, 2009), 303.
2. Sasha Issenberg, "How President Obama's Campaign Used Big Data to Rally Individual Voters," *Technology Review*, December 19, 2012, http://www.technologyreview.com/featured-story/509026/how-obamas-team-used-big-data-to-rally-voters/.
3. Sasha Issenberg, *The Victory Lab: The Secret Science of Winning Campaigns* (New York: Crown, 2012).
4. Politico Bookshelf: "The Victory Lab: The Secret Science of Winning Campaigns, Written by Sasha Issenberg," *Politico*, http://www.politico.com/bookshelf/books/details/9780307954794/the-victory-lab-by-sasha-issenberg.
5. Michael Lewis, *Moneyball: The Art of Winning an Unfair Game* (New York and London: W. W. Norton, 2003).
6. Quoted in Frank J. Luntz, *Candidates, Consultants, and Campaigns: The Style and Substance of American Electioneering* (New York: Blackwell, 1988), 22; also quoted in Issenberg, *The Victory Lab*, 11.
7. Stuart Stevens, "Mitt Romney: A Good Man. The Right Fight," *Washington Post*, November 28, 2012, http://www.washingtonpost.com/opinions/a-good-man-the-right-fight/2012/11/28/5338b27a-38e9-11e2-8a97-363b0f9a0ab3_story.html.
8. Ibid.
9. Kevin Robillard, "Stuart Stevens: Obama Ground Game Overrated," *Politico*, November 29, 2011, http://www.politico.com/story/2012/11/84381.html.
10. "Narwhal, Monodon Monoceros," *National Geographic*, http://animals.nationalgeographic.com/animals/mammals/narwhal/.
11. "Killer Whale (Orca) Orcinus Orca," *National Geographic*, http://animals.nationalgeographic.com/animals/mammals/killer-whale/.
12. Alexis C. Madrigal, "When the Nerds Go Marching in," *Atlantic*, November 16, 2012, http://www.theatlantic.com/technology/archive/2012/11/when-the-nerds-go-marching-in/265325/.
13. Ibid.
14. Ibid.

15. Michael Kranish, "For Romney Camp, a High-Tech Meltdown on Election Day," *Boston Globe*, November 10, 2012, http://www.bostonglobe.com/news/nation/2012/11/10/orca-mitt-romney-high-tech-get-out-vote-program-crashed-election-day/6Oyavmi6V94dZbqRhPucrO/story.html.
16. "Thank You for Your Help With Project ORCA," a video uploaded by the Romney Campaign, YouTube.com, October 31, 2012, http://www.youtube.com/watch?v=328p5tM2OGg&feature=youtu.be.
17. Jerome R. Corsi, "Romney Foiled by Computers, Consultants?" WND.com, November 29, 2012, http://www.wnd.com/2012/11/romney-foiled-by-computers-consultants/.
18. Ibid.
19. John Ekdahl, "The Unmitigated Disaster Known as Project ORCA," *Ace of Spades HQ*, November 8, 2012, http://ace.mu.nu/archives/334783.php.
20. Michael Kranish, "ORCA, Mitt Romney's high-tech get-out-the-vote program, crashed on Election Day," November 9, 2012, http://www.boston.com/news/politics/2012/president/candidates/romney/2012/11/10/orca-mitt-romney-high-tech-get-out-the-vote-program-crashed-election-day/gflS8VkzDcJcXCrHoV0nsI/story.html.
21. Ibid.
22. Madrigal, "When the Nerds Go Marching in."
23. Patrick Brennan, "How Narwhal Beat Orca," *The Corner*, a blog of *National Review*, November 26, 2012, http://www.nationalreview.com/corner/334035/how-narwhal-beat-orca-patrick-brennan.
24. Josh Peterson, "Who's responsible for Project ORCA? Romney campaign silent," *Daily Caller*, November 16, 2012, http://dailycaller.com/2012/11/16/whos-responsible-for-project-orca-romney-campaign-silent/.
25. Adam Mazmanian, "Republicans Flame Romney's Digital Team," *National Journal*, November 16, 2012, http://www.nationaljournal.com/politics/republicans-flame-romney-s-digital-team-20121116.
26. Issenberg, *The Victory Lab*, 246.
27. Donald P. Green and Alan S. Gerber, *Get Out the Vote: How to Increase Voter Turnout*, 2nd ed. (Washington, DC: Brookings Institution, 2008).
28. Issenberg, "How President Obama's Campaign Used Big Data."
29. According to a ninety-three page analysis titled "*Inside the Cave: An In-Depth Look at the Digital, Technology, and Analytic Operations of Obama for America*," published by Engage Research, a Republican Party-oriented competitor in the field of technology-based political marketing. The analysis is available at http://engagedc.com/download/Inside%20the%20Cave.pdf. This statistic is found on page 19.
30. Ibid., 31.
31. Katrina Trinko, "In E-mail, Obama Laments 'I Will Be Outspent,'" *The Corner* a blog of *National Review* Online, June 26, 2012, http://www.nationalreview.com/corner/304031/e-mail-obama-laments-i-will-be-outspent-katrina-trinko.
32. Engage Research, "*Inside the Cave*," 35.
33. Ibid., 37.
34. Ibid., 44.
35. Matt Cover, "$5 Raffle Ticket Buys Dinner with Obama," CNS News, June 15, 2011, http://cnsnews.com/news/article/5-raffle-ticket-buys-dinner-obama.
36. "George Clooney's Obama Fundraiser Dinner: How to Attend," Huffington Post, April 19, 2012, http://www.huffingtonpost.com/2012/04/19/george-clooney-obama-fundraiser_n_1439162.html.
37. Amy Bingham and Jilian Fama, "Celeb Couple Host Obama Fundraiser in NYC," ABC News, September 18, 2012, http://abcnews.go.com/Politics/OTUS/jay-beyonce-celeb-couple-host-nyc-fundraiser-obama/story?id=17261740.

38. Matt Negrin, "What You Get at a Fundraiser with Anna Wintour and Sarah Jessica Parker," ABC News, June 14, 2012, http://abcnews.go.com/Politics/OTUS/fundraiser-sarah-jessica-parker-anna-wintour/story?id=16567579.
39. Douglas Schoen, "The truth about 2012 polls," FoxNews.com, September 27, 2012, http://www.foxnews.com/opinion/2012/09/27/truth-about-2012-polls/.
40. John Giokaris, "Presidential Polls 2012: Skewed Polling and Biased Media Coverage Give Obama False Advantage over Romney," *Townhall.com*, September 26, 2012, http://townhall.com/columnists/johngiokaris/2012/09/26/presidential_polls_2012_skewed_polling_and_biased_media_coverage_give_obama_false_advantage_over_romney/page/full/.
41. Mike Flynn, "CBS Poll: GOP Has Huge Turnout Edge over Dems," Breitbart.com, September 19, 2012, http://www.breitbart.com/Big-Government/2012/09/19/cbs-poll-gop-voters-getting-more-enthusiastic-about-election-huge-edge-over-democrats.
42. Sarah Dutton et al., "Poll: Obama Leads in Virginia, Wisconsin; Tight in Colorado," CBS News, September 19, 2012, http://www.cbsnews.com/8301-250_162-57515519/poll-obama-leads-in-virginia-wisconsin-tight-in-colorado/?pageNum=4&tag=contentMain;contentBody.
43. Dan McLaughlin, "On Polling Models, Skewed & Unskewed," *RedState* (blog), October 31, 2012, http://www.redstate.com/2012/10/31/on-polling-models-skewed-unskewed/.
44. Jonathan Easley, "GOP Takes Aim at 'Skewed' Polls," *The Hill*, September 25, 2012, http://thehill.com/homenews/campaign/251413-gop-takes-aim-at-skewed-polls.
45. Nate Silver, "Which Polls Fared Best (and Worst) in the 2012 Presidential Race," *New York Times*, January 10, 2013, http://fivethirtyeight.blogs.nytimes.com/2012/11/10/which-polls-fared-best-and-worst-in-the-2012-presidential-race/.
46. Issenberg, *The Victory Lab*, 270. This paragraph is based on Issenberg's description of the Obama internal voter-monitoring process.
47. Ibid., 271.
48. Mark Blumenthal, "Obama Campaign Polls: How the Internal Data Got It Right," Huffington Post, November 21, 2011, http://www.huffingtonpost.com/2012/11/21/obama-campaign-polls-2012_n_2171242.html.
49. Ibid.
50. Michael Scherer, "Inside the Secret World of the Data Crunchers Who Helped Obama Win," *Time*, November 7, 2012, http://swampland.time.com/2012/11/07/inside-the-secret-world-of-quants-and-data-crunchers-who-helped-obama-win/2/.
51. Blumenthal, "Obama Campaign Polls."
52. Marcus Stern and Tim McLaughlin, "Analysis: Obama's Ad Team Used Cable TV to Outplay Romney," Reuters, January 5, 2013, http://www.reuters.com/article/2013/01/05/us-usa-politics-cabletv-idUSBRE90406820130105. Much of this paragraph is drawn from this source.
53. Engage Research, "*Inside the Cave*," 35. Much of this paragraph is drawn from this source.
54. Stern and McLaughlin, "Analysis."
55. Jim Rutenberg and Jeremy W. Peters, "Obama Outspending Romney on TV Ads," *New York Times*, October 2, 2012, http://www.nytimes.com/2012/10/03/us/politics/obama-outspending-romney-on-tv-ads.html?_r=0.
56. Lindsay Young, "Outside Spenders' Return on Investment," Sunlight Foundation, December 17, 2012, http://reporting.sunlightfoundation.com/2012/return_on_investment/.
57. Julie Bykowicz and Alison Fitzgerald, "Rove Biggest Super-PAC Loser, Trump Says Waste of Money," Bloomberg, November 8, 2012, http://www.bloomberg.com/news/2012-11-08/rove-biggest-super-pac-loser-trump-says-waste-of-money.html. Brent Bozell is also the founder and president of the Media Research Center and Cybercast News Service.
58. David Freelander, "Is the Cult of Karl Rove Over?" *Daily Beast*, November 10, 2012, http://www.thedailybeast.com/articles/2012/11/10/is-the-cult-of-karl-over.html.

CHAPTER 4: THE NEW DEAL COALITION RIDES AGAIN

1. Jean Edward Smith, *FDR* (New York: Random House, 2007), 374.
2. Ibid., 375.
3. Ibid.
4. Joint Center for Political and Economic Studies, cited in "Blacks and the Democratic Party," FactCheck.org, April 18, 2008, http://www.factcheck.org/2008/04/blacks-and-the-democratic-party/.
5. Amity Shlaes, *The Forgotten Man: A New History of the Great Depression* (New York: HarperCollins, 2007), 251.
6. Burton Folsom Jr., *New Deal or Raw Deal? How FDR's Economic Legacy Has Damaged America* (New York: Threshold, 2008), 206–9.
7. David Plouffe, *The Audacity to Win: The Inside Story and Lessons of Barack Obama's Historic Victory* (New York: Viking, 2009), 98.
8. Josephine Hearn, "Black Caucus Divided over Obama," *Politico*, January 17, 2008, http://www.politico.com/news/stories/0108/7948.html.
9. David Paul Kuhn, "Exit polls: How Obama Won," *Politico*, November 5, 2008, http://www.politico.com/news/stories/1108/15297.html.
10. Nate Cohn, "What Black Turnout for Obama in 2012 Means for the GOP in 2016," *New Republic*, November 13, 2012, http://www.tnr.com/blog/electionate/110068/the-overlooked-question-2016-the-future-black-turnout#.
11. "2012 Fox News Exit Polls," FoxNews.com, http://www.foxnews.com/politics/elections/2012-exit-poll?intcmp=related.
12. Jill Lawrence, "Obama Voters Shake GOP Vision of Electorate," Joint Center for Political and Economic Studies, published in *National Journal*, November 7, 2012, http://www.nationaljournal.com/politics/obama-voters-shake-gop-vision-of-electorate-20121107. Remaining quotes in this and subsequent paragraphs attributed to the Joint Center for Political and Economic Studies come from this source.
13. Editorial, "Mr. Obama and Rev. Wright," *New York Times*, April 30, 2008, http://www.nytimes.com/2008/04/30/opinion/30wed1.html?_r=0.
14. John H. McWhorter, "Black Americans Must Stop Voting as a Monolith," *Dallas Morning News*, November 9, 2004, http://www.manhattan-institute.org/html/_dmn-black_americans.htm.
15. Michael Fletcher, "E. W. Jackson calls for Christians to make a mass exodus from Democratic Party," *Examiner.com*, September 19, 2012, http://www.examiner.com/article/e-w-jackson-calls-for-christians-to-make-a-mass-exodus-from-democratic-party.
16. Ibid.
17. Gerry Hudson, "Why African Americans Have to Prove the Pollsters Wrong," Huffington Post, November 5, 2011, http://www.huffingtonpost.com/gerry-hudson/black-vote-2012_b_2060120.html.
18. Ibid.
19. Mark Hugo Lopez and Paul Taylor, "Latino Voters in the 2012 Election," Pew Research Hispanic Center, November 7, 2012, http://www.pewhispanic.org/2012/11/07/latino-voters-in-the-2012-election/.
20. "Remarks by the President on Immigration," Rose Garden, White House, Press Release, Office of the Press Secretary, June 15, 2012, http://www.whitehouse.gov/the-press-office/2012/06/15/remarks-president-immigration.
21. John Morton, director, U.S. Immigration and Customs Enforcement, Memorandum, "Exercising Prosecutorial Discretion Consistent with the Civil Immigration Enforcement Priorities of the Agency for Apprehension, Detention, and Removal of Aliens," June 17, 2011, http://www.ice.gov/doclib/secure-communities/pdf/prosecutorial-discretion-memo.pdf.

22. Conor Friedersdorf, "Tiny Explainer: President Obama's DREAM Act Executive Order," September 6, 2012, http://www.theatlantic.com/politics/archive/2012/09/tiny-explainer-president-obamas-dream-act-executive-order/262041/.
23. Elise Foley, "Obama Administration to Stop Deporting Younger Undocumented Immigrants and Grant Work Permits," Huffington Post, June 15, 2012, http://www.huffingtonpost.com/2012/06/15/obama-immigration-order-deportation-dream-act_n_1599658.html.
24. Elise Foley, "DREAM Act Vote Fails in Senate," Huffington Post, December 18, 2010, http://www.huffingtonpost.com/2010/12/18/dream-act-vote-senate_n_798631.html.
25. Reid J. Epstein, "Obama Pressed on Failures at Univision Forum," *Politico*, September 20, 2012, http://www.politico.com/news/stories/0912/81470.html.
26. Barack Obama, quoted at http://www.gop.com/news/research/obamas-biggest-mistake/.
27. Barack Obama, quoted in Frank James, "Despite Obama's High Latino Support, Univision Puts Him on Hot Seat," NPR, September 10, 2012, http://www.npr.org/blogs/itsallpolitics/2012/09/20/161495589/despite-obamas-high-latino-support-univision-puts-him-on-hot-seat.
28. Jennifer Epstein, "Obama Attacks 'Nominee' Romney on Immigration," *Politico*, April 13, 2012, http://www.politico.com/politico44/2012/04/obama-attacks-nominee-romney-on-immigration-120503.html.
29. Julia Preston, "Romney's Plan for 'Self-Deportation' Has Conservative Support," *New York Times*, January 24, 2012, http://thecaucus.blogs.nytimes.com/2012/01/24/romneys-plan-for-self-deportation-has-conservative-support/.
30. Elsie Foley, "Mitt Romney: Arizona Immigration Law 'Underscores the Need' for President to Act," Huffington Post, June 25, 2012, http://www.huffingtonpost.com/2012/06/25/mitt-romney-arizona-immigration-law-sb1070-scotus_n_1624618.html.
31. "2012 Fox News Exit Polls."
32. "Fox Exit Poll Summary – 2012: Presidential Election," FoxNews.com, November 7, 2012, http://nation.foxnews.com/2012-presidential-election/2012/11/07/fox-exit-poll-summary-2012-presidential-election.
33. Anne Kim and Stefan Hankin, "Union Voters and Democrats," Progressive Policy Institute, May 2011, http://progressivefix.com/wp-content/uploads/2011/05/05.2011-Kim_Hankin_Union-Vote-and-Democrats.pdf.
34. Bureau of Labor Statistics, U.S. Department of Labor, "Union Members Summary," January 27, 2012, http://www.bls.gov/news.release/union2.nr0.htm.
35. Steven Greenhouse, "Labor Unions Claim Credit for Obama's Victory," *The Caucus* (the politics and government blog of the *New York Times*), November 7, 2012, http://thecaucus.blogs.nytimes.com/2012/11/07/labor-unions-claim-credit-for-obamas-victory/.
36. Ibid.
37. Ibid.
38. Dave Jamieson, "Labor Unions Deliver for Obama with Post-Citizens United Ground Game," Huffington Post, November 7, 2012, http://www.huffingtonpost.com/2012/11/07/labor-unions-deliver-for-obama_n_2089430.html.
39. Ibid.
40. Sarah Butrymowicz, "With time running out, teachers push pro-Obama message in swing states," The Hechinger Report, October 24, 2012, http://hechingerreport.org/content/with-time-running-out-teachers-push-pro-obama-message-in-swing-states_10064/.
41. Ibid.
42. Tom Curry, "Voters Back Obama Despite Economic Concerns, Exit Polls Show," NBC News, November 6, 2012, http://nbcpolitics.nbcnews.com/_news/2012/11/06/14979402-voters-back-obama-despite-economic-concerns-exit-polls-show?lite.

43. Stan Greenberg et al., "Winning 'the 47 Percent,': Recommendations based on major new research" (memorandum), Democracy Corps; Women's Voices Women Vote Action Fund; Greenberg Quinlan Rosner Research, October 9, 2012, http://www.wvwvaf.org/wp-content/uploads/2012/10/Memo.pdf.
44. Dante Chinni, "Women Are Not a Unified Voting Bloc," *Atlantic*, November 9, 2012, http://www.theatlantic.com/sexes/archive/2012/11/women-are-not-a-unified-voting-bloc/265007/.
45. Josh Voorhees, "GOP Blasts 'Obama's War on Women,'" *The Slatest*, March 19, 2012, http://slatest.slate.com/posts/2012/03/19/rnc_ad_blasts_obama_s_war_on_women_by_focusing_on_bill_maher.html.
46. Pauline Arrillaga, "'War on Women' 2012: Amid Controversy, Women Ponder How They Became Campaign Issue," Huffington Post, May 12, 2012, http://www.huffingtonpost.com/2012/05/12/war-on-women-2012_n_1511785.html.
47. *Wikipedia*, s.v. "Sandra Fluke," http://en.wikipedia.org/wiki/Sandra_Fluke.
48. "Proof of the GOP War on Women," PoliticusUSA.com, http://www.politicususa.com/proof-war-women-2.
49. Guttmacher Institute, "States Enact Record Number of Abortion Restrictions in 2011," January 5, 2012, http://www.guttmacher.org/media/inthenews/2012/01/05/endofyear.html.
50. Shaila Dewan, "In Weak Economy, an Opening to Court Votes of Single Women," *New York Times*, August 7, 2012, http://www.nytimes.com/2012/08/07/us/politics/in-weak-economy-an-opening-to-court-votes-of-single-women.html?pagewanted=all.
51. See, for instance, Sara McLanahan and Gary Sandefur, *Growing Up with a Single Parent: What Hurts, What Helps* (Cambridge, MA: Harvard University Press, 1997).
52. Frances Fox Piven and Richard A. Cloward, "Globalizing Capitalism and the Rise of Identity Politics" (essay dated 1995) in Piven and Cloward, *The Breaking of the American Social Compact* (New York: New Press, 1998), 56.
53. Micah Cohen, "Gay Vote Proved a Boon for Obama," *New York Times*, November 15, 2012, http://www.nytimes.com/2012/11/16/us/politics/gay-vote-seen-as-crucial-in-obamas-victory.html.
54. Timothy Stenovec, "Legal Weed: Marijuana More Popular Than Barack Obama in Colorado," Huffington Post, November 7, 2012, http://www.huffingtonpost.com/2012/11/07/legal-weed-marijuana-more-popular-than-obama-amendment-64_n_2090109.html.
55. "2012 Fox News Exit Polls."
56. Jason Mattera, *Obama Zombies: How the Liberal Machine Brainwashed My Generation* (New York: Threshold, 2010), xii, xiii.
57. Terence Grado, "New December Jobs Report, Same Bleak Story," GenerationOpportunity.org, January 4, 2013, http://generationopportunity.org/2013/01/04/new-december-jobs-report-same-bleak-story/.
58. CIRCLE (The Center for Information and Research on Civic Learning and Engagement), "At Least 80 Electoral Votes Depended on Youth," November 7, 2012, http://www.civicyouth.org/at-least-80-electoral-votes-depended-on-youth/.
59. Sam Roberts, "Projections Put Whites in Minority in U.S. by 2050," *New York Times*, December 17, 2009, http://www.nytimes.com/2009/12/18/us/18census.html?_r=0.
60. Samuel P. Jacobs, "Romney Relies on Shrinking Pool of White Male Voters," Reuters, October 11, 2012, http://www.reuters.com/article/2012/10/11/us-usa-campaign-whites-idUSBRE89A07C20121011.
61. David Corn, "SECRET VIDEO: Romney Tells Millionaire Donors What He REALLY Thinks of Obama Voters," *Mother Jones*, September 17, 2012, http://www.motherjones.com/politics/2012/09/secret-video-romney-private-fundraiser.
62. Jeanne Sahadi, "47% Will Pay No Federal Income Tax," CNN Money, October 2, 2009, http://money.cnn.com/2009/09/30/pf/taxes/who_pays_taxes/?postversion=2009093012.

63. Paul Taylor et al., "A Bipartisan Nation of Beneficiaries," Pew Research Center, December 18, 2012, http://www.pewsocialtrends.org/files/2012/12/Benefits_FINAL_12-20.pdf, 4.
64. Debate Club, "Did the '47 Percent' Video Sink Romney 's Campaign?" *U.S. News & World Report*, http://www.usnews.com/debate-club/did-the-47-percent-video-sink-romneys-campaign.
65. Frank James, "Comparing Romney's '47 Percent' Remark and Obama's 'Cling to Guns' Comments," National Pubic Radio, September 18, 2012, http://www.npr.org/blogs/itsall-politics/2012/09/18/161335578/the-difference-between-romneys-mooching-47-and-obamas-bitter-votersi.
66. Rich Robinson, "Top 10 PR Blunders of 2012," Huffington Post, December 18, 2012, http://www.huffingtonpost.com/rich-robinson/top-pr-blunders-of-2012_b_2316961.html.
67. See, for instance: Kirk Hallahan, "Seven Models of Framing: Implications for Public Relations," *Journal of Public Relations Research* 11, no. 3 (1999): 205–42, https://umdrive.memphis.edu/cbrown14/public/Mass%20Comm%20Theory/Week%203%20Agenda%20Setting%20and%20Framing/framing%20and%20public%20relations.pdf.
68. Jim Rutenberg and Jeremy W. Peters, "Obama Outspending Romney on TV Ads," *New York Times*, October 2, 2012, http://www.nytimes.com/2012/10/03/us/politics/obama-outspending-romney-on-tv-ads.html.
69. Glenn Kessler, "Romney and Bain Capital: The Obama Campaign's Newest Ad," in The Fact Checker (blog), *Washington Post*, May 15, 2012, http://www.washingtonpost.com/blogs/fact-checker/post/romney-and-bain-capital-the-obama-campaigns-newest-ad/2012/05/14/gIQAxCP3PU_blog.html.
70. Mark Maremont, "Romney at Bain: Big Gains, Some Busts," *Wall Street Journal*, January 9, 2012, http://online.wsj.com/article/SB10001424052970204331304577140850713493694.html.

CHAPTER 5: THE BATTLEGROUND STATES TIP THE BALANCE

1. Karl Rove, *Courage and Consequence: My Life as a Conservative in the Fight* (New York: Threshold Editions, 2010), 398–99.
2. Ibid., 399.
3. Timothy Burke, "Karl Rove in Denial Melts Down on Fox News, Attempts to Get Network to Rescind Calling Election," Gawker.com, November 7, 2012, embedded video at http://gawker.com/5958381/karl-rove-in-denial-melts-down-on-fox-news-attempts-to-get-network-to-rescind-calling-election.
4. Michael Simon, lead target analyst of the Obama presidential campaign in 2004, quoted in Issenberg, *The Victory Lab*, 275–76. This paragraph is paraphrased directly from this source.
5. Ohio 2008 presidential election voting totals were taken from the U.S. Election Atlas, drawing from the state and county tabulations, http://uselectionatlas.org/RESULTS/.
6. U.S. Census Bureau, U.S. Department of Commerce, Cuyahoga County, Ohio, in State and County Quick Facts, http://quickfacts.census.gov/qfd/states/39/39035.html.
7. City Planning Commission, City of Cleveland, "Population," http://planning.city.cleveland.oh.us/cwp/pop_trend.php.
8. Rich Exner, "Barack Obama Carried Ohio's Big Counties; John McCain Won the Small-County Vote: Statistical Snapshot," Cleveland *Plain Dealer*, October 29, 2012, http://www.cleveland.com/datacentral/index.ssf/2012/10/barrack_obama_carried_ohios_bi.html.
9. Keith Koffler, "Obama Has Made Two Dozen Visits to Ohio," White House Dossier, August 1, 2012, http://www.whitehousedossier.com/2012/08/01/obama-dozen-visits-ohio/. All Koffler and Carney quotes in this section are from this source.
10. Tracy Jan and Bryan Bender, "Auto Bailout in '09 Key to Obama's Survival in Ohio," *Boston Globe*, October 30, 2012, http://www.bostonglobe.com/news/politics/2012/10/29/barack-obama-bailout-auto-industry-looms-large-ohio-which-has-many-auto-jobs/UP7AmBAiWvK-wXLKctgABcK/story.html.

11. Kathryn A. Wolfe and Jessica Meyers, "Auto Bailout May Have Saved Obama," *Politico,* November 7, 2012, http://www.politico.com/news/stories/1112/83511.html.
12. Jeff Green and Mark Niquette, "Obama Leverages Auto Bailout for Crucial Midwest Wins," Bloomberg Businessweek, November 7, 2012, http://www.businessweek.com/news/2012-11-07/obama-leverages-auto-bailout-for-crucial-midwest-wins.
13. Mitt Romney, "Let Detroit Go Bankrupt," *New York Times,* November 18, 2008, http://www.nytimes.com/2008/11/19/opinion/19romney.html.
14. James Sherk and Todd Zywicki, "Auto Bailout or UAW Bailout? Taxpayer Losses Came from Subsidizing Union Compensation," The Heritage Foundation, June 13, 2012, http://www.heritage.org/research/reports/2012/06/auto-bailout-or-uaw-bailout-taxpayer-losses-came-from-subsidizing-union-compensation.
15. Jake Miller, "Romney Cites Incorrect Auto Manufacturing Claim in Ohio," CBS News, October 26, 2012, http://www.cbsnews.com/8301-34222_162-57541359/romney-cites-incorrect-auto-manufacturing-claim-in-ohio/.
16. Craig Trudell, "Fiat Says Jeep Output May Return to China as Demand Rises," Bloomberg, October 22, 2012, http://www.bloomberg.com/news/2012-10-21/fiat-says-china-may-build-all-jeep-models-as-suv-demand-climbs.html.
17. Gualberto Ranieri, "Jeeps in China," Chrysler blog, October 25, 2012, http://blog.chryslerllc.com/blog.do?id=1932&p=entry. Italics in original.
18. John Ward, "Mitt Romney Adviser Says Jeep Jobs Added in China Are Jobs Not Added in U.S.," Huffington Post, October 30, 2012, http://www.huffingtonpost.com/2012/10/30/mitt-romney-jeep-china-jobs_n_2045988.html.
19. Michael Dorstewitz, "Romney was right: Chrysler will build Jeeps in China," *Bizpac Review,* January 15, 2013, http://www.bizpacreview.com/2013/01/15/romney-was-right-chrysler-will-build-jeeps-in-china-14820.
20. Zeke Miller, "Romney Camp Defends Auto Bailout Ad: 'What Is There That's False?'" BuzzFeed, October 29, 2012, http://www.buzzfeed.com/zekejmiller/romney-camp-defends-auto-bailout-ad.
21. Sabrina Siddiqui, "Obama Jeep Ad Hits Back at Romney's Misleading Claims," Huffington Post, October 29, 2012, http://www.huffingtonpost.com/2012/10/29/obama-jeep-ad_n_2040851.html?1351541544. A video of the ad can be viewed in this article.
22. David Shepardson, "Chrysler to Build Jeeps in China," *Detroit News,* January 14, 2013, http://www.detroitnews.com/article/20130114/AUTO04/301140373/Chrysler-build-Jeeps-China?odyssey=tab|topnews|text|FRONTPAGE. No longer accessible.
23. Stephen Koff, Rich Exner, and James Owens, "Keys to Victory in Ohio," Cleveland *Plain Dealer,* November 7, 2012, http://media.cleveland.com/pdgraphics_impact/photo/08cganalysisoljpg-614e52de1e6ad826.jpg.
24. Matthew Yglesias, "The Auto Bailout Didn't Save Obama," *Money Box* (blog), November 13, 2012, http://www.slate.com/blogs/moneybox/2012/11/13/did_obama_win_because_of_the_auto_bailout_evidence_suggests_otherwise.html.
25. Nate Cohn, "The Auto Bailout Didn't Decide Ohio," *New Republic,* November 12, 2012, http://www.tnr.com/blog/electionate/109972/the-auto-bailout-didnt-decide-ohio#.
26. Ibid.
27. Monica Davey and Michael Wines, "Getting Out the Ohio Vote, Campaigns Are a Study in Contrasts," *New York Times,* November 3, 2012, http://www.nytimes.com/2012/11/04/us/politics/in-ohio-2-campaigns-offer-a-study-in-contrasts.html?pagewanted=all.
28. Ibid.
29. Population statistics for Florida, including county statistics, are taken from the U.S. Census Bureau, U.S. Department of Commerce, Florida, in State and County Quick Facts, http://quickfacts.census.gov/qfd/states/12000.html.
30. Jeremy Wallace, "Five Counties to Watch in Florida," *Herald-Tribune,* (Sarasota, FL) November 6, 2012, http://politics.heraldtribune.com/2012/11/06/five-counties-to-watch-in-florida/.

31. Brenda Farrington, "Jacksonville Area May Be Key to Victory in Florida," Real Clear Politics, October 6, 2012, http://www.realclearpolitics.com/articles/2012/10/06/jacksonville_area_may_be_key_to_victory_in_florida_115697.html.
32. Florida 2008 presidential election voting totals were taken from the U.S. Election Atlas, drawing from the state and county tabulations, http://uselectionatlas.org/RESULTS/.
33. "Emergency Lawsuit Filed in Florida over Long Lines at Early Voting," Huffington Post, November 4, 2012, http://www.huffingtonpost.com/2012/11/04/florida-early-voting-lawsuit_n_2072435.html?utm_hp_ref=miami.
34. Posted by Marc Caputo, "Why Obama Wins Florida," *Miami Herald*, November 8, 2012, http://miamiherald.typepad.com/nakedpolitics/2012/11/why-obama-wins-florida.html.
35. Marc Caputo and Scott Hiaasen, "President Barack Obama's Ground Game Delivers in Florida," *Miami Herald*, November 7, 2012, http://www.miamiherald.com/2012/11/06/3085117/exit-polls-florida-too-close-to.html.
36. Guest Blogger, "Not a Dream: Romney's Top 5 Comments on Immigration During the Republican Primary," *ThinkProgress* (blog), June 15, 2012, http://thinkprogress.org/election/2012/06/15/500607/mitt-romney-immigration-primary/?mobile=nc.
37. "TRANSCRIPT: Fox News – Google GOP Debate," FoxNews.com, September 22, 2011, http://www.foxnews.com/politics/2011/09/22/fox-news-google-gop-2012-presidential-debate/. The Perry quotes in the following paragraph is also from this transcript.
38. Susan Page and Jackie Kucinich, "Perry, Romney and Others Wrangle over Immigration in Debate," *USA Today*, September 23, 2011, http://usatoday30.usatoday.com/news/politics/story/2011-09-22/gop-debate-florida/50518542/1.
39. "Romney – I Would Veto the DREAM Act," YouTube.com, loaded on December 31, 2011, updated on January 1, 2012, http://www.youtube.com/watch?v=RJC1Mn8Pxg8&feature=youtu.be. See also "Gov. Romney Was Very Clear, He Would Veto the DREAM Act," Politifact.com, June 22, 2012, http://www.politifact.com/truth-o-meter/statements/2012/jun/22/david-plouffe/mitt-romney-said-he-would-veto-dream-act-says-davi/.
40. Jon Ward, "Mitt Romney Interview with the Huffington Post: Full Transcript," Huffington Post, December 31, 2011, http://www.huffingtonpost.com/2011/12/31/mitt-romney-interview-transcript_n_1177598.html.
41. Amy Gardner and Rosalind S. Helderman, "Gingrich Mocks Romney's 'Self-Deportation' Plan for Illegal Immigrants," *Washington Post*, January 25, 2012, http://articles.washingtonpost.com/2012-01-25/politics/35440222_1_cayman-island-accounts-illegal-immigrants-obama-level-fantasy.
42. Elise Foley, "Immigrant Groups Call for Romney to Take Down Ad," Huffington Post, October 18, 2012, http://www.huffingtonpost.com/2012/10/18/immigration-romney-television-ad_n_1981091.html.
43. U.S. Census Bureau, U.S. Department of Commerce, North Carolina, in State and County Quick Facts, http://quickfacts.census.gov/qfd/states/37000.html.
44. Elizabeth Hartfield, "Move the Democratic Convention From Charlotte? Not Likely," ABC News, May 11, 2012, http://abcnews.go.com/blogs/politics/2012/05/move-the-democratic-convention-from-charlotte-not-likely/.
45. John Frank, "N.C. House Asks DNC Not to Require Unions," *Charlotte Observer*, November 30, 2011, http://www.charlotteobserver.com/2011/11/30/2813233/nc-house-to-dnc-no-unions.html.
46. Bureau of Labor Statistics, U.S. Department of Labor, "Union Members Summary," January 27, 2012, http://www.bls.gov/news.release/union2.nr0.htm.
47. David Lauter, "Romney Bests Obama in North Carolina," *Los Angeles Times*, November 6, 2012, http://articles.latimes.com/2012/nov/06/news/la-pn-romney-wins-north-carolina-election-20121106.

48. U.S. Census Bureau, U.S. Department of Commerce, Colorado, in State and County Quick Facts, http://quickfacts.census.gov/qfd/states/08000.html.
49. John Ingold, "Colorado Presidential Election Poll Shows Obama, Romney Tied," *Denver Post*, Sept. 16, 2012, http://www.denverpost.com/nationalpolitics/ci_21553979/colorado-presidential-election-poll-shows-obama-romney-tied.
50. U.S. Census Bureau, U.S. Department of Commerce, Nevada, in State and County Quick Facts, http://quickfacts.census.gov/qfd/states/32000.html.
51. John Dickerson, "How Obama Defies Gravity," Slate.com, July 20, 2012, http://www.slate.com/articles/news_and_politics/politics/2012/07/nevada_is_suffering_economically_but_barack_obama_may_beat_mitt_romney_there_because_of_hispanics_and_superior_organization_.single.html.
52. U.S. Census Bureau, U.S. Department of Commerce, Iowa, in State and County Quick Facts, http://quickfacts.census.gov/qfd/states/19000.html.
53. "Romney Edges Out Santorum to Win Iowa Caucuses," FoxNews.com, January 4, 2012, http://www.foxnews.com/politics/2012/01/03/gop-candidates-await-iowa-verdict/.
54. "Iowa GOP Now Says Santorum Won Iowa Caucuses," KCCI-TV News, Des Moines, January 23, 2012, http://www.kcci.com/Iowa-GOP-Now-Says-Santorum-Won-Iowa-Caucuses/-/9357770/10379562/-/lhnq4iz/-/index.html.
55. Chris Cillizza, "Mitt Romney, Iowa Frontrunner," *Washington Post*, December 30, 2011, http://www.washingtonpost.com/blogs/the-fix/post/mitt-romney-iowa-frontrunner/2011/12/29/gIQAnbZ1OP_blog.html.
56. U.S. Census Bureau, U.S. Department of Commerce, Iowa, in State and County Quick Facts, http://quickfacts.census.gov/qfd/states/51000.html.
57. "Fox News Exit Poll Summary: Obama's Key Groups Made the Difference," FoxNews.com, November 7, 2012, http://www.foxnews.com/politics/2012/11/07/fox-news-exit-poll-summary/.

CHAPTER 6: THE ESTABLISHMENT CANDIDATE VERSUS THE CELEBRITY

1. Richard Ben Cramer, *What it Takes: The Way to the White House*, 1st Vintage Books ed. (New York: Random House, 1992), vii–viii.
2. See the C-Span broadcast of the dinner, embedded in the article at http://news.investors.com/politics-andrew-malcolm/101912-629999-mitt-romney-and-obama-roast-themselves-and-each-other-at-al-smith-event-video.htm?p=full.
3. Wendell Willkie, *One World* (New York: Simon and Schuster, 1943).
4. Phyllis Schlafly, *A Choice, Not an Echo* (Alton, IL: Pere Marquette, 1964).
5. Ibid., 48.
6. Ibid., 49.
7. Ibid., 49–50.
8. Joan Vennochi, "Romney's Revolving World," *Boston Globe*, March 2, 2006, http://www.boston.com/news/globe/editorial_opinion/oped/articles/2006/03/02/romneys_revolving_world/.
9. Quotations in this section are drawn from David Corn, "SECRET VIDEO: Romney Tells Millionaire Donors What He REALLY Thinks of Obama Voters," *Mother Jones*, September 17, 2012, http://www.motherjones.com/politics/2012/09/secret-video-romney-private-fundraiser. For the full transcript, see: "Full Transcript of the Mitt Romney Secret Video," *Mother Jones*, September 19, 2012, http://www.motherjones.com/politics/2012/09/full-transcript-mitt-romney-secret-video.

10. Michael Barbaro, "After a Romney Deal, Profits and Then Layoffs," *New York Times*, November 12, 2011, http://www.nytimes.com/2011/11/13/us/politics/after-mitt-romney-deal-company-showed-profits-and-then-layoffs.html.
11. "The Real Romney Record: Dade International," from opposition research website http://www.realromneyrecord.com/cases/dade-international.
12. Michael Barbaro and Ashley Parker, "Image Expert Shapes Romney (His Hair, Anyway)," *New York Times*, November 24, 2011, http://www.nytimes.com/2011/11/25/us/politics/romneys-image-expert-the-one-for-his-hair-anyway.html?pagewanted=all.
13. Ibid.
14. Michael Barbaro, "Republicans Urge Romney to Promote Positive Vision," *New York Times*, April 25, 2012, http://www.nytimes.com/2012/04/26/us/politics/republicans-urge-romney-to-promote-positive-vision.html?pagewanted=all.
15. William Kristol, "President Romney," *Weekly Standard*, April 30, 2012, http://www.weeklystandard.com/articles/president-romney_640520.html.
16. Ibid.
17. "Transcript and Audio: First Obama-Romney Debate," NPR.com, October 3, 2012, http://www.npr.org/2012/10/03/162258551/transcript-first-obama-romney-presidential-debate.
18. Michael Shepard and Kristin Jensen, "Romney Won First Debate, 67 Percent of Voters Tell CNN," Bloomberg, October 3, 2012, http://www.bloomberg.com/news/2012-10-04/romney-won-first-debate-67-percent-of-voters-tell-cnn.html.
19. Jeff Zeleny and Jim Rutenberg, "Obama and Romney, in First Debate, Spar over Fixing the Economy," *New York Times*, October 3, 2012, http://www.nytimes.com/2012/10/04/us/politics/obama-and-romney-hold-first-debate.html?pagewanted=all.
20. "Transcript and Audio: Third Presidential Debate," NPR.com, October 22, 2012, http://www.npr.org/2012/10/22/163436694/transcript-3rd-obama-romney-presidential-debate.
21. Ariel Edwards-Levy, "Obama Won Third Debate, Poll Says," Huffington Post, October 25, 2012, http://www.huffingtonpost.com/2012/10/25/obama-debate-poll_n_2019172.html.
22. Louis Jacobson, "Did the U.S embassy in Cairo make an apology?" PolitiFact.com, September 12, 2012, http://www.politifact.com/truth-o-meter/article/2012/sep/12/romney-says-us-embassy-statement-was-apology-was-i/.
23. Gregory J. Krieg, "Obama Says Romney 'Shoots First and Aims Later' in Embassy Attack Comments," ABC News, September 12, 2012, http://abcnews.go.com/Politics/OTUS/obama-romney-shoots-aims-embassy-attack-comments/story?id=17219337.
24. Erik Wemple, "Kurtz: Romney Gaffe Coverage 'Overshadowed' Benghazi Tragedy," *Washington Post*, September 17, 2012, http://www.washingtonpost.com/blogs/erik-wemple/post/kurtz-romney-gaffe-coverage-overshadowed-benghazi-tragedy/2012/09/17/7a491a06-00ba-11e2-b260-32f4a8db9b7e_blog.html.
25. Donovan Slack, "Obama visits Hoover Dam," *Politico*, October 2, 2012, http://www.politico.com/politico44/2012/10/obama-visits-hoover-dam-137280.html.
26. Toby Harnden, "Obama 'Believed He Had BEATEN Romney' in Denver Debate – After Ignoring Advice of Top Aides on Preparation," *Daily Mail*, October 9, 2012, http://www.dailymail.co.uk/news/article-2215173/Obama-believed-beaten-Romney-Denver-debate-ignoring-advice-aides.html.
27. Adam Nagourney et al., "How a Race in the Balance Went to Obama," *New York Times*, November 7, 2012, http://www.nytimes.com/2012/11/08/us/politics/obama-campaign-clawed-back-after-a-dismal-debate.html?pagewanted=all&_r=0.
28. Ron Fournier, "Obama Wins Third Debate but Romney Wins Debate Season," *National Review*, October 22, 2012, http://www.nationaljournal.com/2012-presidential-campaign/obama-wins-third-debate-but-romney-wins-debate-season-20121022.
29. Stephanie Condon, "Romney Takes Slight Lead in New Gallup Poll," CBS News, October 9, 2012, http://www.cbsnews.com/8301-250_162-57528936/romney-takes-slight-lead-in-new-gallup-poll/.

30. Jake Miller, "Polls: Gallup Still Has Romney Up, Marist Shows Obama Leads in Two Swing States," CBS News, October 19, 2012, http://www.cbsnews.com/8301-250_162-57536261/polls-gallup-still-has-romney-up-marist-shows-obama-leads-in-two-swing-states/.
31. Jon Ward, "Mitt Romney Benghazi Exchange Allows Obama to Dodge Questions until Third Debate," Huffington Post, October 17, 2012, http://www.huffingtonpost.com/2012/10/17/mitt-romney-benghazi-attack-debate_n_1973226.html.
32. Mark Landler and Jeremy W. Peters, "Rice Concedes Error on Libya, G.O.P. Digs In," *New York Times*, November 27, 2012, http://www.nytimes.com/2012/11/28/us/politics/after-benghazi-meeting-3-republicans-say-concerns-grow-over-rice.html.
33. Lucy Madison, "Richard Mourdock: Even Pregnancy from Rape Something 'God Intended,'" CBS News, October 23, 2012, http://www.cbsnews.com/8301-250_162-57538757/richard-mourdock-even-pregnancy-from-rape-something-god-intended/.
34. Jerome R. Corsi, "Romney playing for keeps on Obama's turf," WND, November 2, 2012, http://www.wnd.com/2012/11/romney-playing-for-keeps-on-obamas-turf/.
35. "Romney Delivers Rip-Roaring Speech in Wisconsin," Fox Nation, November 2, 2012, http://nation.foxnews.com/mitt-romney/2012/11/02/romney-delivers-rip-roaring-speech-wisconsin.

CHAPTER 7: OBAMA'S AMERICA VERSUS ROMNEY'S AMERICA

1. Transcript, "President Obama's Second Inaugural Address," *Wall Street Journal*, January 21, 2013, http://blogs.wsj.com/washwire/2013/01/21/president-obamas-second-inaugural-address/.
2. Penny Starr, "6,125 Proposed Regulations and Notifications Posted in Last 90 Days – Average 68 per Day," CNSNews.com, November 9, 2012, http://cnsnews.com/news/article/6125-proposed-regulations-and-notifications-posted-last-90-days-average-68-day.
3. Tony Lee, "'Tsunami' of Regulations Expected after Obama Re-election," Breitbart.com, November 9, 2012, http://www.breitbart.com/Big-Government/2012/11/09/Tsunami-Of-Regulations-Expected-After-Obama-Reelect.
4. Conn Carroll, "Obama EPA Kills Power Plant, 3,900 Jobs in Texas," *Washington Examiner*, January 24, 2013, http://washingtonexaminer.com/obama-epa-kills-power-plant-3900-jobs-in-texas/article/2519575#.UQaNm0qjfN.
5. Franklin Foer and Chris Hughes, "Barack Obama Is Not Pleased: The President on His Enemies, the Media, and the Future of Football," *New Republic*, January 27, 2013, http://www.newrepublic.com/article/112190/obama-interview-2013-sit-down-president.
6. Brian Sussman, *Climategate: A Veteran Meteorologist Exposes the Global Warming Scam* (Washington, D.C.: WND Books, 2010).
7. "FULL SPEECH: Watch Romney's Major Economic Speech in Ames, Iowa," The Right Scoop, October 26, 2012, http://www.therightscoop.com/watch-live-mitt-romneys-big-economic-speech-in-ames-iowa/. Written transcript presented by Romney campaign to WND in Ames, Iowa, October 26, 2012.
8. Nicholas Kristof, "Nicholas D. Kristof: How Would Romney Plan Work? See Europe," *Daily News* (L.A.), October 26, 2012, http://www.dailynews.com/opinions/ci_21862277/nicholas-d-kristof-how-would-romney-plan-work. All Kristof quotes in this section are from this article.
9. Molly Ball, "Romney's Major Economic Speech That Wasn't," *Atlantic*, October 26, 2012, http://www.theatlantic.com/politics/archive/2012/10/romneys-major-economic-speech-that-wasnt/264172/. All Ball quotes in this section are taken from this article.
10. Rachel Streitfeld, "Romney Pledges 'Big Change' But Offers Few Specifics," CNN, October 26, 2012, http://politicalticker.blogs.cnn.com/2012/10/26/romney-pledges-big-change-but-offers-few-specifics/.

11. Ibid.
12. "Remarks by the President at a Campaign Event in Roanoke, Virginia," Roanoke Fire Station #1, Roanoke, Virginia, White House website, July 13, 2012, http://www.whitehouse.gov/the-press-office/2012/07/13/remarks-president-campaign-event-roanoke-virginia.
13. Rush Limbaugh, "The Most Telling Moment of Obama's Presidency: 'You Didn't Build That,'" RushLimbaugh.com, July 24, 2012, http://www.rushlimbaugh.com/daily/2012/07/24/the_most_telling_moment_of_obama_s_presidency_you_didn_t_build_that.
14. Natalie Gewargis, "'Spread the Wealth'?" ABC News, October 14, 2008, http://abcnews.go.com/blogs/politics/2008/10/spread-the-weal/.
15. "Remarks by the President at the National Prayer Breakfast," Washington Hilton, Washington, D.C., White House website, February 2, 2012, http://www.whitehouse.gov/the-press-office/2012/02/02/remarks-president-national-prayer-breakfast.
16. Barack Obama, "The 2012 State of the Union Speech," January 25, 2012, WhiteHouse.gov, http://www.whitehouse.gov/photos-and-video/video/2012/01/25/2012-state-union-address-enhanced-version#transcript.
17. Paul Roderick Gregory, "Warren Buffett's Secretary Likely Makes Between $200,000 and $500,000/year," *Forbes*, January 25, 2012, http://www.forbes.com/sites/paulroderickgregory/2012/01/25/warren-buffetts-secretary-likely-makes-between-200000-and-500000year/.
18. Obama, "The 2012 State of the Union Speech."
19. Editorial, "Warren Buffett, Hypocrite," *New York Post*, August 28, 2011, http://www.nypost.com/p/news/opinion/editorials/warren_buffett_hypocrite_E3BsmJmeQVE38q2Woq9yjJ.
20. Congressional Budget Office, "Average Federal Taxes by Income Group," June 2010, http://www.cbo.gov/publications/collections/collections.cfm?collect=13.
21. Steve McCann, "Confiscate Americans' Wealth to Pay Government Workers?" *American Thinker*, March 9, 2011, http://www.americanthinker.com/2011/03/confiscate_americans_wealth_to.html.
22. Sara Murray, "Nearly Half of U.S. Lives in Household Receiving Government Benefit," *Wall Street Journal*, October 5, 2011, http://blogs.wsj.com/economics/2011/10/05/nearly-half-of-households-receive-some-government-benefit/.
23. Charles Gasparino, "Adding Up to Nothing: O's Fast Talk on the Economy," *New York Post*, January 26, 2012, http://www.nypost.com/p/news/opinion/opedcolumnists/adding_up_to_nothing_8K1eBN3afYXNELupfK8tRL.
24. Juan Williams, "Obama'ss Class Warfare Strategy Is Working with Americans," FoxNews.com, October 4, 2011, http://www.foxnews.com/opinion/2011/10/04/obamas-class-warfare-strategy-is-working-with-americans/.
25. Peter R. Orszag, Memorandum for Heads of Executive Departments and Agencies, Executive Office of the President, Office of Management and Budget, December 18, 2009, http://www.whitehouse.gov/sites/default/files/omb/assets/memoranda_2010/m10-08.pdf.
26. Kristina Wong, "Farewell 'Saved or Created': Obama Administration Changes the Counting of Stimulus Jobs," ABC News, January 11, 2010, http://abcnews.go.com/blogs/politics/2010/01/farewell-saved-or-created-obama-administration-changes-the-counting-of-stimulus-jobs/.
27. William McGurn, "The Media Fall for Phony 'Jobs' Claims," *Wall Street Journal*, June 10, 2009, http://online.wsj.com/article/SB124451592762396883.html.
28. Kristof, "Nicholas D. Kristof: How Would Romney Plan Work? See Europe."
29. McGurn, "The Media Fall for Phony 'Jobs' Claims," quoting Senator Baucus.
30. Jeffrey H. Anderson, "What Stimulus?" *Weekly Standard*, May 21, 2012, http://m.weeklystandard.com/articles/what-stimulus_644424.html.
31. Terence P. Jeffrey, "Obama's Trillion Dollar Lies," CNSNews.com, August 29, 2012, http://cnsnews.com/blog/terence-p-jeffrey/obamas-trillion-dollar-lies.

32. Terence P. Jeffrey, "First Term: Americans 'Not in Labor Force' Increased 8,332,000," CNSNews.com, January 20, 2013, http://cnsnews.com/news/article/first-term-americans-not-labor-force-increased-8332000.
33. "Remarks by the President at Ohio University, Athens, Ohio," White House website, October 17, 2012, http://www.whitehouse.gov/the-press-office/2012/10/17/remarks-president-ohio-university-athens-oh. All quotes in this section from the Ohio University speech are from this website.
34. Saul D. Alinsky, *Rules for Radicals: A Pragmatic Primer for Realistic Radicals* (New York: Vintage, 1971).
35. Associated Press, "Detroit Wants to Save Itself by Shrinking," NBC News, March 8, 2010, http://www.nbcnews.com/id/35767727/ns/us_news-life/#.UQgGukqjfN8.
36. Alex P. Kellogg, "Detroit Shrinks Itself, Historic Homes and All," Wall *Street Journal*, May 14, 2010, http://online.wsj.com/article/SB10001424052748703950804575242433435338728.html.
37. Yves Marchand and Romain Meffre, *The Ruins of Detroit* (London: Steidl, 2011).
38. Khalil AlHajal, "Numbers Expert Says Detroit Population below 700,000 but Is Starting to Turn Corner," Michigan Live, September 27, 2012, http://www.mlive.com/news/detroit/index.ssf/2012/09/numbers_expert_says_detroit_po.html.
39. U.S. Census Bureau, State & County QuickFacts, "Detroit, Michigan," http://quickfacts.census.gov/qfd/states/26/2622000.html.
40. Ibid.
41. Data Driven Detroit, "State of the Detroit Child: 2012 Report," January 2013, http://datadrivendetroit.org/projects/2012-state-of-detroits-child/, or for the complete report, http://datadrivendetroit.org/wp-content/uploads/2013/01/D3_2012_SDCReport_Hotfix.pdf.
42. Ben Rooney, "Michigan Approves Plan to Close Half of Detroit Schools," CNN Money, February 22, 2011, http://money.cnn.com/2011/02/22/news/economy/detroit_school_restructuring/index.htm.
43. Terrence P. Jeffrey, "Only 7 Percent of Detroit Public-School 8th Graders Proficient in Reading," CNSNews.com, December. 11, 2012, http://cnsnews.com/news/article/only-7-detroit-public-school-8th-graders-proficient-readinG.
44. Ping Zhou, "The Geography of Detroit's Decline," About.com, December 17, 2012, http://geography.about.com/od/urbaneconomicgeography/a/geography-detroit-decline.htm.
45. Leonard N. Fleming, "Detroit Offers Cops Incentives to Buy Homes in the City," *Detroit News*, February 8, 2011, http://www.detroitnews.com/article/20110208/METRO01/102080375/1409/METRO/Detroit-offers-cops-incentives-to-buy-homes-in-the-city.
46. Ibid.
47. Janell Ross, "Black Unemployment at Depression Level Highs in Some Cities," Huffington Post, April 27, 2011, http://www.huffingtonpost.com/2011/04/27/black-unemployment-remain_n_853571.html.
48. Mark V. Levine, Center for Economic Development, University of Wisconsin-Milwaukee, Working Paper, "Race and Male Employment in the Wake of the Great Recession: Black Male Employment Rates in Milwaukee and the Nation's Largest Metro Areas, 2010," January 2012, at Table 8, "Change in Black Male Employment Rates in Selected Metropolitan Areas: 1970–2010," http://www4.uwm.edu/ced/publications/black-employment_2012.pdf, p. 14.
49. Bruce A. Dixon, "Why Record Black Male Unemployment Remains Invisible to the First Black President," *Black Agenda Report*, February 1, 2012, http://blackagendareport.com/content/why-record-black-male-unemployment-remains-invisible-first-black-president.
50. "Presidential Exit Polls," *New York Times*, n.d., http://elections.nytimes.com/2012/results/president/exit-polls.

51. Jon Wiener, "The Bad News about White People: Romney Won the White Vote Almost Everywhere," *The Nation*, November 7, 2012, http://www.thenation.com/blog/171093/bad-news-about-white-people-romney-won-white-vote-almost-everywhere#.
52. Tom Scocca, "Eighty-Eight Percent of Romney Voters Were White," *Slate*, November 7, 2012, http://www.slate.com/articles/news_and_politics/scocca/2012/11/mitt_romney_white_voters_the_gop_candidate_s_race_based_monochromatic_campaign.html.
53. Tom Scocca, "Why Do White People Think Mitt Romney Should Be President?" *Slate*, November 2, 2012, http://www.slate.com/articles/news_and_politics/scocca/2012/11/mitt_romney_white_vote_parsing_the_narrow_tribal_appeal_of_the_republican.html. Remaining Scocca quotes in this section are from this article.
54. John B. Judis and Ruy Teixeira, *The Emerging Democratic Majority* (New York: Scribner, 1972, 2002), 35. Citations refer to the 2002 edition.
55. Ibid., 6.
56. Barbara Vobejda, "Clinton Signs Welfare Bill amid Division," *Washington Post*, August 23, 1996, http://www.washingtonpost.com/wp-srv/politics/special/welfare/stories/wf082396.htm.
57. Robert Rector, "An Overview of Obama's End Run on Welfare Reform," The Heritage Foundation, September 20, 2012, http://www.heritage.org/research/reports/2012/09/an-overview-of-obama-s-end-run-on-welfare-reform.
58. Statistics in this paragraph are from Robert Rector and Amy Payne, "Morning Bell: Welfare Spending Shattering All-Time Highs," *The Foundry*, a publication of the Heritage Foundation, October 18, 2012, http://blog.heritage.org/2012/10/18/morning-bell-welfare-spending-shattering-all-time-highs/.
59. John Melloy, "Welfare State: Handouts Make Up One-Third of U.S. Wages," CNBC, March 8, 2011, http://www.cnbc.com/id/41969508/Welfare_State_Handouts_Make_Up_OneThird_of_US_Wages.
60. Becket Adams, "The Welfare Spending Chart You Won't Want to See," *The Blaze*, December 7, 2012, http://www.theblaze.com/stories/2012/12/07/the-welfare-spending-chart-you-wont-want-to-see/.
61. Murray Rothbard, *Making Economic Sense* (Auburn, AL: Ludwif von Mises Institute, 1995), chap. 13, "Economic Incentives and Welfare," http://mises.org/econsense/ch13.asp.
62. Liz Farmer, "More Than Half of all Prince George's, DC Families Headed by Single Parents," *Washington Examiner*, December 27, 2010, http://washingtonexaminer.com/more-than-half-of-all-prince-georges-dc-families-headed-by-single-parents/article/108845.
63. Office of Policy Planning and Research, U.S. Department of Labor, *The Negro Family: The Case for National Action* (Washington, D.C.: Government Printing Office, 1965).
64. U.S. Census Bureau, *The 2009 Statistical Abstract*, (Washington, D.C.: U.S. Government Printing Office, 2009), Table 85, "Births to Teens and Unmarried Women, and Births with Low Birth Weight, by Race and Hispanic Origin: 1990 to 2006," as drawn from the U.S. National Center for Health Statistics, *National Vital Statistics Reports (NVSR), Births: Final Data for 2005*, vol. 56, no. 6, December 5, 2007, and *Births: Preliminary Data for 2006*, vol. 56, no. 7, December 5, 2007, at http://www.census.gov/compendia/statab/cats/births_deaths_marriages_divorces/births.html.

CHAPTER 8: WHO VOTED, WHO DIDN'T

1. John Fund, *Stealing Elections: How Voter Fraud Threatens Our Democracy* (San Francisco: Encounter Books, 2004), 5.
2. David Kupelian, "Rob the Vote: How Obama Plans to Win a Second Term as President," *Whistleblower*, August 2012, 4–7.

3. Joseph Farah, "The Election Fraud Lobby: Vast Network Obsessed with Winning 'By Any Means Necessary,'" *Whistleblower*, August 2012, 4–5.
4. Fund, *Stealing Elections*, 4–5.
5. Aaron Klein, "Did This Dirty Trick Get Obama Elected?" WND.com, November 8, 2012, http://www.wnd.com/2012/11/did-this-dirty-trick-get-obama-elected/.
6. James Simpson, "The Left 's National Vote-Fraud Strategy Exposed," *Whistleblower*, August 2012, 11–16.
7. Matthew Vadum, *Subversion Inc.: How Obama's ACORN Red Shirts Are Still Terrorizing and Ripping Off American Taxpayers* (Washington, D.C.: WND Books, 2011), 97.
8. Ibid., 101.
9. Simpson, "The Left 's National Vote-Fraud Strategy Exposed," 11.
10. Whistleblower Editors, "SURPRISE! Taxpayers Still Paying for 'Defunct' Criminal Vote-Fraud Group," *Whistleblower*, August 2012, 15.
11. "Weary Activist Group ACORN Changes Affiliate Names," *Washington Times*, March 16, 2010, http://www.washingtontimes.com/news/2010/mar/16/weary-activist-group-acorn-changes-affiliate-names/?page=all.
12. Vadum, *Subversion Inc.*, 273–74.
13. Brayden Goyette, "1.8 MILLION Dead People Still Registered to Vote in the U.S., Study Says," *New York Daily News*, February 14, 2012, http://www.nydailynews.com/news/politics/1-8-million-dead-people-registered-vote-u-s-study-article-1.1022389.
14. "Election Fraud," Pew Center on the States, August 30, 2012, http://www.pewstates.org/research/analysis/election-fraud-85899414756.
15. Corbin Carson, comp., "Election Fraud in America," News21, August 12, 2012, http://votingrights.news21.com/interactive/election-fraud-database/.
16. Associated Press, "High Court Rejects GOP in Ohio Voting Dispute," October 17, 2008, http://www.nbcnews.com/id/27238980/ns/politics-decision_08/t/high-court-rejects-gop-ohio-voting-dispute/#.UQqZ1FqjfN8.
17. Steve Bousquet, "List of 180,000 Suspect Florida Voters to Be Made Public," *Miami Herald*, *Naked Politics* (blog), July 10, 2012, http://miamiherald.typepad.com/nakedpolitics/2012/07/list-of-180000-suspect-florida-voters-to-be-made-public.html.
18. "Gov. Rick Scott 'Tried to Kick 180,000 People off the Voters Rolls,'" PolitiFact.com, June 27, 2012, http://www.politifact.com/florida/statements/2012/jul/10/moveon/moveon-says-gov-rick-scott-tried-kick-180000-peopl/.
19. Michael Peltier, "Florida Voter Purge Draws New Legal Challenge after State Officials Release Different List," Huffington Post, September 27, 2012, http://www.huffingtonpost.com/2012/09/27/florida-voter-purge-challenge_n_1920826.html.
20. Mark Caputo, "DOJ to Florida: Stop Noncitizen Voter Purge. Will FL Fight DOJ?" *Miami Herald*, *Naked Politics* (blog), May 31, 2012, http://miamiherald.typepad.com/nakedpolitics/2012/05/doj-to-florida-stop-noncitizen-voter-purge.html.
21. Florida Department of State, "Secretary of State Ken Detzner Files Lawsuit against U.S. Department of Homeland Security, Seeks Access to Database of Non-Citizens to Ensure Accuracy of Florida Voter Rolls," press release, June 11, 2012, http://www.dos.state.fl.us/news/communications/pressRelease/pressRelease.aspx?id=583.
22. Steve Bousquet, "Judge Halts Federal Attempt to Block Florida's Voter Purge," *Miami Herald*, June 27, 2012, http://www.miamiherald.com/2012/06/27/2871392/judge-halts-federal-attempt-to.html.
23. The Editors, "Voter ID Is Not Jim Crow," *National Review Online*, December 16, 2011, http://www.nationalreview.com/articles/285835/voter-id-not-jim-crow-editors.
24. "BREAKING: Supreme Court Rejects Challenge to Indiana Voter ID Law," RedState.com, n.d., http://archive.redstate.com/stories/the_courts/breaking_supreme_court_rejects_challenge_to_indiana_voter_id_law/.

25. Ethan Bronner, "Voter ID Rules Fail Court Tests across Country," *New York Times*, October 2, 2012, http://www.nytimes.com/2012/10/03/us/pennsylvania-judge-delays-implementation-of-voter-id-law.html?_r=0.
26. Ryan J. Reilly, "Romney Co-Chair: Voter ID Would Have Won Us Wisconsin," TPM, November 13, 2012, http://tpmmuckraker.talkingpointsmemo.com/2012/11/romney_wisconsin_voter_id.php.
27. Patrick Marley, "State Supreme Court Declines to Take up Voter ID, for Now," *Milwaukee Journal-Sentinel*, September 27, 2012, http://www.jsonline.com/news/statepolitics/state-supreme-court-declines-to-take-up-voter-id-for-now-8371acv-171594631.html.
28. Aaron Gardner, "Colorado Counties Have More Voters Than People," Media Trackers, September 4, 2012, http://colorado.mediatrackers.org/2012/09/04/colorado-counties-have-more-voters-than-people/.
29. Earl F. Glynn, "Colorado: Comparison of Registered Voter Counts to Census Voting Age Population," WatchdogLabs.org, August 21, 2012, http://watchdoglabs.org/blog/2012/08/21/colorado-comparison-of-registered-voter-counts-to-census-voting-age-population/.
30. Sam Levin, "Romney Votes in Colorado Might Count for Obama? RNC, Officials on Computer Glitch," *Westword* (blog), November 2, 2012, http://blogs.westword.com/latestword/2012/11/romney_votes_obama_voting_machine_error_rnc.php.
31. "Clerk Pulls Voting Machine after Mack Man Has Problems with It," *Daily Sentinel* (Grand Junction, CO), October 23, 2012, http://www.gjsentinel.com/news/articles/clerk-pulls-voting-machine-after-mack-man-has-prob.
32. "SEIU Launches Largest Field Campaign in Union's History for 2012 Election," SEIU press release, June 19, 2012, http://www.seiu.org/2012/06/seiu-launches-largest-field-campaign-in-unions-his.php. SEIU quotes up to the next note number are all from this press release.
33. "SEIU Paid Anti-Romney Protestors $11/Hour in Ohio," *Daily Caller*, September 27, 2012, http://dailycaller.com/2012/09/27/seiu-paid-anti-romney-protesters-11hour-in-cleveland-video/.
34. Michelle Cottle, "SEIU, AFL-CIO Driving Obama 's Ground Game," *Daily Beast*, November 1, 2012, http://www.thedailybeast.com/articles/2012/11/01/seiu-afl-cio-driving-obama-s-ground-game.html.
35. Bureau of Labor Statistics, U.S. Department of Labor, "Union Members – 2012," press release, January 23, 2013, http://www.bls.gov/news.release/pdf/union2.pdf.
36. Michelle Malkin, *The Culture of Corruption: Obama and His Team of Tax Cheats, Crooks, and Cronies* (Washington, D.C.: Regnery, 2009), 196.
37. Diana Furchtgott-Roth, "Why the Unions Are Shrinking," *Washington Examiner*, January 22, 2013, http://washingtonexaminer.com/furchtgott-roth-why-the-unions-are-shrinking/article/2519391.
38. James Sherk and Todd Zywicki, "Auto Bailout or UAW Bailout? Taxpayer Loses Came from Subsidizing Union Compensation," Heritage Foundation, June 13, 2012, http://www.heritage.org/research/reports/2012/06/auto-bailout-or-uaw-bailout-taxpayer-losses-came-from-subsidizing-union-compensation.
39. Michael P. McDonald, "Early Voting Mesmerizing," Huffington Post, October 26, 2012, http://www.huffingtonpost.com/michael-p-mcdonald/early-voting-mesmerizing_b_2027200.html.
40. United States Election Project, "2012 Early Voting Statistics," upd. November 6, 2012, http://elections.gmu.edu/early_vote_2012.html.
41. Office of Nevada Secretary of State Ross Miller, "2012 General Election: Early Voting Absent/Mail-in, Election Day Turnout," upd. 4:30 pm, November 6, 2012, http://nvsos.gov/Modules/ShowDocument.aspx?documentid=2500.
42. N. Robbins Northeast Ohio Voter Advocates, "Effects of legislation and Directives on Early In-Person (EIP) Voting in Ohio in 2012, as of Aug. 17, 2012," http://nova-ohio.org/Effects%20of%20legislation%20and%20Directives%20on%20early%20in-person%20(EIP)%20voting%20in%20Ohio%20in%202012.pdf.

43. Luke Johnson, "Ohio Early Voting: Long Lines Reported outside Polling Places," Huffington Post, November 4, 2012, http://www.huffingtonpost.com/2012/11/04/ohio-early-voting_n_2073287.html.
44. Ann Sanner, "High Court Won't Block Early Voting in Ohio," Huffington Post, October 16, 2012, http://www.huffingtonpost.com/huff-wires/20121016/us-supreme-court-ohio-early-voting/.
45. James O'Keefe, "Voter Fraud," Project Veritas, https://www.theprojectveritas.com/civicrm/contribute/transact?reset=1&id=103.
46. Erin Haust, "Vote Early Vote Often," *Conservative Daily News*, October 10, 2012, http://www.conservativedailynews.com/2012/10/vote-early-vote-often/.
47. James O'Keefe, Project Veritas, "NC Non-Citizens Voting, Dead Offered Ballots, UNC Officials Embrace Voter Fraud," YouTube.com, May 15, 2012, https://www.youtube.com/watch?feature=player_embedded&v=ptSrcNvJzBQ#.
48. James O'Keefe, Project Veritas, "EXCLUSIVE: DNC Staffer Assists Double Voting in Support of Obama," YouTube.com, October 10, 2012, https://www.youtube.com/watch?v=q_iJfn-bMzI0.
49. Sean Trende, "The Case of the Missing White Voters," Real Clear Politics, November 8, 2012, http://realclearpolitics.com/articles/2012/11/08/the_case_of_the_missing_white_voters_116106.html. All Trende quotes in this section are from this web page.
50. "2012 Fox News Exit Polls," Fox News, n.d., http://realclearpolitics.com/articles/2012/11/08/the_case_of_the_missing_white_voters_116106.html.
51. Byron York, "York: In Ohio, the GOP Puzzles over Missing White Voters," *Washington Examiner*, November 12, 2012, http://washingtonexaminer.com/york-in-ohio-the-gop-puzzles-over-missing-white-voters/article/2513293. Additional York quotes and statistics in this section are from this article.
52. Craig L. Foster, *A Different God? Mitt Romney, the Religious Right and the Mormon Question* (Salt Lake City: Greg Kofford, 2008), 121.
53. Ibid.
54. For a discussion of the Associate Press story, see James Joyner, "AP Smears Romney with 155-Year-Old Family Story," *Outside the Beltway*, February 24, 2007, http://www.outsidethebeltway.com/ap_smears_romney_with_155-year-old_family_history/.
55. Travis Waldron and Scott Keyes, "Prominent Perry Endorser Robert Jeffress Calls AIDS a 'Gay Disease,' Claims 70 Percent of Gays Have AIDS," *ThinkProgress* (blog), October 7, 2011, http://thinkprogress.org/politics/2011/10/07/339299/video-prominent-perry-endorser-robert-jeffress-says-voting-for-romney-would-give-credibility-to-a-cult/.
56. Christopher Hitchens, "Romney 's Mormon Problem," *Slate*, October 17, 2011, http://www.slate.com/articles/news_and_politics/fighting_words/2011/10/is_mormonism_a_cult_who_cares_it_s_their_weird_and_sinister_beli.html.
57. Executive Summary, "Romney 's Mormon Faith Likely a Factor in Primaries, Not in a General Election," Pew Forum on Religion & Public Life, a project of the Pew Research Center, November 23, 2011, http://www.pewforum.org/Politics-and-Elections/Romneys-Mormon-Faith-Likely-a-Factor-in-Primaries-Not-in-a-General-Election.aspx.
58. Peter Hamby, "Romney Chides Reporter at New Hampshire Event," *Political Ticker* (blog), October 10, 2011, http://politicalticker.blogs.cnn.com/2011/10/10/romney-no-press-questions-allowed-until-the-campaign-says-so/.
59. Michelle Boorstein and Scott Clement, "Romney Won over White Evangelicals, Catholics, but They Weren't Enough to Win Race," *Washington Post*, November 7, 2012, http://articles.washingtonpost.com/2012-11-07/local/35506630_1_catholic-vote-catholic-bishops-religious-liberty.
60. "Billy Graham, Mitt Romney Meet," Billy Graham Evangelistic Association, October 11, 2012, http://www.billygraham.org/articlepage.asp?articleid=8983.

61. Ed O'Keefe, "Billy Graham to Mitt Romney: 'I'll Do All I Can to Help You,'" *Washington Post*, October 11, 2012, http://www.washingtonpost.com/blogs/post-politics/wp/2012/10/11/billy-graham-to-mitt-romney-ill-do-all-i-can-to-help-you/.
62. Eugene Burdick, *The 480: A Novel of Politics* (New York: McGraw-Hill, 1964), ix.
63. Quoted in: Issenberg, *The Victory Lab*, 122.
64. John F. Kennedy, "I Believe in an America Where the Separation of Church and State Is Absolute," address to the Greater Houston Ministerial Association, Beliefnet, http://www.beliefnet.com/News/Politics/2000/09/I-Believe-In-An-America-Where-The-Separation-Of-Church-And-State-Is-Absolute.aspx.
65. Kathryn Lofton, "Mormonism Cost Romney the Election (But It's Not What You Think)," *Religious Dispatches* magazine, November 6, 2012, http://www.religiondispatches.org/archive/election2012/6578/mormonism_cost_romney_the_election__but_it_s_not_what_you_think_/.
66. Jim Meyers, "Newsmax/Insider Advantage Poll: Trump Gains Slim Lead in 2012 GOP Race," Newsmax, April 26, 2011, http://www.newsmax.com/Headline/DonaldTrump-MikeHuckabee-SarahPalin-/2011/04/26/id/394126.
67. James M. Perry, "Americans Continue to Believe in Nonsense," *Toledo Blade*, September 4, 2012, http://www.toledoblade.com/politicalconventions/2012/09/04/Americans-continue-to-believe-in-nonsense.html.
68. Joel B. Pollak, "The Vetting – Exclusive – Obama's Literary Agent in 1991 Booklet: 'Born in Kenya and Raised in Indonesia and Hawaii,'" Breitbart.com, May 17, 2012, http://www.breitbart.com/Big-Government/2012/05/17/The-Vetting-Barack-Obama-Literary-Agent-1991-Born-in-Kenya-Raised-Indonesia-Hawaii; and Drew Zahn, "Shocker! Obama Still 'Kenyan-Born' in 2007," WND.com, May 18, 2012, http://www.wnd.com/2012/05/shocker-obama-was-still-kenyan-born-in-2003/.
69. Shawna Thomas, NBC News, "Trump 'Proud of Himself, Takes Credit for Birth-Certificate Release," MSNBC News, April 27, 2011, http://firstread.nbcnews.com/_news/2011/04/27/6542314-trump-proud-of-himself-takes-credit-for-birth-certificate-release?lite.
70. Steve Fries, "Ron Paul Delegates Get Nosebleed Seats," *Politico*, August 26, 2012, http://www.politico.com/news/stories/0812/80168.html. The reporting in this source is the basis of information contained in this paragraph and the next several.
71. Drew Zahn, "GOP Patriarch Rises to Challenge Establishment," WND.com, January 21, 2013, http://www.wnd.com/2013/01/gop-rebel-rises-to-challenge-party-establishment/.
72. Muriel Kane, "Rule Changes Forced through by Romney Campaign at RNC Provoke Grassroots Backlash," *Business Insider*, August 26, 2012, http://www.rawstory.com/rs/2012/08/26/rule-changes-forced-through-by-romney-campaign-at-rnc-provoke-grassroots-backlash/.
73. Zeke Miller, "Romney Campaign Radically Changes GOP Nominating Process after Ron Paul Takeovers," BuzzFeed, August 24, 2012, http://www.buzzfeed.com/zekejmiller/romney-campaign-radically-changes-gop-nominating-p.
74. Zeke Miller, "Romney Executes Republican Party Power Grab," BuzzFeed, August 24, 2012, http://www.buzzfeed.com/zekejmiller/romney-executes-republican-party-power-grab.
75. Miller, "Romney Campaign Radically Changes GOP Nominating Process after Ron Paul Takeovers."
76. Liz Halloran, "With a Roar and Some Rage, Ron Paul Rallies His Faithful," NPR, August 26, 2012, http://www.npr.org/blogs/itsallpolitics/2012/08/26/160082270/with-a-roar-and-some-rage-ron-paul-rallies-his-faithful.
77. Hamdan Azhar, "The Ron Paul Effect: How the GOP Threw the Election by Disenfranchising Ron Paul Supporters," Policymic.com, n.d., http://www.policymic.com/articles/18815/the-ron-paul-effect-how-the-gop-threw-the-election-by-disenfranchising-ron-paul-supporters. Discussion here adjusted for final election results from the five states involved in the analysis.

78. Felicia Sonmez, "Romney Ohio Campaign Event Turns into Storm Relief Effort," *Washington Post*, October 30, 2012, http://www.washingtonpost.com/blogs/post-politics/wp/2012/10/30/mixed-messages-at-romney-storm-relief-event-in-ohio/.
79. Russell Goldman, "Obama and Christie Tour Sandy's Devastation," ABC News, October 31, 2012, http://abcnews.go.com/Politics/OTUS/president-obama-jersey-gov-christie-tour-superstorm-sandy/story?id=17606560.
80. "CBS News Early Exit Poll Information Says 60 Percent of Voters Consider Economy Most Important Issue," WKZO.com, November 6, 2012, http://wkzo.com/news/articles/2012/nov/06/cbs-news-early-exit-poll-information-has-economy-at-60-percent-as-voters-most-important-issue/; and Climate Guest Blogger, "Exit Polls 2012: Hurricane Sandy Was a Deciding Factor for Millions of Voters in the Election," *ThinkProgress* (blog), November. 6, 2012, http://thinkprogress.org/climate/2012/11/06/1152421/exit-polls-2012-hurricane-sandy-was-a-deciding-factor-in-the-election/.
81. Gallup Editors, "Romney 49%, Obama 48% in Gallup's Final Election Survey," Gallup.com, November 5, 2012, http://www.gallup.com/poll/158519/romney-obama-gallup-final-election-survey.aspx.

CHAPTER 9: A NATION DIVIDED AGAINST ITSELF

1. Abraham Lincoln, "A House Divided against Itself Cannot Stand," June 17, 1858, acceptance speech, Illinois Republican Party Nomination for U.S. Senate, Illinois State Capitol, Springfield, IL, June 17, 1858, NationalCenter.org, http://www.nationalcenter.org/HouseDivided.html.
2. President Barack Obama, quoted in Jonathan Horn, "Obama Runs from His Failed Presidency as Fast as He Can," *Forbes*, June 5, 2012, http://www.forbes.com/sites/jonathanhorn/2012/06/05/obama-runs-from-his-failed-presidency-as-fast-as-he-can/.
3. Davison M. Douglas, "The End of Busing?" *Michigan Law Review* 95, 1715–37, 1996–97, http://scholarship.law.wm.edu/cgi/viewcontent.cgi?article=1116&context=facpubs.
4. William H. Frey, "Race, Immigration and America's Changing Electorate," in Ruy Teixeira, ed., *Red, Blue & Purple America: The Future of Election Demographics* (Washington, D.C.: Brookings Institution Press, 2008), 79–108, at 81.
5. U.S. Census Bureau, Department of Commerce, "U.S. Census Bureau Projections Show a Slower Growing, Older, More Diverse Nation a Half Century from Now," press release, December 12, 2012, http://www.census.gov/newsroom/releases/archives/population/cb12-243.html.
6. Nina Golgowski, "California's Hispanic Population to Outnumber Whites by the End of 2013," *Daily Mail*, January 19, 2013, http://www.dailymail.co.uk/news/article-2265134/California-Hispanic-population-exceed-whites-end-2013.html.
7. Ruy Teixeira, ed., *America's New Swing Region: Changing Politics and Demographics in the Mountain West* (Washington, D.C.: Brookings Institution, 2012).
8. Alan Abramowitz and Ruy Teixeira, "The Decline of the White Working Class and the Rise of a Mass Upper-Middle Class," in Teixeira, *Red, Blue & Purple America*, 109–43.
9. Tom W. Smith, "Changes in Family Structure, Family Values, and Politics, 1972–2006," in ibid., 147–93.
10. John C. Green and E. J. Dionne Jr., "Religion and American Politics: More Secular, More Evangelical, or Both?" in ibid., 194–224.
11. Ruy Teixeira, "Demographic Change and the Future of the Parties," Center for American Progress Action Fund, June 2010, http://www.americanprogress.org/wp-content/uploads/issues/2010/06/pdf/voter_demographics.pdf.
12. Ibid.

13. John Halpin and Karl Agne, "State of American Political Ideology: A National Study of Political Values and Beliefs," Center for American Progress, March 2009, http://www.americanprogress.org/wp-content/uploads/issues/2009/03/pdf/political_ideology.pdf.
14. Ruy Teixeira and John Halpin, "The Return of the Obama Coalition," *American Progress*, November 8, 2012, http://www.americanprogress.org/issues/progressive-movement/news/2012/11/08/44348/the-return-of-the-obama-coalition/.
15. Sam Fahmy and Jeff Humphreys, "Despite Recession, Hispanic and Asian Buying Power Expected to Surge in U.S., According to Annual UGA Selig Center Multicultural Economy Study," Terry College of Business, University of Georgia, news release, November 4, 2010, http://www.terry.uga.edu/news/releases/2010/minority-buying-power-report.html.
16. "Latino Gang Members Accused of Terrorizing Compton Black Family," *Los Angeles Times*, January 25, 2013, http://latimesblogs.latimes.com/lanow/2013/01/compton-gang-members-arrested-in-alleged-hate-campaign-against-black-familly.html.
17. Teresa Watanabe, "Crimes rooted in hatred increase," *Los Angeles Times*, July 25, 2008, http://articles.latimes.com/2008/jul/25/local/me-hatecrime25.
18. John Rudolf, "NYPD Report Says 96 Percent of Shooting Victims Are Black or Latino," Huffington Post, September 7, 2012, http://www.huffingtonpost.com/2012/09/06/nypd-report-details-crime_n_1862771.html.
19. Study published by LSU sociology professor Edward Shihadeh and PhD candidate Raymond Barranco, published in the journal *Social Forces*, as reported by WDSU-TV, Baton Rouge, Louisiana, "LSU Study: Latino Immigration Creates Problems in Black Community," April 12, 2012, http://www.wdsu.com/LSU-Study-Latino-Immigration-Creates-Problems-In-Black-Community/-/9854144/10988072/-/15jvsnu/-/index.html.
20. Colin Flaherty, "Black Mob Violence and the Media Silence," WND.com, September 19, 2012, http://www.wnd.com/2012/09/black-mob-violence-and-the-media-silence/.
21. "Flash Mob Mayhem: Violent Groups of Teens Leave NYC Businesses in Ruins," CBS News Channel 2, New York, February 4, 2013, http://newyork.cbslocal.com/2013/02/04/flash-mob-mayhem-violent-groups-of-teens-leave-nyc-neighborhoods-in-disarray/.
22. "Chicago Police Changing Response Plan for Some 911 Calls," CBS Chicago Channel 2, February 4, 2013, http://chicago.cbslocal.com/2013/02/04/chicago-police-changing-response-plan-for-some-911-calls/.
23. Don Babwin, "Rahm Emanuel Pushes Police Budget Cuts Despite Campaign Pledge to Add Cops," Huffington Post, September 2, 2011, http://www.huffingtonpost.com/2011/09/03/emanuel-pushes-police-bud_0_n_947885.html.
24. Erica Goode, "Crime Increases in Sacramento after Deep Cuts to Police Force, *New York Times*, November 3, 2012, http://www.nytimes.com/2012/11/04/us/after-deep-police-cuts-sacramento-sees-rise-in-crime.html?pagewanted=all&_r=0.
25. Los Angeles County District Attorney 's Office, "Gang Crimes," upd., April 5, 2012, http://da.co.la.ca.us/gangs.htm.
26. John McWhorter, "How the War on Drugs Is Destroying Black America," *Cato's Letter* 9, no. 1 (Winter 2011), http://www.cato.org/sites/cato.org/files/pubs/pdf/catosletterv9n1.pdf.
27. Abramowitz and Teixeira, "The Decline of the White Working Class," in Teixeira, *Red, Blue & Purple America*, 118–19.
28. Executive Summary, "Young, Unemployed and Optimistic: Coming of Age, Slowly, in a Tough Economy," Pew Research Social & Demographic Trends, February 9, 2012, http://www.pewsocialtrends.org/2012/02/09/young-underemployed-and-optimistic/.
29. Ibid.
30. Chris Miles, "Are Millennials a Lost Generation? Report Shows Job Gap between Young and Old Widest Ever," PolicyMic.com, February 2012, http://www.policymic.com/articles/4055/are-millennials-a-lost-generation-report-shows-job-gap-between-young-and-old-widest-ever.

31. Audrey Farber, "Millennial Nomads: Did We Peak in College?" PolicyMic.com, February 2012, http://www.policymic.com/articles/3926/millennial-nomads-did-we-peak-in-college/category_list.
32. Kim Parker, "The Big Generation Gap at the Polls Is Echoed in Attitudes on Budget Tradeoffs," Pew Research Social & Demographic Trends, December 20, 2012, http://www.pewsocialtrends.org/2012/12/20/the-big-generation-gap-at-the-polls-is-echoed-in-attitudes-on-budget-tradeoffs/.
33. Don Peck, "How a New Jobless Era Will Transform America," *Atlantic*, March 2010, http://www.theatlantic.com/magazine/archive/2010/03/how-a-new-jobless-era-will-transform-america/307919/.
34. Greg Giroux, "Obama's 81% New York City Support Is Best in 114 Years," Bloomberg.com, January 10, 2013, http://www.bloomberg.com/news/2013-01-09/obama-s-81-support-in-new-york-city-is-best-in-114-years.html.
35. Josh Margolin, "'Wall St.' Flees NY for Tax-Free Fla.," *New York Post*, January 28, 2013, http://www.nypost.com/p/news/local/wall_st_flees_ny_for_tax_free_fla_Q6e4qSDMUethpylfznC4tO.
36. David Kerr, "Pope Warns of 'Grave Threat' to Religious Freedom in US," Catholic News Agency, January 19, 2012, http://www.catholicnewsagency.com/news/pope-warns-of-grave-threat-to-religious-freedom-in-us/.
37. Matthew Larotonda, "Catholic Churches Distribute Letter Opposing Obama Healthcare Rule," ABC News, January 29, 2012, http://abcnews.go.com/blogs/politics/2012/01/catholic-churches-distribute-letter-opposing-obama-healthcare-rule/.
38. Jonathan V. Last, "Obamacare vs. Catholics," *Weekly Standard*, February 13, 2012, http://www.weeklystandard.com/articles/obamacare-vs-catholics_620946.html.
39. Mark Tooley, "Religion and Voters in 2012," *American Spectator*, November 8, 2012, http://spectator.org/archives/2012/11/08/religion-and-voters-in-2012.
40. "How the Faithful Voted: 2012 Preliminary Analysis," The Pew Forum on Religion & Public Life, November 7, 2012, http://www.pewforum.org/Politics-and-Elections/How-the-Faithful-Voted-2012-Preliminary-Exit-Poll-Analysis.aspx.
41. Billy Hallowell, "Blaze Analysis: The Catholic Vote Went to Obama over Romney Despite Contraception & Religious Freedom Debates," *The Blaze*, November 8, 2012, http://www.theblaze.com/stories/2012/11/08/blaze-analysis-catholic-voters-chose-obama-over-romney-despite-contraception-religious-freedom-debate/.
42. Last, "Obamacare vs. Catholics."
43. "Convention Floor Erupts as Dems Restore References to God, Jerusalem in Platform," Fox News, September 5, 2012, http://www.foxnews.com/politics/2012/09/05/democrats-restore-references-to-god-jerusalem-in-platform/.
44. Ibid., as seen in video embedded in article.
45. Evan McMorris-Santoro, "Utah Delegates Help Launch a Democratic Insurrection over Platform Changes," TPM.com, September 5, 2012, http://2012.talkingpointsmemo.com/2012/09/democrats-vote-no-charlotte.php.
46. Omar Sacirbey, Religion News Service, "Muslim Delegates at Democratic Convention Quadrupled Since 2004," *Washington Post*, September 5, 2012, http://www.washingtonpost.com/national/on-faith/muslim-delegates-at-democratic-convention-quadrupled-since-2004/2012/09/05/58216ce8-f797-11e1-a93b-7185e3f88849_story.html.
47. Daniel Greenfield, "Muslims Have More DNC Delegates Than Montana, Utah and Oklahoma Put Together," FrontPageMag.com, September 7, 2012, http://frontpagemag.com/2012/dgreenfield/muslims-have-more-dnc-delegates-than-montana-utah-and-oklahoma-put-together/.

48. David Jackson, "Obama: Boy Scouts Should Allow Gays," *USA Today*, February 4, 2013, http://www.usatoday.com/story/theoval/2013/02/04/obama-boy-scouts-gays/1890065/.
49. Abramowitz and Teixeira, "The Decline of the White Working Class," in Teixeira, *Red, Blue & Purple America*, 116–17.
50. CNN Wire Staff, "Thousands Rally, Greece Brought to Standstill by Anti-Austerity Strike," *CNN.com*, October 18, 2012, http://www.cnn.com/2012/10/18/world/europe/greece-strike-austerity.
51. Sean Sullivan, "The Republican Party's Big State-Level Advantage, in One Chart," *The Fix* (blog), February 4, 2013, http://www.washingtonpost.com/blogs/the-fix/wp/2013/02/04/the-republican-partys-big-state-level-advantage-in-one-chart/; see also, "Infographic: 2013 Governors, Legislative Sessions, and Control," Pew State and Consumer Initiatives, January 22, 2013, http://www.pewstates.org/research/data-visualizations/infographic-2013-governors-legislative-sessions-and-control-85899444219.
52. Aaron Blake, "Why Winning Back the House Is a Tough Task for Democrats," *The Fix* (blog), January 25, 2013, http://www.washingtonpost.com/blogs/the-fix/wp/2013/01/25/beyond-the-beltway-gop-remains-in-very-good-shape/.
53. Grover G. Norquist and Patrick Gleason, "GOP's Untold Gains on State Level," *Politico*, November 18, 2012, http://www.politico.com/news/stories/1112/84006.html.
54. Ken Thomas and Steve Peoples, "Republican Governors Lead Charge on Rewriting GOP Blueprint after 2012 Election Drubbing," Huffington Post, January 25, 2013, http://www.huffingtonpost.com/2013/01/25/republican-governors_n_2552494.html. The information in the next paragraph is also drawn from this source.
55. Dana Ford, "GOP Expands Majority in Governors' Mansions, CNN Projects," CNN, November 7, 2012, http://www.cnn.com/2012/11/06/politics/governor-races.
56. NBC News staff and news service, "Judge Strikes Down Wisconsin Law Restricting Union Rights," NBC News, September 14, 2012, http://usnews.nbcnews.com/_news/2012/09/14/13868190-judge-strikes-down-wisconsin-law-restricting-union-rights?lite.
57. Steven Greenhouse, "In Indiana, Clues to Future of Wisconsin Labor," *New York Times*, February 26, 2011, http://www.nytimes.com/2011/02/27/business/27collective-bargain.html?pagewanted=all.
58. Sean Cavanagh, "Daniels Signs Collective Bargaining Restrictions into Law," *State EdWatch* (blog) April 20, 2011, http://blogs.edweek.org/edweek/state_edwatch/2011/04/daniels_signs_limits_on_collective_bargaining_into_law.html.
59. Tom LoBianco, Associated Press, "Indiana a Changed State after Mitch Daniels' 8 Years," *Washington Times*, January 2, 2013, http://www.washingtontimes.com/news/2013/jan/2/indiana-changed-state-after-mitch-daniels-8-years/?page=all.
60. Tom Davies, Associated Press, "Taxpayers Net $111 Credit from State Surplus," *Post-Tribune*, November 21, 2012, http://posttrib.suntimes.com/news/16544005-418/indiana-taxpayers-to-see-111-credit-from-surplus.html.
61. Lesley Weidenbener, "Daniels Transfers $360 Million of Indiana Surplus into Pension Funds," *Courier Press*, October 4, 2012, headline.

CONCLUSION: A CHOICE, NOT AN ECHO

1. Schlafly, *A Choice, Not an Echo*, 29.
2. Lauren Fox, "Conservative Groups Admonish GOP Leadership for Ousting Members from Committees," *U.S. News & World Report*, December 4, 2012, http://www.usnews.com/news/articles/2012/12/04/conservative-groups-admonish-gop-leadership-for-ousting-members-from-committees.

3. Kate Nocera, "Tim Huelskamp, Justin Amash Rip Republican Leaders," *Politico*, December 4, 2012, http://www.politico.com/story/2012/12/tim-huelskamp-justin-amash-rip-republican-leaders-84571.html.
4. David Weigel, "The Tea Party Purge of 2012," *Slate*, December 4, 2012, http://www.slate.com/articles/news_and_politics/politics/2012/12/tim_huelskamp_and_the_tea_party_post_2012_election_john_boehner_strips_outspoken.html.
5. William Saletan, "Todd Akin's Rape Fiasco," *Slate*, August 20, 2012, http://www.slate.com/articles/news_and_politics/frame_game/2012/08/todd_akin_s_legitimate_rape_gaffe_shows_how_abortion_can_be_a_crime_issue_.html.
6. Josh Voorhees, "GOP Senate Candidate Suggests Pregnancy from Rape Is 'Something that God Intended,'" *Slate*, October 24, 2012, http://www.slate.com/blogs/the_slatest/2012/10/24/richard_mourdock_rape_comment_gop_senate_hopeful_says_rape_is_something.html.
7. Katia McGlynn, "The Craziest Things Christine O'Donnell Has Ever Said," Huffington Post, May 25, 2011, http://www.huffingtonpost.com/2010/09/27/christine-odonnell-craziest-quotes_n_718328.html#s145707&title=Bedknobs__Broomsticks.
8. David Kurtzman, "The 10 Most Ridiculous Sharron Angle Quotes (So Far)," About.com, n.d., http://politicalhumor.about.com/od/republicanquotes/a/Sharron-Angle-Quotes.htm ; see also, Sam Stein, "Sharron Angle Floated '2nd Amendment Remedies' as a 'Cure' for 'The Harry Reid Problems,'" Huffington Post, June 16, 2010, http://www.huffingtonpost.com/2010/06/16/sharron-angle-floated-2nd_n_614003.html.
9. Jeff Zeleny, "Top Donors to Republicans Seek More Say in Senate Races," *New York Times*, February 2, 2013, http://www.nytimes.com/2013/02/03/us/politics/top-gop-donors-seek-greater-say-in-senate-races.html?hp&_r=2&.
10. David Bossie, "The Civil War Has Begun," Breitbart.com, February 6, 2013, http://www.breitbart.com/Big-Government/2013/02/06/The-Civil-War-Has-Begun. Bossie quotes in this section are all from this article.
11. Larry O'Connor, "Bozell Pushes Back Hard against Rove War on Tea Party," Breitbart.com, February 5, 2013, http://www.breitbart.com/Big-Government/2013/02/05/Bozell-Pushes-Back-Hard-Against-Rove-War-On-Tea-Party.
12. Kathleen Walter and Cyrus Afzall, "Brent Bozell: Rove Attacking Reagan Base of GOP," Newsmax.com, February 5, 2013, http://www.newsmax.com/Newsfront/rove-bozell-gop-base/2013/02/05/id/489053. Quotations in the next two paragraphs are also taken from this source.
13. Larry O 'Connor, "Rove Aide Calls Bozell 'Hater' with 'Weird Axes to Grind,'" Breitbart.com, February 6, 2013, http://www.breitbart.com/Big-Government/2013/02/06/Rove-Aide-Calls-Bozell-Hater-Weird-Axes-To-Grind.
14. Jeffrey Lord, "Rove Spokesman Apologizes to Bozell," *American Spectator*, February 6, 2013, http://spectator.org/blog/2013/02/06/rove-spokesman-apologizes-to-b?utm_source=twitterfeed&utm_medium=twitter&nomobile=. The author of this book was a signatory to the letter written by Craig Shirley, addressed to Steven Law.
15. See also: "Rove 's New PAC Is Bad Investment for Conservatives," press release, Citizens for the Republic, February 4, 2013, http://www.cftr.org/press/release43.aspx.
16. David Taintor, "Conservatives Demand Rove Group Fire Aide over 'Hater' Comments," TPM, February 7, 2013, http://livewire.talkingpointsmemo.com/entry/conservatives-demand-rove-group-fire-aide-over-hater.
17. Jeff Zeleny, "New Rove Effort Has G.O.P. Aflame," *New York Times*, February 6, 2013, http://www.nytimes.com/2013/02/07/us/politics/new-rove-effort-has-gop-aflame.html.
18. Angela Terkel, "Karl Rove, American Crossroads Spin GOP Election Losses," Huffington Post, November 8, 2012, http://www.huffingtonpost.com/2012/11/08/karl-rove-american-crossroads_n_2092523.html.

19. Karl Rove, "The President's 'Grand Bet' Pays Off," *Wall Street Journal*, opinion, November 7, 2012, http://online.wsj.com/article/SB10001424127887323894704578105153335057318.html?mod=googlenews_wsj.
20. Sheelah Kolhatkar, "Exclusive: Inside Karl Rove's Billionaire Fundraiser," Bloomberg *Businessweek*, August 31, 2012, http://www.businessweek.com/printer/articles/69276-exclusive-inside-karl-roves-billionaire-fundraiser.
21. "Turnabout: Now Calls for Rove to Go!" WND.com, September 1, 2012, http://www.wnd.com/2012/09/turnabout-now-calls-for-rove-to-go/.
22. Schlafly, *A Choice, Not an Echo*, 86.
23. Michael Patrick Leahy, "Caddell Unloads on 'Racketeering GOP Consultants,'" Breitbart.com, March 14, 2013, http://www.breitbart.com/Big-Government/2013/03/14/Caddell-Blows-the-Lid-Off-CPAC-With-Blistering-Attack-on-Racketeering-Republican-Consultants.
24. Kidron K. Skinner, Annelise Anderson and Martin Anderson, eds., *Reagan in His Own Hand: The Writings of Ronald Reagan That Reveal His Revolutionary Vision for America* (New York: Free Press, 2001), "Government Cost II," 271.
25. "Big Bird in the Presidential Debate: Mitt Romney Advocates Cutting Funding for Sesame Street, PBS," *Washington Post*, October 4, 2012, http://articles.washingtonpost.com/2012-10-04/politics/35502193_1_big-bird-presidential-debate-pbs.

INDEX

G

H

I

J

K

L

M

N

O

P–Q

R

Y

Z